Praise for Why Literacy Matters

"Building upon a solid base of research, this thought-provoking book provides strong arguments on why literacy matters, both for individuals and for societies. Clearly written throughout, the book is essential reading for anyone involved in adult literacy education."

David Barton, Professor of Language and Literacy and Director of the
Lancaster Literacy Research Centre, Lancaster University, UK

"Ralf St. Clair offers practitioners, students, researchers and policy makers a strong, sober and clear argument, offering ample evidence of the value and meanings of literacy to people throughout their lives. He reveals the multifarious ways in which learning and using literacy matters to people across the world. Using capability as the harnessing concept enables St Clair to examine conflicting and contested views of literacy and associated research and scholarship. He does so in ways which both critique and positively connect diverse approaches. This book will be a valuable, rich resource for those new to the field and contribute to continuing debates."

Dr Ursula Howard, Visiting Professorial Fellow,
Institute of Education, University of London, UK

"As we move into the second decade of the 21st century, we need to ask if anything will be different for the millions who struggle every day with limited literacy. We also need to question the value of what we have learned from the massive human effort and public expenditures on adult literacy education in the Global North over the past fifty years and more. With this timely book, Ralf St. Clair brings his international experience and insight to some of the most pressing issues we face in literacy education. His capabilities model is but one example of the new clarity he brings to the ways literacy is being understood – and misunderstood. With practical suggestions for improving the lasting effects of literacy education, this book should be of interest to anyone concerned about the future of adult literacy and learning."

B. Allan Quigley, Ed.D, Professor of Adult Education,
St. Francis Xavier University, Nova Scotia, Canada

"A welcome addition to the basic skills literature – reflective, accessible and concise. Anchoring the meaning of literacy on Amartya Sen's concept of capability appeals particularly. This makes the point that that literacy is a form of competence that cannot sensibly be separated from its function in the achievement of individual and collective goals in the cultural context in which they are set – in Sen's terms 'freedom to achieve'. Adult literacy education developed in this framework realises most fully its potential for matching provision to need."

John Bynner, Emeritus Professor of Social Sciences in Education,
of London, UK

D0273370

Why Literacy Matters

Understanding the Effects of Literacy
Education for Adults

promoting adult learning

Published by

© 2010 National Institute of Adult Continuing Education
(England and Wales)

21 De Montfort Street
Leicester
LE1 7GE

Company registration no. 2603322
Charity registration no. 1002775

NIACE has a broad remit to promote lifelong learning opportunities for
adults. NIACE works to develop increased participation in education and
training, particularly for those who do not have easy access because of class,
gender, age, race, language and culture, learning difficulties or disabilities,
or insufficient financial resources.

You can find NIACE online at www.niace.org.uk

Cataloguing in Publications Data
A CIP record for this title is available from the British Library

ISBN 978-1-86201-450-3

Cover design by Book Production Services.
Designed and typeset by Avon DataSet Ltd, Bidford on Avon, Warwickshire, UK.
Printed and bound in the UK by Page Bros, Norwich.

Contents

Acknowledgements

I would like to acknowledge the support of the University of Glasgow, who permitted me to take some study leave to get the book project started, and the anonymous reviewer whose suggestions improved the manuscript a great deal. My editors at NIACE were Alec McAulay and David Shaw, who were both eternally supportive and patient. The mistakes and badly worded phrases remain, of course, all my own doing.

The book was inspired by the learners and practitioners I meet on my travels around the world of literacies. Thank you – I hope you find it useful.

Finally I have to thank my partner for providing somewhere to work, loads of intellectual and personal support, and an apparently inexhaustible supply of good German chocolate.

This book is dedicated to Grant.

Ralf St. Clair
Konstanz, 2010

Introduction

The topic of this book is the significance of adult literacy education for adults, but to really understand this topic we have to start off with a slightly broader perspective. In the last few years there have been remarkable changes in the attention given to questions of literacy for children and adults, and equally important developments in the way people think about literacy. Many of these developments span across literacy in all its forms, and call for adult literacy education to be seen as part of a far wider ecosystem of literacy learning and application.

One significant change has been the development of theories grounded in the new literacy studies, which challenge the idea of a single form of literacy and suggest that we are better to think of diverse literacies practised in specific social contexts. Another important change is that our new understanding of literacy makes it more sensible to think about literacy as an aspect of people's entire lives rather than as two separate elements of school literacy and adult literacy. This does not mean that adults and children need to learn the same things or learn in the same way, but that it makes sense to acknowledge the lifelong continuities of literacy. As will be discussed more fully later in this volume, people's literacy lives tend to follow fairly consistent trajectories from early childhood well into adulthood, with the same sorts of factors affecting their relationships with reading and writing.

There have been several international surveys designed to assess skills of entire populations since the early 1990s and huge UNESCO and World Bank investments in the creation of literacy programmes for less developed nations. The economic concepts of human capital theory have caught on, making skills – including the literacy skills of the adult population – a key concern for policymakers. Funding for adult literacy programmes, while still a tiny fraction of the educational budget of most countries, has become a little more stable. Overall, what was a relatively marginal field now sits far nearer to the centre of educational policy and practice.

Not surprisingly, these developments have strengthened the field enormously, but they have also changed its orientation. There are substantial moves towards professionalism of the adult literacy education field in many countries and general indications of integration into broader educational systems. There are discussions about public investment in adult literacy, including where investment can best be placed and where it should be found given the zero sum game of government funding. There are also substantial amounts of new data to draw upon about the effects and outcomes of literacy education at any age.

For these reasons, this seems like a good time to pause and think a little about what we are trying to do in adult literacy education. It seems that the recurrent crises in adults' and children's literacy may be passing, replaced by a steady commitment to supporting people's ability to use written language. Alongside these developments has come some inflation of the claims about the benefits of literacy education: economic prosperity, individual income, healthy lives, smarter children and so on. As a long time adult literacy educator and researcher, my concern is that these claims will prove to be unfounded, or at least these outcomes will prove to be prohibitively expensive to reach, and that the commitment to literacy education will erode. It seems really important to be clear and realistic about what adult literacy education can offer, and what expectations it can be measured against. Overclaiming for the effects of policy investment can lead to rapid disillusionment and reduction of political and financial support. Perhaps the clearest case is schools, which operate within a consistent context of critique largely because expectations are so high. If possible, literacy education for adults needs to avoid ending up in a similar situation. There is a need to take a look at the rapidly accruing evidence and ask a number of hard questions:

- How can we think and talk about literacy in a way that is theoretically rich yet precise enough to support a clear policy message?
- What kind of impact does literacy learning have on adult's lives?
- What can instructors learn from the existing evidence?

In looking at these questions, I go back and forth between the impact of literacy practices as a set of human activities and the impact of learning literacy as a specific educational enterprise. When I started planning this book I intended to look primarily at literacy learning rather than literacy practices, but as I worked through the evidence and developed a framework for discussion it became clear to me that this was, in many ways, an artificial distinction. There are two reasons for this. The first is that adults learn literacy in all sorts of ways, from initial schooling to adult education classes to college preparation to chatting with their family. Trying to draw a line between acquisition and use of literacy is unconvincing and not very helpful. The second point is that what matters is the use people make of their literacy capabilities, and how those capabilities play out in their lives. Understanding the effects of literacy learning involves clarifying the effects of literacy as a part of people's lives as a whole.

I am not going to spend very much time in this book on the question of whether literacy and literacy education matter. It is a question that cannot really be answered meaningfully through data analysis, and I believe that anybody who has ever walked into a literacy programme for adults already knows one answer to the question. To the people who are learning, literacy education matters very much indeed, for a whole host of reasons – if it did not, they would not be there. It seems to me that the more challenging and helpful questions are around the *ways* in which literacy matters, and how we can understand and acknowledge those more deeply.

There are some very obvious gaps in the discussion in this book, and many people who have been around literacy education will be able to identify them and say 'what about the effect on people's diet, or the ability to budget?' for example. My intention is not to dismiss those outcomes – as an educator I know that literacy learning can have a huge impact on all sorts of areas. However, there are problems with trying to include everything in any discussion. For example, there are some areas of outcome where there simply is not a lot of evidence, while other areas have some evidence but are of limited relevance to any broad policy discussion on literacy learning. The five areas included in this book are a selection of possible outcomes, though I have tried to select in the most responsible way possible.

I am also not going to talk a great deal about numeracy. This is not because numeracy is unimportant – as we shall see, there are some areas in which numeracy matters a great deal more than literacy – but numeracy is its own concept with its own set of concerns. Rather than engage with numeracy intensively, I have decided to touch on it where necessary and leave substantive discussion to those who look at numeracy more closely in their work.

My approach to literacy has always been driven by a humanist commitment to reducing inequity in whatever form it appears and I stand by that commitment. That does not blind me to the need to be more careful about what we claim literacy can do for people, and what they can do with it. This is a great moment for lifelong literacy, and another may not come along for a while. So let's use it in the best way we possibly can, with reflection and with care, with recognition of literacy's limits and the enormity of human potential.

Initial approaches to literacy

Literacy is not a simple term; there is no agreed definition of what makes a person literate, or what a literate person ought to be able to do. But in a book about the effects of literacy in the lives of adults it is important to have a clear understanding of the concept, if only for the purposes of this discussion. The way that literacy is conceived affects where we look for it, how we measure it, and what other factors may influence it. Each of these makes a difference to how we think about the effects of literacy in people's lives.

Literacy is such a commonplace word in today's conversations about education, economy and jobs that it seems odd to suggest it is also a slippery and difficult term to define, and that authors need to develop and justify their own approach. Often, newspaper articles and television sound bites give the impression that literacy is something that people either have or do not have, and that it is easy to tell the difference. And perhaps in some circumstances it is. When it comes to filling in forms, people may be able to grasp the questions or not. The written portions of the driving test will be understood and passed by some people and not by others. A letter written home by a daughter may be enjoyed and shared, or may be appreciated simply as a gesture. The tricky thing about these observations, though, is that they are not just about some abstract ability called literacy, they are about the ways people use and apply that ability or group of abilities. It is important to be cautious about oversimplifying the nature of literacy as it is practised in real life settings. Graff (1994) argues the view:

4

That subjects such as literacy, learning, schooling, and education are simple, unproblematic notions is a further historical myth. Experience, historical and more recent, to the contrary jointly underscores their fundamental complexity – practically and theoretically – their enormously complicated conceptual and highly problematic nature. (p. 44)

Given this complexity, it is worthwhile spending some time being clear about what we mean by literacy. It is not very helpful to point to the things that are taught by literacy education programmes (including schools) and say 'isn't that literacy?' The problem is that programmes vary a great deal in what they teach; even if they didn't, their approach might well only be one among many possible approaches. It is important to peel back the layers of practice as we know it and look at the idea of literacy in a broader form.

Perhaps the first thing to say is that literacy is all about language use. Language, at the level we use it, is a uniquely human trait (as far as we know). As Deacon (1997) puts it:

As our species designation – sapiens – suggests, the defining attribute of human beings is an unparalleled cognitive ability. We think differently from all other creatures on earth, and we can share those thoughts with each other in ways that no other creature even approaches. In comparison, the rest of our biology is almost incidental. (p.21)

Language can be seen as a defining characteristic of our species. Pinker (1994) expresses the remarkable nature of the human language ability even more strongly than Deacon, and makes language use begin to sound a little bit like telepathy. Here he is talking about the way humans can construct meaning from the written word:

As you are reading these words, you are taking part in one of the wonders of the natural world. For you and I belong to a species with a remarkable ability: we can shape events in each other's brains with exquisite precision. (p.15)

Pinker is pointing towards a phenomenon as mysterious as language use itself – the way that symbols can be used to share meanings. When considered from an evolutionary perspective it seems quite remarkable that humans have this ability. It is quite intuitively sensible that being able to communicate across distances by speaking and shouting would be a huge advantage for a fairly weak and slow species of scavengers living on the African plains, but why would the ability to represent those utterances with symbols be useful? The general consensus at the moment appears to be that literacy was not a specifically evolved ability, but a by-product of the way our brains developed under other influences. Our ability to work with language, our phonological ability to interpret sounds, and our visual processing (amongst other traits) came together to allow us to represent language through symbols. This is a remarkable circumstance – our human ability to turn inky blobs into meaning, emotion and understanding would be completely astonishing if so many of us did not constantly do it.

The idea that we evolved for oral language and just happen to be able to use written language could be taken to mean that spoken language is natural whereas written language is essentially cultural. This argument is equivalent to saying that running is something our species does naturally but 100 metre Olympic sprints are a cultural artefact. It is important to be careful with such arguments as natural and cultural phenomena tend to be very tightly wrapped up together. While it is true that sprints are social inventions, they would be very dull if humans could not run. Finding ways to take advantage of something our species does inherently and well is hardly unnatural. Written language is not purely an invention, but a highly developed application of a set of human abilities.

In discussions of literacy it used to be very common to preserve a strong division between spoken and written language. Recently, there has been growing agreement that this distinction is unhelpful, and that oral and written language are very substantially mingled in the actions of individuals. Talking about the Middle Ages, Chinca and Young (2005) argue that literacy cannot be defined:

> . . . *without taking into account the many ways in which the written word was embedded in orality. Written texts might be dictated, communicated and discussed orally; even reading to oneself could involve vocalising the words on the page . . . Emphasising this opens the way for fresh research whose basic assumption is the interplay . . . between the written word and oral networks of communication.* (p. 4)

This same interplay is a feature of contemporary literacy use in everyday life. For example, we write down a phone message for a colleague or a friend, or we read out notes in a meeting. Perhaps we see something on television and walk to the computer to search for more information in written form. In these and many other ways we slip between spoken and written forms of language. There is no set of things we do that can be considered as pure literacy. This makes an important difference to how we theorise, measure and value literacy by challenging the idea that there can ever be a strongly bounded set of actions that are literate and that are set apart from non-literate or pre-literate actions. It seems that there is a fuzzy boundary around the origins and nature of written language use. Literacy is part of a larger set of cognitive features unique to humans, and is deeply embedded within our ways of thinking about the world.

For the discussion in this book it is helpful to hold on to one distinction, however. The ways in which the term 'literacy' can be used are proliferating, and it seems to have become a synonym for 'understanding of,' so that 'emotional literacy' means 'understanding emotions' and so on. This discussion specifically uses literacy to refer to engagement with language in textual form. There are several reasons for this. The first is that the scope of the book would be simply unmanageable if every form of literacy were considered. The second is that literacy learning, including schooling, primarily deals with textual engagement. The third is that the evidence we have about literacy and its effects mostly concerns text literacy. Other applications of the word are simply too recent for a lot of data to have built up.

At the broad level, this discussion concerns people's engagement with text, both as consumers (readers) and producers (writers). Most current views of literacy tend to view reading and writing as equally important aspects of the whole, but historically this is far from the norm. At some times the emphasis has been on reading, often so that individuals could read religious tracts. This was a particularly important motivation in Germany, Sweden and Scotland from the middle of the sixteenth century (Graff, 1995). Writing was of far less interest in these locations – what mattered was the ability of individuals to read the Bible as part of the Protestant relationship with God, hence diminishing the temptation to rely on priests to interpret the Gospel. At other times, as least for the purposes of historical analysis, the ability to write is more important. One of the standard methods of assessing literacy in Western Europe during the nineteenth and twentieth centuries is to look at marriage and birth registers and see who could sign their name (Mace, 2001). These examples remind us that what we may think of as the 'normal' way to act as literate people within the developed parts of the twenty-first century world has been very unusual historically. In the present moment, both reading and writing are seen as key attributes, and my own view of literacy is that both production and consumption are vital and inter-related aspects of text use. However, as will be discussed later, there is still a considerable imbalance in the amount of data available about the two aspects, with much more evidence about reading than writing.

It is obvious that literacy is a tricky thing to talk about, with lots of fuzzy boundaries; between literate and not literate, between writing and speech, between reading and writing, and between schooling and adult literacy. This could either be a cause for despair or, as I prefer to think about it, an intriguingly broad canvas upon which to work. In this book I describe the 'capabilities' model of literacy and use it to analyse the evidence about literacy outcomes. The idea of capabilities is based upon the key insights of three approaches to understanding literacy that have been extremely influential over the last fifty years: the functional approach, literacy as a set of cognitive skills, and literacies as social practices. There is a tendency to view these three approaches as leading to different conclusions – I argue, however, that they are fundamentally compatible if we accept that literacy is a complex, multi-faceted phenomenon. The capabilities model brings the three approaches together to illustrate the different factors influencing literacy and the different manifestations it may have in the lives of individuals. The definition of literacy used in this book is 'the ability to achieve a desired purpose by applying appropriate skills in a specific situation of engagement with texts.'

The format of this book

This book is structured in three sections. In the first four chapters I look at current models of literacy, present the capabilities model and the idea of literacy capabilities, discuss evaluation of social and economic programmes (how do we know an 'impact' when we see one?) and look at measurement of literacy. This is a lot of preparatory discussion, but it is key to understanding the rest of the book and also reflects the difficult questions currently circulating within literacy. Questions such as what we mean by literacy and how we recognise changes in it are subtle and difficult, and take some discussion. The second section lays out the evidence on the impacts of literacy in five domains of human life: psychological, economic, family, health and social/political. These chapters suggest what kind of impact we might theoretically expect, and then look at the evidence for that kind of impact. The final section of the book summarises the evidence and discusses the instructional and policy implications.

Throughout the book I do not distinguish strongly between adult literacy and schooling as a source of data. Where evidence from one area seems to offer an interesting or valuable insight, I use it. The division between initial literacy for children and literacy for adults is more a product of our current schooling systems rather than a well-evidenced divide. There are differences, naturally, to do with expectations, life experience, and compulsory attendance, but these may not necessarily be very significant in addressing the central questions of this book. It is both more realistic and more helpful to take a lifelong approach and leave the age and situation of learners more open. However, when I move on to look at the implications I do bring my comments back to adult literacy learning in particular, because this is a specific form and location for learning. Even though the insights come from a broad perspective, I believe it's important to see how they play out in this specific context.

A lot of the research in this book is derived from the global North, though I will incorporate more diverse perspectives whenever possible. The main challenge is the relative lack of research based in the global South. This makes sense on one level, in that countries with fewer resources for education are likely to spend less on research, but is unfortunate in that there will be extremely valuable insights from these regions missing from the discussion. I hope that in the future these contexts will receive the attention they deserve.

I would like this discussion to contribute something to our understanding of literacy and to the reasons why it matters. Our field could be well served by a shared perspective on the significance of our work and the benefits and challenges of reading and writing as they are used by people throughout their lives. My hope is that the ideas in this book, as well as the broad survey of evidence around literacy education, might prove to be useful in building such a perspective.

PART ONE

HOW CAN WE THINK ABOUT THE EFFECTS OF LITERACY EDUCATION?

CHAPTER ONE

Three ways to look at literacy: A brief review

Before we can understand the potential outcomes of learning literacy, it is important to be clear about what we mean when we talk about literacy. There are a couple of reasons why this is so important. The first is that our conception of literacy makes a difference to where we look for its effects, so it matters a great deal how it is framed. The second is that a great deal of the evidence for the effects of literacy education is built on the effects of literacy itself. For example, if stronger literacy skills are linked to higher income it makes sense to look at the evidence that involvement in adult literacy education can improve an individual's income. Literacy is not a simple idea, and the specific view taken upon it influences the nature of the questions to be discussed quite profoundly.

This chapter looks at three of the most influential perspectives upon literacy, and the next chapter draws on these perspectives to offer the model that drives the discussions in this book. The three perspectives of functional literacy, mental operations and social practices have been selected because they offer the clearest and most developed insights into the conception of literacy, and underpin most of the pragmatic approaches applied in educational settings. I have made no attempt to be inclusive of all possible views even within these perspectives, but tried to focus discussion upon the key points. Other authors might have made different selections and drawn different boundaries, but these three particular perspectives have both a relatively long pedigree and a wide range of influence on the field.

Each of the three perspectives has a huge amount of work associated with it, so the presentation here is necessarily selective. The objective of the chapter is to provide an understanding of the main claims and insights offered by each of the three in order to understand how they fit together and how they differ. This understanding underpins the working model of literacy capabilities presented in the next chapter. For more detailed discussion of each perspective, I would encourage interested readers to follow up the references. There is a lot of excellent writing on the processes, contexts and significance of literacies viewed from each of the three perspectives discussed here.

What works: the functional view

For many people, one of the most intuitively appealing approaches to literacy is functional literacy. In very simple terms, functional literacy is being able to read and write well enough to be able to function in everyday life. This leads to a definition of literacy based on the reading and writing that occurs 'naturally' in our lives. For example, people living in the developed economies in the early years of the twenty-first century might be expected to be able to read a newspaper, have some knowledge of using a computer, be able to understand a bus timetable, create a basic household budget and so on. The notion of functional literacy has a strong pragmatic appeal – after all, it is based on the abilities people are said to need.

The idea of functional literacy arose out of progressive educational thought in the first half of the twentieth century. One of the most influential individuals was Illinois educator and professor William Gray, who trained as a teacher at Illinois State Normal University and was strongly influenced by the Herbartian ideas of child-centred and inductive approaches to teaching (Lauritzen, 2007). By the 1950s Gray was retired and UNESCO asked him to conduct a review of literacy around the world, which took four years to complete and was published in 1956. In this work, he presents one of the most influential definitions of literacy ever written:

> *A person is functionally literate when he has acquired the knowledge and skills in reading and writing which enable him to engage in all those activities in which literacy is normally assumed in his culture or group. (Gray, 1956, p. 24)*

At the time, this was a groundbreaking way to think about literacy because

14

it suggests that literacy is both relativistic and contextual. Gray avoids setting a universal standard against which people had to perform irrespective of their situation, as would have fit with the dominant views of literacy at that time. Instead he reflects his philosophical and theoretical commitment to learner-centred processes in literacy learning by making individuals' use of text the key concern. It is an active view of reading and writing that starts to push towards the notion of literacy as an activity rather than an abstract form of knowledge.

Fifty years later, very similar ideas are still driving UNESCO's literacy programmes. Their current working definition of literacy suggests that:

> *A person is functionally literate who can engage in all those activities in which literacy is required for effective function of his or her group and community and also for enabling him or her to continue to use reading, writing and calculation for his or her own and the community's development. (UNESCO, 2002)*

Similar ideas can be found within some national approaches to literacy, such as the philosophy driving the adult literacy and numeracy education system in Scotland:

> *The ability to read, write and use numeracy, to handle information, to express ideas and opinions, to make decisions and solve problems, as family members, workers, citizens and lifelong learners. (Scottish Executive, 2001)*

These deliberately open and pragmatic ways of looking at literacy do not address two important questions, however. One is how we know whether people are functionally literate. If we followed the philosophical base of the definition the only way would be to ask each person whether they felt they could use texts in a functional way. This is clearly not very efficient, and also raises the question of whether people might see themselves as functionally literate by definition because they adjust what they *do* to match what they *can do*. For example, people who are good at maths but less comfortable with poetry are not going to study or work in English literature. If it is necessary to understand the patterns of literacy engagement across a society this is quite an important problem, as will be discussed in more depth in chapter four.

The second question is what functions people should be literate for. Is there a key set of functions common to most people in any given society, or must literacy usage remain completely eclectic and individual? If there are common functions, are they common to all societies, to developed economies, to specific nation-states or to smaller units within them?

The openness of the original functional literacy approaches has also proven to be their central vulnerability. Because they do not tie down what sort of functions (and to what level) should be the central concerns of literacy measurement and teaching, there has been a tendency to fill the gap with work-orientated measures and teaching approaches (Barton, 2007). The degree to which instrumental economic concerns have the potential to dominate discussions of literacy is a recurring topic throughout this book, but it is perhaps most obviously demonstrated in the development of ideas around functional literacy.

One example will suffice to illustrate this potential. As noted above, Scotland has an extremely open definition of literacy underpinning its educational provision for adults. The 2007 'Scotland Performs' framework lays out a series of 45 indicators of well-being for the Scottish population (Scottish Government, 2007). One of these is directly related to literacy: 'Reduce number of working age people with severe literacy and numeracy problems.' This indicator is seen as important because:

> *If an individual has a weakness in these skills, they are less likely to make an effective contribution to Scotland's economy. Evidence of the scale of the problem is currently limited and dated (though currently being updated) but suggests that 20–25 per cent of the working age population may have very low literacy and numeracy skills. That is potentially an enormous drag on Scotland's economic capacity. It is also a social issue, because parents who are unable to read are less able to support their children's learning, putting at risk the next generation's capacity to engage in lifelong learning. (Scottish Government, 2007)*

In addition, there is a proposed level of education (Scottish Credit and Qualifications Framework Level 4) above which people's skills are regarded as sufficiently developed for the needs of the current Scottish economy. On the one hand, Scottish policy sets out an open and relativistic agenda around literacy and its value in a wide range of contexts, but on the other it shuts literacy down again to a particular form and level of literacy that is seen as economically valuable.

It is very easy to suggest that this is bad policymaking, but from the policymakers' perspective it is quite the opposite. Policy needs a clear objective against which its success can be measured, and if an area of policy such as literacy does not have clear outcomes they may often be externally imposed simply to allow some degree of policy control (St.Clair and Belzer, 2007). If functional models of literacy are dominant in policymaking without a clear notion of what 'functional' actually means, it can lead both to conservatism and to lack of protection from prevailing political forces. In the real world of literacy programmes this means that programmes can find themselves being strongly influenced by political imperatives such as the recent interest in phonics-based instruction or the emphasis on adult education for work. One degree of insulation that can be offered from these broad contextual pressures can come from a clear view of the purposes of adult literacy programmes. The danger of the open functional definition is that the original values associated with functional literacy approaches – of learner-centeredness, flexibility and recognition of context – can easily be lost.

There are a number of further issues with functional approaches. There is often an implied assumption that functional literacy levels are easy to teach and learn, to some extent because they are so strongly based in 'real life.' The idea is that it should be simpler to learn abilities that will be used every day for practical reasons – after all, 'everybody can do it.' This view is strongly challenged by researchers who are interested in the nature of literacy practices, who argue that learning any form of literacy involves getting to know an enormous range of meanings and activities (Blanche-Benveniste, 1994). It is important to ask whether adopting a functional view of literacy really helps us to simplify ideas around reading and writing, since the range of skills to be learned is just as extensive as any other form of literacy.

Functional literacy also seems to assume that the relationship between an individual's textual engagement and their context runs in one direction, from environment to practice. It is quite likely, however, that the two influence each other. The types of literacy used in a given social context may well be strongly shaped by what people can actually do. A really simple example is the way the prices of fruit are displayed. In Canada, when you walk into a supermarket, fruit prices should be listed only in metric measures – metric has been standard legal practice in Canada for over thirty years. Quite often, however, prices are listed only in pounds. I believe that this is because people are used to pounds of fruit and can conceive of them more easily than kilograms (I know I can). So the customers' adherence to imperial measures influences the literacy and numeracy practices of the shopping context.

If the literacy demands of a given situation adjust themselves to match the available abilities, then the utility of the functional view as a guide to measurement and assessment is seriously compromised. People's skills and the literacy practices required to function within a given society will tend to converge. Some people will not meet the demands of a given society, but those demands are flexible to some degree and it is perfectly logical to argue that it makes more sense to lower the literacy demands of a specific context rather than raise the literacy abilities of millions of individuals. If a workplace, for example, requires workers to handle sophisticated written information and this is difficult for employees, it is likely more effective to simplify the text rather than to educate the workers.

While the notion of functional literacy was inspired by good intentions and admirable commitment to individuals' learning, in the end it does not help a great deal with understanding what literacy is. Any functional definition of literacy will tend to collapse into circularity – literacy is that which you have to do to be literate. So the notion of functional literacy is more useful from a descriptive point of view than as an analytical tool. Nonetheless, functional approaches underline two critical aspects of literacy that are important to bear in mind. The first of these is the relativism inherent to literacy. No one measure or indicator of literacy will be appropriate to every context, and so the definition of the broad concept must have room to recognise this. The second is that the use of literacy is an important consideration. People are interested in engaging with texts because of what this allows them to do, and any definition that moves too far from the application of these abilities is likely to lose some value.

Literacy as a set of cognitive processes

There is a huge amount of work, both theoretical and practical, holding that literacy can best be understood as a set of cognitive practices performed by an individual. Psychology has a long-standing fascination with the mental operations of reading – if we are trying to understand literacy, the argument goes, then we must understand more about the cognitive apparatus that allows us to turn marks on a page into meaningful language. This work has attracted many brilliant and imaginative researchers

18

over the years, and thanks to their efforts we have some sort of framework for understanding the processes underlying literacy.

In psychological research, the emphasis has generally lay more on reading processes than on writing (Verhoeven, 1994). One of the effects of this emphasis is to bring back the notion that reading and writing are somewhat separate functions, though there seems to be little hard evidence on whether they are in fact separate or embedded within each other. Writing has mechanical aspects (though less so with a keyboard than a pencil), and the flow from thought to written word goes in the opposite direction from reading, but this does not imply that the fundamental processing demands are necessarily distinct. Currently, we simply do not know very much about this process. The discussion here is concerned mainly with reading due to the balance of available research even though textual production is likely to be as important in most people's lives as textual consumption.

The work on reading as a set of mental operations tends to separate reading into two aspects, both of which involve awe-inspiring and complex mental operations. The first aspect is the processes involved in moving between squiggles on the page and a set of words in the mind of the reader. These are generally referred to as lexical processes. People who suffer from visual dyslexia may find this aspect difficult, but all sorts of other factors can get in the way of lexical access, such as vision problems, high distractibility and so on. The second aspect of reading is comprehension. Apart from anything else, comprehension requires remembering a great deal of information, including the words that have just been read, the context of the text and intertextual links (how the text relates to other texts the reader is familiar with). Even in relatively simple reading, there is a great deal of mental work being done.

The following diagram, from Perfetti (1985) and based on the work of Rumelhart and McClelland (1981) shows a simple layout of the lexical processes.

The processes begin with the visual input, what is actually seen on the page. This then leads to examination of the features of the visual input. These features can 'turn on' certain possible letters and 'turn off' others, as shown by the arrowheaded lines and circle-headed lines respectively. So the shape I turns on capital E, capital N and so on, while turning off capital S. The lack of any other further lines or shapes then turns off everything except capital I to provide accurate letter identification.

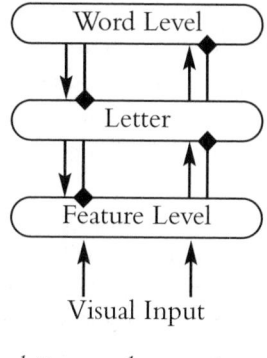

Diagram 1: From letters on the page to words in the mind.

The same process occurs at the word level, with an initial *I* turning on 'Istanbul' and turning off 'sheepdog.' Word identification also gets some help from context. Readers hold recently read words in their working memory, and use them to predict what is likely to come next. So as a reader comes across the capital *I* they may already have created the context 'I remember the first time I saw the Bosporus, as the plane swept low across the ancient city of I . . .' The lexical processes are highly interactive, working together to make word recognition as efficient and accurate as possible (Perfetti, 1985).

Lexical processes have two levels to them. After the word has been recognised as 'Istanbul' a second process called lexical access comes into play. This is very crudely analogous to looking up the word in a mental dictionary that each of us carries around. Readers work out if the word is in their language and if they recognise it at all. This process sits between the compilation of letters into words and the next step in understanding a text, which is creating comprehension.

Comprehension involves building a mental representation of the meaning of a text. One part of this process is semantic encoding of the words as they are recognised. A number of resources have to be brought to bear on the words in order to make this happen. Firstly, 'what a reader must have at the outset is an entry for each word in semantic memory. Such a semantic memory may be conceived as a network that links word concepts to abstracted meaning features and to other word concepts' (Perfetti, 1985, p. 33). The meanings are assembled into propositions, stored in working memory, and then integrated into a whole meaning. It is well established that comprehension works 'downwards' in the reading process as well as upwards – what readers understand the text to mean influences what they look for as they decode letters and words. It follows from this that knowledge of a subject and the appropriate vocabulary does not just ease comprehension – the entire set of reading processes becomes more efficient.

The broadest level of process is the creation of a text model. Here the propositions are filled out through knowledge and inference, as well as the reader's own frameworks of thought, known as schemata. For example, the phrase 'four kings beats a full house' may make little sense on its own. If you understand conventional Western playing cards it makes more sense. If you are a poker ace, it is blindingly obvious what the phrase refers to. What you know when you approach a particular text, from experience, previous texts or otherwise, makes a substantial difference to the ease of comprehension. It may also alter the depth of comprehension, as people with highly refined schemata are likely to pull a great deal more out of a given sequence of words. When I read Shakespeare I quite enjoy it, but do not get nearly as much out of it as somebody who studies English literature. They will make connections I remain oblivious to, and get references to historical events and jokes that I simply do not see. Reading is a constructive task, building on the perceived text and the individual's knowledge to create meaning.

What should be obvious from this discussion is how much goes on when a person reads and comprehends a text. The way that I have laid out the processes here is purely schematic – there is no implied chronology. In other words, there is no evidence that the various processes occur in the order logic suggests they should. It seems quite likely that somebody who is used to reading has developed an integrated and interactive set of processes, and that a number of interconnected systems are pulling together simultaneously to turn the marks on the page into meaning. For people who find reading more challenging, it is possible that any one (or more) of these processes may not be integrating into the whole, and slowing the system down.

Reading, according to this description, would be an exhausting task if it were not for the automaticity of certain processes. This means that the processes are not consciously performed, and that they consequently use fewer mental resources than processes that are not automatic. There are certain limits to the mental processing a human can do, such as a limit to the number of chunks of information that can be held in short-term memory, so the more that can be made automatic the better. Fluency in reading, the ability to move through a text at a good speed and comprehend it well, depends on automaticity of the various processes involved. It should be obvious that if somebody has to stop and identify each letter it will slow down their reading; similarly, if they have to pause and remember what each word means it will take a while to get through a text. Lacking context is another interesting case. In my experience, it often takes adult postgraduate students a great deal of time to get through the first few readings they encounter, but as they get more used to the language and the common ideas of the field their pace and their comprehension increases. With increased automaticity reading takes a great deal less effort and works better. It is quite possible that there is a text processing speed people have to achieve for reading to become almost effortless because reading more slowly means that the reader has to hold words in their working memory longer before putting them together. When reading reaches a certain pace words and phrases do not have to be retained as long and the processing capacity required to read actually drops.

People who have difficulty reading, whether because of visual acuity issues, dyslexia, or simply lack of practice, may have specific challenges in only one stage of reading, but the interlocked nature of the processes leads to a cascade effect influencing their reading as a whole. For example, to make sense of a word readers rely on the context in which it appears, using working memory to hold a picture of the text they are working through. If their lexical processes are slowed because of difficulty in focusing on the page to identify letters, then it may be that the larger context passes out of their working memory before it can be applied to the word when it is retrieved. There is also evidence that people may have more than one problematic process underlying their reading difficulties, such as linking the written word to the pronounced word and retrieving the meaning of that word (Wolf and Bowers, 1999). It seems that the sophisticated models of the mental processes of reading do not always provide clear implications for understanding reading difficulties or how people learn to read.

There are many specific and quite important questions that remain to be answered regarding the mental operations of literacy. One of the most interesting is the role of phonological strategies, or the ways in which readers connect written language to spoken language. It is not clear whether these are an intrinsic part of the reading process. On the one hand, there is evidence that readers may access their phonological strategies only when they are working through text that is difficult for them, whatever their reading ability (Perfetti, 1985). For example, even though I am reasonably used to reading, when I am trying to figure out a foreign language or an area I know little about, I may sound out the words or even read aloud. On the other hand, there is quite compelling evidence that phonological strategies come into play every time a person reads. Van Orden (1991) describes a proofreading task where the errors may be homophones of the correct word (sleat versus sleet) or spelling errors (speet versus sleet), and suggests that homophone substitution was caught considerably less often by the proofreaders than straight spelling errors. Similarly, Perfetti (1988) describes an experiment in which subjects were shown words for a very brief period before they were masked by a non-word. He found that the initial words were remembered more accurately when the masking non-word was phonologically similar (that is, when HERE was followed by HEER rather than HEOR), and suggested that there was a 'backward priming' effect at play – in other words, a reinforcement of the phonological processing of the first word. These experiments suggest that the sounds of language matter a great deal in reading.

It is tempting to make too much of these experiments and models, and perhaps claim that we know more about the internal mental processes of reading than we really do. The idea that phonological operations are fundamental to reading (rather than something we bring out when we are uncertain about a word or phrase) lies behind the current fashion for teaching phonics in schools. The basic claim is that difficulty with the phonological connection between print and spoken language slows down the transformation of visual input into meaning, and that explicit instruction in this connection will lead to automaticity, therefore freeing up processing space for the other processes involved in reading. However, it seems that the situation is more complex than this claim suggests. One of the biggest problems is that the experiments are often conducted in English, and English is not really a well developed alphabetic language. In many ways, English resembles a logographic language, where the specific word represented by the symbol affects the sound of the components (for example, thorough versus rough). There is regularity to these relationships, but the rules required to represent them are cumbersome and there are very many of them. In addition, approaches that privilege phonological strategies so strongly do not really explain why logographic languages work, or indeed why the measured results for phonics instruction are not more convincing (Strauss and Altwerger, 2007; Thompson and Johnston, 2007).

The recent interest in educational research as a scientific endeavour, with robust evidence used as the basis for practical decision-making, has encouraged educators to look once more at teaching approaches based on mental process perspectives on literacy (Belzer and St.Clair, 2005). For example, the report of the National Reading Panel in the United States (NICHD, 2000) conducted a meta-analysis of published research and demonstrated that explicit instruction in phonological strategies helped with learning to read. It is important to be cautious about such meta-analyses, however. One reason is that they tend to overlook the politics of publishing, which dictate that it is hard to publish studies showing very little difference whatever educators do – there is a tendency to publish only studies that clearly identify an effect. Most responsible researchers in the field of reading processes would be a great deal more cautious about the implications of their findings for teaching and learning reading than many publications claiming to define 'best practices' tend to be.

As we try to understand more about the mental operations of reading it is possible that new technologies, such as PET scans, will provide a way to understand the workings of the brain in more depth. In the meantime, there are three central lessons to be derived from current knowledge. The first is that reading is a complex set of mental operations that interlink very tightly and support each other. Difficulty with any one of these operations will have a significant impact on reading, suggesting that many things can go wrong in the reading process but the outward signs, such as miscues and slow reading, may well look very similar. The second lesson is that there are key processes involved in reading. The separation of word recognition, lexical access and text comprehension, for example, is generally agreed by most researchers to make sense. Even though we are uncertain of the details, this does seem to be a relatively well-supported framework that applies to reading in any language. Thirdly, we can say that these mental operations improve with practise, as they must if automaticity is the goal. Even though it is too simple to consider the cognitive processes of reading purely as skills, they do resemble skills in a number of ways. Initially they are performed deliberately and hesitatingly, but over time they become faster and require less effort. The final lesson is that we are not yet certain enough about many of the fundamental psychological questions of reading to make fully informed decisions about teaching and learning.

The comprehension of text is not a stand-alone process, as psychological researchers would readily admit. The path from printed symbols to words has strong cognitive, internal aspects, but moving from words to meaning requires bridging out in two directions. One is intertextuality, the process of linking texts to other texts, and the other is placing the text in a social context. The social practices perspective has a great deal to offer in understanding these dimensions of literacy.

The social practices of reading and writing

Approaches to literacy based on examination of mental processes provide many useful insights into reading, clarifying what happens in the initial stages of turning text into meaningful language. As we move further away from the initial encounter with the text and deeper into the process of creating meaning the approach starts to throw up as many questions as it does answers. For example, where do meaning schemes, or schemata, come from? How do readers choose between the array of interpretive perspectives available to them? How far down into the mental processes do the meaning-making structures reach – that is, to what extent is letter identification affected by our understanding of what we are reading and what it is trying to say? Does it make sense to talk of a single set of universal reading processes, as much of the psychological literature does, or is there a variety of contextualised approaches? These and similar questions led to the development of a different approach to understanding literacy, often called the social practices perspective.

Historically, mental processes approaches to literacy tended to focus very strongly on psychologically based, testable propositions about the cognitive mechanics of reading, and seemed less interested in the social aspects. When the social sciences turned towards more relativistic and culturally shaped ways of looking at the world in the 1970s and 1980s, approaches focusing on mental operations were seen to have a number of flaws. Basically process approaches, as psychological models, tend to assume that the act of reading is the same for everybody regardless of background, and that reading 'skill' is a single variable that can be arranged along a scale with no real problems. In an era that was interested in challenging and dismantling such over-simplified ideas of human ability, the reductionist aspects of the mental process approaches did not seem very helpful to understanding the complexity and range of behaviours associated with literacy.

The work that was done at that time became the foundation for the new literacy studies, a cross-disciplinary approach to literacy emphasising the social aspects of textual production and use. A key argument of social practices perspectives is that it simply does not make sense to view literacy separately from the communicative context in which it is used. More than this, it challenges the notion of literacy skills, seeing these as an attempt to define artificial context-free components of what is an essentially embedded process.

Analysts within the new literacy studies would generally accept the idea that textual technology develops in response to social, economic and political demands. One of the most influential writers on the relationship between social formations and text use is Brian Street. His work (1984, 2003, 2006) sets out to challenge the idea that literacy springs up on its own as an autonomous activity that then changes society, as was the case in older theories (see Chapter Five). Instead, he argues, there is a need for an ideological model of literacy including the following characteristics (1984, p.8):

- It assumes that the meaning of literacy depends upon the social institutions in which it is embedded.
- Literacy can only be known to us in forms which already have political and ideological significance.
- The processes whereby reading and writing are learnt are what construct the meaning of it for particular practitioners.
- We would probably more appropriately refer to 'literacies' than to any single literacy.

These claims presented a considerable challenge to the views of literacy prevalent at that time, and also seem quite counter-intuitive. The notion that literacy is a single set of skills that you can be better or worse at putting into practice is quite appealing and easy to understand for many people. This more complex, contextualised view, as with many sociological theories, seems to not only challenge but contradict our everyday experience. After all, can reading a report at work really be that different from reading a newspaper at home, or reading a blog on the Internet?

One of the most controversial features is the idea that it makes more sense to talk about 'literacies' than 'literacy,' as a way to reflect the enormous diversity of social practices around text production and consumption. This has become known as the 'multi-literacies' approach, and contains within it the implicit argument that the various forms of literacy have equal worth. They do not vary in their sophistication or communicative ability, but in their appropriateness to a given context. So the forms of literacy valued in schools are valued because that is what school literacy usually looks like, rather than because they are fundamentally better. An example is the language people use when explaining why foods go together (Bernstein, 1990). School-based literacy values language that is very explicit, making clear which foods go together and why (vegetable versus fruit, make a meal, etc.). It is designed to communicate abstract meaning between people who may not share very much common knowledge. Other forms of literacy may not be so explicit, perhaps because it represents communication between two people who eat together every night and who have common understandings. In this case, sticking a note on the fridge saying 'Get toms and stuff' might be enough, working as a clear code to inform one person that they have to stop at the shop on the way home from work and pick up a range of salad ingredients. Within a multi-literacies approach both the explicit school-based literacy and the brief note are important and interesting manifestations of literacy use.

It is worth noting that the social practices approach to literacies does have an implicit political commitment. It resists the idea that any form of reading and writing is inherently more valuable than any other, challenging the elitism of the idea that there is one best way to write English, for example. This argument is consistent with Labov's (1972) work on spoken language, which showed that allegedly 'degenerate' forms of language based in regional or ethnic communities were as capable of supporting complex ideas as standard forms of language, and that language users shift between different versions of speech depending on context. Extending this idea to literacy is both intriguing and challenging in the light of one key difference between spoken and written language – with spoken language there is generally an opportunity to ask clarifying questions, unlike written language.

Since Street's work of the mid-1980s, this perspective on literacy has been explored and expanded a great deal. There has been a huge amount of work looking at the way literacies function in different contexts to produce different outcomes, and the consequences for individuals. This work has spanned many settings around the world and has addressed a repeated concern about the ways that some literacies are seen as more desirable and powerful than others (Crowther, Hamilton and Tett, 2001). Some of the new literacy studies have worked to expand the meaning of literacy, such as Gee's increasing interest in online communities and their ways of communicating, including multi-user computer games and Second Life (St.Clair and Phipps, 2008).

A group of researchers based at the Institute for Advanced Studies at the University of Lancaster in the UK has spent many years building on the initial insights of new literacy studies. In particular, the Lancaster School has helped to build up a library of ethnographic descriptions of the way people actually use reading and writing in their everyday lives (Barton and Hamilton, 1998; Barton, Hamilton and Ivanic, 2000). They have explored two key concepts of new literacy studies in particular depth. One is 'literacy events,' or occasions where the written word has a part to play, such as reading a story to children or the shopping reminder mentioned above. The second is 'literacy practices' or the 'common patterns in using reading and writing in any situation and people bring their cultural knowledge to an activity' (Barton, 1994, p. 188). People draw from their literacy practices in any given literacy event, such as the exaggerated tones people use when reading to children. This distinction usefully breaks down the larger concept of literacy into smaller chunks that can be analysed and understood within a specific context.

Coming back to the question of whether reading a report at work is different from reading the newspaper at home, the social practices approach suggests that the answer is very positively yes. First of all, they are clearly different literacy events, taking place in a different context for a different purpose and with a different expected outcome. In the case of the report, the aim is to gather information to be acted upon in a work setting, so identifying and retaining the main information is crucial. When reading a newspaper the reader can be driven far more strongly by their own interests, and it is less important to filter and remember particular aspects of the information. This suggests that the literacy practices used may be significantly different. When I read a report at work, for example, I tend to have a pencil to mark particular sections and to use the indexing regularly. Reading a newspaper I often talk to people around me, skip parts, and also tend to read the comics first. So while the broadest notion of getting meaning from written language is shared by both examples, the actual processes and approaches are quite distinct.

As mentioned earlier, the social practices approach to literacy, even though it dismisses the notion that some types of literacy are inherently more valuable than others, does recognise that some forms have more social power than others (Crowther, Hamilton and Tett, 2001). Being able to write in perfect 'reportese' enhances the probability that an individual's writing will be taken seriously, as does correct spelling and grammar. Despite the growing acceptance of non-standard English in novels, films and plays, it still seems to carry little weight with policymakers. There are also pragmatic concerns – if I were to write this book in a language based on my native Glaswegian it might well seriously impact the ability of readers to plough through it. Similarly, when reading, there are many examples of language designed to function as a coded representation of the intended meaning, such as the use of the word 'interesting' to mean 'incredibly dull and badly expressed.' Readers who do not have access to the coding schema appropriate to the specific context are likely to miss a great deal of what is being said.

One implication of the social practices approach is that the idea of a single continuum of literacy skill does not work very well. It makes more sense to think of a set of skills that are relevant to a given situation. In the United States, there was an interesting attempt to take this insight seriously in the assessment of literacy learning. The Equipped for the Future (EFF) initiative was developed in response to a General Accounting Office report on adult literacy programmes that suggested the field lacked clearly defined purposes and outcomes (EFF, 2004). The people involved in creating the Equipped for the Future initiative were interested in seeing if it were possible to come up with a set of agreed standards for what an adult should be able to do to be considered literate. They talked to over one thousand literacy learners and many academics involved in the field, ending up with a series of role maps going far beyond traditional views of literacy as reading and writing. The key roles were adult as worker, adult as citizen and community member and adult as parent and family member. Each of these roles had a broad set of responsibilities associated with it, such as 'promote family members' growth and development: family members support the growth and development of all family members, including themselves' within the parent and family member role. The responsibilities had key activities associated with them, with five in the case of promoting family members' growth.

Equipped for the Future recognises many of the central values of the social practices approach. It clearly responds to the importance of multi-literacies, and leads with the idea of what people want to be able to do rather than suggesting that there is a linear, abstract continuum between illiteracy and literacy in adults. EFF breaks down literacy into four major domains and a number of sub-domains, arguing that literacy abilities can be present in each of these different domains in a different form and with a different degree of competence. The notion that responsibilities and activities can be identified in advance for all adults is less compatible with the new literacy studies perspective, but nonetheless the EFF framework and materials represent a concrete attempt to put social practices into action. Unfortunately, when the US Federal government wanted to develop a national system of literacy progress indicators, they turned away from Equipped for the Future to a mechanism that simply collates test results, and Equipped for the Future has languished since the early 2000s.

Social practices perspectives on literacies have been around for about thirty years now, and it seems reasonable to take stock of the work that has been done. There have been a number of important analytical insights developed within this field building on the political commitments discussed earlier. One is a set of ideas around the communicative orders arising from modern capitalism, such as a new work order (Gee, Hull and Lankshear, 1996), a new communicative order (Street, 2004) and new ways to look at the demands of academic literacies (Lea and Street, 2006). A key part of these analyses has been the increasing inclusion of semiotic markers within the fold of literacy studies, so that computer icons, graffiti and everyday graphics are seen as a form of written language.

Social practices perspectives have a great deal to offer our understanding of literacies as they are experienced by the individuals who use them, and have underpinned the creation of extensive ethnographic accounts of literacies in practice. It remains almost silent, however, on the questions surrounding how people actually consume and produce text. Social practice approaches remain uninterested in the mechanics of reading and writing, generally treating these areas as 'black boxes' about which it is difficult to know anything. In doing so, I believe that social practices approaches perpetuate the very division between individuals and social factors that they are designed to erase.

This can create problems for educators who wish to adopt a social practices approach as it does not really address how literacy practices are learned and developed at any length nor provide any guidance on effective teaching. Even when social practices researchers attempt explicitly to tackle this issue head on, they often end up restating their perspective and presenting models rather than providing educators with clear guidance. For example, Street, writing about academic literacies, suggests that

> . . . if subject tutors address the apparent common-sense discourses of their
> own discipline, they may come to question what remains taken for granted

whilst hidden. Teaching writing becomes not just a technical aside, to be dealt with before the real work of developing disciplinary knowledge can proceed but instead becomes part of the reflection upon and change in disciplinary knowledge itself. (2004, p. 16)

It is not clear how this differs from what good tutors teaching critical awareness would already be doing with their students. I am sure that many educators would point out that this is really a restatement of the key ideas of content area literacy, a subject that has been included in teacher education for many years. Finally, it provides limited guidance on how teachers take themselves and students through the reflective process.

While issues of power are recognised in the new literacy studies, the implications of these issues for the theorisation of literacy seem to be quite underdeveloped. For example, should all literacy learners, at any stage of life and from any social background, have a chance to learn narrowly defined high status forms of literacy, or should the notion of high status literacy be broadened or perhaps resisted? The tendency not to develop clear approaches to such issues can be seen as a weakness of much social practice theorising.

What social practices views do extremely well is emphasise the variety of ways to use literacy and the diversity of values underpinning them. In these aspects they can be seen to reflect the linguistic orientation of the early years. Potentially literacy practices could provide enormously valuable insights into the way people create meanings from texts and create their schemata, though this has been rarely addressed directly. Where the new literacy studies has been less successful is making the move from linguistic theory to educational framework, and it follows from this that the social practices theories tend to be less useful for thinking through the outcomes of learning literacy.

Conclusion

The three views presented here are, on first glance, not very compatible. The functional view is designed to be highly pragmatic, respectful of people and what they want to do with literacy. Functional views are less interested in what literacy is, and more concerned with what can be done with it. They usefully emphasise the relativism of literacy and its contextual nature, and remind us that application matters. At the same time, functional views are extremely open to domination by ideas that probably are not compatible with its original conception, such as the notion that 'functional' means 'employment-focused.'

The mental operations view offers some fascinating and important insights – not least into the number of complex manipulations that have to come together to enable a person to make sense of text. There is a troubling tendency to overlook the processes involved in writing, and also a huge range of unanswered questions about the step between perception and understanding. The insights that effective literacy requires a degree of automaticity between mutually supportive operation, and that fluent reading uses a high degree of prediction are critical reminders that there is a substantial component of specific, learnable activity in literacy.

The social practices view underlines the way in which literacy, or literacies, operate in different contexts. To some extent, the social practices view is starting to answer some of the questions associated with the mental operations and the functional view by focusing so strongly on the way that meaning develops within a context. There is a tendency in some social practice writing to underemphasise the part that mental operations play in literacy, and the instructional implications have not yet been fully worked out. The idea that literacy is irreducibly social is an insight with implications across the literacy field.

The next chapter presents a model of literacy that builds on each of these views, pulling them together and showing how the strengths and weaknesses of each are complementary. I call this model the 'capabilities' approach to literacy, and will be applying it throughout the rest of the book.

CHAPTER TWO

Literacies as capabilities

The ideas around literacy are highly contested, which makes it difficult to adopt any existing approach as a way to understand the effects of literacy learning in a theoretically robust way that is underpinned by good evidence from existing research. To address this, I have developed a model I call the 'capabilities approach,' with the aim of bringing together the key ideas from the functional, mental operations and social practices perspectives into a single well-informed way to think about the outcomes of literacy education. This model is only a heuristic for thinking about why literacy matters – it is not meant as an attempt to build a unified theory of literacy.

Creating a universal theory of literacy would be very challenging given the many layers of subtle difference between the three perspectives. The less ambitious desire to create a model to capture how literacies play out in people's lives can be achieved, however, by combining their insights to create a well-informed and coherent model of the ways cognitive skills help people to work meaningfully with written texts in different social settings. I have adopted the term 'capability' to emphasise the pragmatic nature of the outcomes to be discussed, which are focused on what people can do and achieve with their literacies. Based on this idea, the definition of a literacy capability used throughout this discussion is 'the ability to achieve a desired purpose by applying appropriate skills in a specific situation of engagement with texts.'

The idea of capabilities has become quite popular in social theory over the last few years, largely because of the work of Sen (1979). Walker (2005) summarises Sen's capability approach very well:

33

> *Put simply, the capability approach is about freedom and the development of an environment suitable for human flourishing. Capability refers to what people are actually able to be and do, rather than to what resources they have access to. It focuses on developing people's capability to choose a life that they have reason to value. Freedom and capabilities cannot be separated. The opportunities to develop capabilities and the process of deciding collectively on valuable capabilities both require and produce freedom (pp. 103–104).*

There are two aspects of the literacy capability model that reflect Sen's approach. The first is the view that capabilities are concerned with what people – individual and collectively – can actually do. The second is that literacy capabilities can contribute to the quality of people's lives, and freedom is a critical aspect of that contribution. So while the approach to literacy described here is not based on Sen's work, it is certainly consistent with it.

The outcomes of literacy discussed in this book are based on capabilities. Where people are able to achieve their purpose then some form of outcome has been achieved. These purposes could range from reading a newspaper to writing a novel to planning a wedding to understanding Kant. Some people could view putting purposes so centrally as making the capabilities model very pragmatic and even functional, but it is intended to recognise the importance of people's desires and aims in their use of literacy skills. All three approaches to literacy discussed in the last chapter have a great deal to offer in creating a rich framework for understanding this use.

This model reflects a growing interest in breaking down the tensions between different views of literacy. Green and Howard (2007) discuss the compatibility of skills-based and social practices approaches to literacy using the English and Scottish literacy systems as examples of each. As with much policy-based analysis, their emphasis is more on skills as demonstrable (and testable) abilities and less on the mental operations underpinning them. However, as they consider approaches to modelling ways of teaching and learning literacy they make it clear that existing ways of thinking about what it means to be literate could benefit from development. One of the key requirements is a way to bridge across different approaches to literacy.

Literacy as capability

A literacy capability is the ability to achieve a desired purpose by apply-ing appropriate skills in a specific situation of engagement with texts. Where there is a capability, the person is able to do what they want to do, whether at home, in the workplace, in a social or political context or as a support to further learning. Put the other way round, lack of capability can prevent people from doing what they want to do. A really simple exam-ple is the experience of being in a country or even an area of a modern city where you cannot read the language. Lacking literacy capability makes it more difficult to find the grocery store or identify a taxi.

This model has several significant characteristics. It attempts to restrict the notion of literacy to written language, because while references to musical literacy or media literacy suggest some interesting possibilities there is not a great deal of research in these areas as yet. It is interesting to note that Street, who was one of the original proponents of a multilit-eracies approach, has recently argued that the notion of literacies has become too diluted, and needs to be pulled back to reading and writing (Street, 2004). The definition applied in this discussion uses the notion of 'engagement with texts' in order to include both the consumption and production of the written word. Individuals engage with texts whenever they read, write or use written calculations.

The capability model also recognises the importance of the context in which text engagement takes place in defining and shaping literacy, and makes no attempt to universalise a particular level or form of per-formance. At the same time, the definition is clear about the existence and importance of skills in supporting text engagement and underlines the importance of learning and practicing specific strategies. The notion of functional literacy provides a background to the definition to the extent that appropriate application will be functional, in the sense of useful, for the individual in question. Literacy that applies skills appropriately is an effective way to communicate ideas, either with others or with yourself in the future.

The capabilities model brings together two key factors in the process of engaging with a text. One is that the reader or writer has the skills necessary to do what they want to do with the text. There are many ways that skills could fall short, ranging from perceptual issues to lack of knowl-edge. For example, I would fall at this hurdle if asked to read Italian or Arabic because I simply do not have the skills. In the first case I would recognise the letters but not get any meaning from the text, in the second the text might as well be purely artistic shapes because I don't know Arabic letter forms. Without a set of skills and mental operations to bring to bear upon the written word the outcome is incomprehension. These skills and operations are not innate to humans and must be learned consciously or unconsciously – probably a bit of both in most cases.

The second factor of the model is the appropriateness of the skills used. In the section on social practices I mentioned Labov's contention that everybody uses multiple forms of language, and this holds true for literacy as well. Engagement with text involves recognition of the context, probably not always on a conscious level, and activation of the set of cognitive skills most likely to achieve the intended purposes. There are different sets of demands and processes involved in reading a report at work and the newspaper at home, or in setting up a lathe and baking a cake. Application of an inappropriate set of skills may lead once more to incomprehension or failure to achieve a desired purpose.

There is no evidence that people go into a situation, analyse it, work out which skills they will need and then call on them. If there is anything we have learned about human literacy use (and thinking in general) over the last few decades it is that processes are complicated, and simple mechanistic models tend not to help very much. However, purely as a metaphor we can imagine a fruit bowl. The fruit are the cognitive literacy skills. At one time somebody might need an apple and a banana to achieve their purpose, and at other times they might need a banana and an orange. If those fruit are present, they have the capability required in that situation; if they are missing for any reason, or the person accidently ends up with two bananas, then they do not have the capability to achieve their purpose. The point of this metaphor is to underline a simple point – the more fruit people have, the more likely they are to have capability in a given situation. In terms of literacies, if a wider a range of literacy practices are available to the individual, the more they will be able to attain their purpose even when faced with novel situations with unpredictable demands.

The capability model can help to explain some of the challenges of second language literacy, where learning the mechanics of a language has to be accompanied by learning the cultural context within which it operates. For many international students in British universities, the difficulty is not necessarily writing in English, but learning the cultural peculiarities that accompany academic writing in that context. This can apply as much to people who have always spoken English as their first language but do not have experience of the appropriate application of that language because of class background or unfamiliarity with the context. People who enter university programmes have to learn a new form of reading and writing to achieve success in the programme, and this can be a central part of learning to navigate the complex university academic and social systems (Tett, 2000; Lea and Street, 2006).

The model provides a concept of literacy rich enough to capture the psycho-social complexity of real-life text use. It does not dismiss or overlook any of the factors contributing to textual engagement – surely one of the most challenging and layered of all human cognitive activities. Instead it attempts to recognise the complexities and work with literacy in its own terms, as an irreducibly complicated, tangled, multi-faceted set of activities.

Capabilities and outcomes

The relationship between capabilities and outcomes in our working model is relatively straightforward, and is shown in Diagram 2.

In the centre of this diagram sit the cognitive processes associated with literacy and the skills they represent. As discussed earlier there are

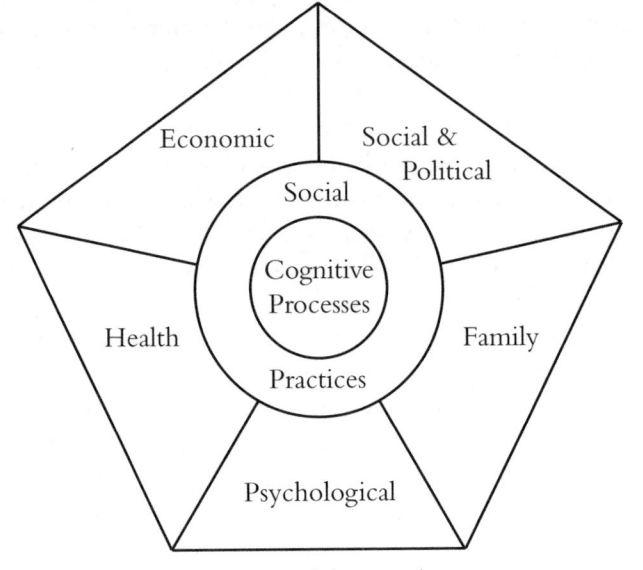

Diagram 2: Capabilities and outcomes

many of these, and they sit in a complex relationship to each other with high degrees of inter-dependence. The next ring out is the situations in which the skills are applied through exercise of social practices. This ring could be divided into different areas, such as home life, work life, and so on, though it probably it does not work in such a clear way. It seems likely that different settings overlap in their demands and that the divisions are very much more fuzzy. These areas do not map clearly onto either the skills in the central ring or the outcome areas in the outer ring. The outer ring is the range of outcomes in given situations, and even though this diagram (and this book) limits outcomes to five areas, there may well be many others and many other ways to divide them up. One of the key points is that capabilities represent pathways through the diagram linking the three layers, and they are far from predictable because they are individual and contextual.

To understand the outcomes of literacy, it is necessary to look at which capabilities are represented in each of the five sectors. The model is a little artificial, in that it is easy to imagine outcomes that could bridge between the sectors, such as economic outcomes that lead to stronger family life. Nonetheless, it is useful to imagine them separately because that is the way the vast majority of evidence is arranged and because even where outcomes are linked there is likely to be a primary outcome leading to others. So, for example, the primary outcome may be attaining new employment due to demonstrating a particular literacy capability, which then leads to the secondary outcome of more family-friendly working conditions.

The model makes the definition and assessment of the effects of literacy learning both more challenging and more intriguing. Analysis becomes much more open and complex than the process of identifying a direct link between literacy learning and a given outcome. The model suggests that literacy learning will not lead to a single outcome, but enhance a pool of literacy practices that are part of a loosely coupled system leading to potential outcomes. To continue with the slightly silly fruit metaphor, adding a banana to the bowl can contribute to a wide range of recipes. This means that the task of examining and understanding the implications of text use means looking at various areas of outcome and trying to understand the effect that literacy learning may have in that area, and the possible strength of these effects. Instead of assuming that literacy leads to a particular outcome in a linear and predictable way, the sort of claim made when people talk about 'better' literacy skills leading to higher wages, it is necessary to consider a range of possible ways the acquisition and application of skills may play out.

It is probably useful to illustrate this more clearly with a concrete example. Suppose that we are interested in people's health outcomes and how literacy learning can improve them, which is an area attracting a lot of interest over the last few years. One way to do this would be to look at people's measured literacy skills and try to link them to health outcomes. For many reasons I'll discuss in the next chapter, this is a deceptively difficult task, but even in a perfect world it is easy to think up a couple of reasons why this relationship might be difficult to pin down. One might be that measured literacy skills are associated with greater income, and people with greater income may have better health outcomes. It is possible to assume that a direct link exists when really it is a common underlying factor at work. Or perhaps there are lots of people who do not use health services very regularly, making it very hard to say anything about their health status. We cannot assume that they are in perfect health, since they might not have health coverage (in the United States in particular) or be self-managing chronic conditions effectively. How would we measure these people's health and the role of literacies within it? It is incredibly difficult to pin down the direct link between text use and health.

However, it is possible to have a look at what happens when people are able to apply the appropriate capabilities to managing their health. We cannot say with any certainty that people with 'higher levels of skills are able to achieve specific health outcomes,' but we can perhaps say something along the lines of 'when they need to apply them to achieve health outcomes, people with stronger capabilities tend to achieve better results.' Of course, this does not address the question of a possible common factor underlying health and literacy, but it does allow for a strong argument to be made that *without* the capability to apply in a specific situation, the outcomes will not be strong. The details of this argument will be explored in more depth in the next chapter, but if it can be accepted provisionally for now, it changes how we think about the effects of literacy learning.

In essence I suggest that different contexts require different sets of abilities. Social practices are the result of specific necessary skills being applied to a specific context. In order to understand the way text use is playing out, it is essential to consider both. An example from my own life can illustrate this. A few years ago, while living in Texas, I was involved in making health decisions for my infant son. I knew very little about American health care and even less about babies, but I am a broad reader and a reasonably well-trained researcher. I was able to take my facility with reading and my familiarity with assessing evidence (both literacy skills) and apply them reasonably effectively to the new domain of infant health. Both the health outcome and my purpose (along with my wife and other family members) were to develop the knowledge needed to ensure my son was safe and well looked after. This purpose was attained partly because I was able to access and apply appropriate skills for the situation.

So when we ask broad questions about the effects of literacy learning we need to know about the potential outcomes in any given area. It is misleading to ask what the outcomes definitely *will* be simply because people may have no need to situate their skills within that context. If my wife and I had not had a child I would not have needed to learn about infant health. The focus must be on what capabilities can bring to outcomes in a given area when the appropriate skills are present and are applied. The potential of literacy can only be understood when what it can bring to a given context is explored and the temptation to look for absolute statements is resisted.

It could be seen as a shortcoming of the approach that no overarching and indisputable cause-effect relationship is being proposed, but I believe that it is important to recognise that there is no pre-determination in the use of literacy by an individual or a group of individuals. When a person learns to read and write, whether as a young person or an adult, the uses they will have for these abilities is unpredictable and depends on the situations they will face in their future life. To base analysis of literacy outcomes in a deterministic framework tends to make the analysis less useful, I suggest, because it implies that every literacy learner will face a standard set of situations in which to apply their abilities. It seems far more reflective of people's life experiences to allow for as much diversity as possible in the need for, and expression of, literacy abilities.

Capabilities in action

A very simplified example of a typical application of this model might be that a person finds themselves in a literacy setting of some sort. They recognise that specific skills and abilities are needed to attain their aims in the specific situation and 'reach' for them. If they are available then the capability is demonstrated and all is well. If not, then the capability does not come about and the person's aims are likely to be unrealised.

As an example, I like to think about a recent experience I had on a train from London to Glasgow. All I had available to read were the sports pages from that day's *Daily Mail*. I think 'well, I'm a reasonably intelligent sort of person, I can make sense of this' and picked it up. For authenticity I have copied a genuine sports headline from the *Daily Mail*: 'Spurs eye Maxi, Everton back in for City's Jo, tug of war for Hammer Ashton, Sol reaches for parasol and who's going Balde?' (Jones, 2009). At this point my decades of reading totally failed me. I genuinely had no idea what this meant, except in the most general sense. Therefore, in this case, I simply could not demonstrate the appropriate literacy skills and could claim no capability whatsoever. While not the end of the world, I did experience a small degree of frustration. It was very possible that somebody else on the train could translate this for me without a second thought, or I could have called my friend Martin who follows English football avidly.

This example illustrates the way that literacy capabilities are not one set of abilities, but a network of diverse capacities or skills driven to some degree by the interests of those who display them. The skills and their application are also learnable – it is likely that if it mattered to me, I could understand the headline with a bit of study. So the acknowledgement that capabilities can be learned if and when the situation calls for them is an important aspect of literacy, and helps to avoid pessimism about people's capabilities. Capabilities are not fixed, but are capable of great change.

The example also hints at another aspect of literacy. People can often adjust their lives to emphasise the literacies that are of interest to them and de-emphasise others. I have reasonably strong capabilities in academic reading and writing because they are a big part of my life, but I am not interested in English football. I have arranged my engagement with text to recognise what I am interested in, and I believe in many contexts this is true of other people. This potentially explains some of the biggest questions of literacy and numeracy work – why do so few people ever say they are unhappy with their capabilities or that they represent a barrier for them? Why do more people not choose to get involved in upgrading their capabilities when many countries have some form of free provision? The answer appears to be that recognition of a capability requiring development only occurs *within* the situation where it is needed. As long as I avoid tabloid sports pages, I need never again think about the appalling gap in my literacy. In other words, people can adjust their engagement with text to match their interests and capabilities.

In some ways this could sound negative, as if people were somehow settling for less than their due, and this is an important political question for educators. If we accept the notion that a larger range of abilities leads to enhanced capability in a range of situations, and therefore to greater ability for individuals and communities to control their lives, it leads to an argument for the value of people working continually on expanding their abilities. As an educator, I find that quite a convincing argument, and would also tend to support the converse position that denying people the chance to expand their abilities is a form of deprivation. However, the step from thinking that learning is a good thing to seeing it as something people have a duty to do is not acceptable, even though it drives a great deal of international adult education policy (Coffield, 1999). It seems to me that educators must avoid hubris, and remember that people are the best judges of their own lives. There is a balance to be struck between making sure that people can get support with literacies when they need and want it and the understanding that some people who could potentially make good use of such support may choose not to take advantage of it.

In general people act purposively whatever their literacy abilities. They call on their friends, colleagues and family for support when they come across a difficulty, and work out how to handle the challenge. As long as they can achieve their goals, one way or another, then why would they attend classes? Over thirty years ago, Knowles (1980) was pointing out that adults need a reason to learn, whether in classes or informal settings. This certainly goes some way to explain the consistent finding within literacy research that people tend to get involved in more formal upgrading when there is a specific need for it (such as a promotion at work) but that people tend to be really quite bad at attending programmes for the length of time necessary to attain the goals educators would like for them (Reder, 2009). Rather than staying until they complete a level or gain a certificate, they often learn what they need to learn and do not come back until the next time they need to learn something. The capabilities model supports this idea, suggesting that people will experience a need to expand their literacy repertoire when they are in a context where their practices do not allow them to achieve their purpose. The driver for literacies learning is dissonance between what is needed in a given situation and what is available to the individual.

It is also very important not to think of Western education and literacy as the global normal. The situation in a place like sub-Saharan Africa is quite different. While the developed economies have a huge diversity of educational opportunities available and a key issue is who benefits from them, in the developing world the supply of education itself is a critical issue. In many developing economies there is seriously limited access to literacy and numeracy capabilities of any sort, partly because primary education is not universal, and this is a particularly important issue for females. In the Central African Republic, the literacy rate is 49 per cent – 65 per cent for males and 33 per cent for females (UNESCO, 2009). While it is not always clear how global reports assess literacy they often rely on years of schooling and given the variable quality of education across the world it is quite possible that the proportion of people who consider themselves literate is lower than these figures suggest. The capabilities model can still be useful here, though the emphasis may be different.

In many developing economies limited literacy capabilities may not necessarily prevent people from achieving their purposes. While the developed economies are often literacy rich, with lots of environmental text, this is not always the case in the developing world. This means that having extensive literacy capabilities may not be as directly useful in this context, and that the dissonance between purpose and abilities may not arise as often as in a more text-based society. However, where texts are used in the developing economies they often function as forms of social control, allowing governments and aid agencies to conduct their work in a less overt fashion than might otherwise be the case. Literacy education in these situations often works within enormous tension between the need to provide people with the ability to act politically, which may require education in a dominant language, and the need to support people's resistance to cultural colonisation, which may require education in a local language (Maruatona and Cervero, 2004). The capabilities model provides a way to think through these complexities a little, and perhaps an opportunity to start to identify the key capabilities and the abilities that support them.

Despite the huge difference in the significance of the examples, I hope that they show that the model of literacy I have discussed has wide applicability, and can help to make some sense of the disparate circumstances in which people recognise a need to strengthen their literacy capabilities.

Conclusion

This chapter has laid out the view of literacy that underpins this book. In some ways, it is a challenging view because it refuses to provide a simple, linear perspective that can be tested with absolute assurance. The view that literacy is the appropriate application of skills in specific situations of engagement with texts leaves many definitional complexities deliberately unresolved, but it does imply very clearly that there are more effective ways to apply skills in any context. The measure of that effectiveness is simply the ability of the person using the skills to achieve their purposes and their communicative goals – their capability.

The capabilities model does not lead to concrete statements about the value of literacy learning in terms of an external measure such as income or productivity. Instead it suggests that the type of questions we have to ask about literacy are 'what does literacy allow us to do?' and 'what does less access to literacy prevent us from doing?' When we look at literacy from this perspective our interest is not a set of rigid outcomes but the potential effects of these capabilities. While this seems very open, it also recognises the complexity and diversity of literacy in use.

In the following chapter we step back from the theorisation of literacy and start to look at the ways in which the outcomes of social programmes are assessed. If we are to understand the effects of literacy, it is important to look at how the effects of programmes more generally are conceived and measured, and what we can learn from this for literacy.

CHAPTER THREE

Understanding outcomes

If we are going to look at questions around the effects of literacy learning we need some way to connect the process of learning to the effects. While this is not necessarily evaluation in the sense of testing the outcomes of a specific activity, many of the same questions arise as in the evaluation of other social programmes. In addition, a great deal of the data that we will be examining over the course of the discussion will be derived from evaluations. Understanding and assessing the meaning of that data will be easier the more we know about the way evaluation works.

Evaluation, at its heart, is the process of assigning value to an activity. For example, we might want to look at book groups and see if they lead people to become interested in continuing their education in some way. This would be an attempt to assess the value of book groups in contributing to that specific outcome. On the face of it, this should be a simple process – it surely cannot be that difficult to take some type of activity and work out how it affects peoples' knowledge and lives. Unfortunately, it is a lot harder than it seems, and there is a large and controversial body of work addressing the problems of evaluation. Knowing a little about this can help us to make sense of the different approaches taken by different evaluation efforts and the claims they make about the effects of programmes.

When people talk about evaluation they use it in a number of distinct ways. One is referring to the effects of learning on an individual – in this case a driving test is an evaluation of the person's ability to complete those tasks. In order to be as clear as possible, I'll refer to this type of evaluation as assessment. There are lots of issues around assessment of literacy usage, and I'll look at them in the next chapter. Another use of evaluation, and the one to be discussed in the present chapter, is to look at the general effect of a given programme. It would be really useful if the assessment results of all the people in a given programme could be added up and produce an overall programme evaluation, but unfortunately this is not a very good way to evaluate programmes, for reasons I'll discuss later.

The interest in looking carefully at the evidence for the effects of social programmes in terms of demonstrable outcomes is relatively recent. For a long time, programmes like education were not especially strongly monitored for their outcomes, and it was assumed that trying to create a high quality process would ensure that the results were acceptable. In other words, far more attention was paid to inputs and process than to the outputs. This is where structures like old-fashioned school inspections came in. Experts would come into classrooms and watch what was going on, and if it seemed to demonstrate competence then the teacher and the school were considered to have met the standards. The exam results at the end of the schooling process were assumed to represent the spread of ability fairly, given that all the students had received relatively equal amounts of good quality teaching. This approach to evaluation valued the professionalism of the teachers and the quality of the instruction they could offer.

This approach relies on a number of assumptions. The first is that educators are reliable and competent people who are capable of doing a good job of teaching the learners. The second is that the test at the end of the programme reflects ability in an unbiased and reasonably accurate way. The third assumption is that the education students receive from school, as reflected in examination outcomes, is socially desirable and useful. In the current climate for social programmes and education, none of these assumptions can really be accepted at face value. They have been replaced with a set of questions: are teachers doing a good job? Are the tests useful? Does this programme teach people what they need to know?

The new approach to social services has resulted in a situation referred to as 'the audit society' (Power, 1999), and can be summarised in the idea that everybody keeps an eye on everybody else's performance. So as a university teacher and writer my performance is reviewed by my colleagues, my students and my line managers, while I review their performance in turn. Among the many effects of this mutual surveillance is a drive towards clarity in expectations. After all, if there is so much judging going on, everybody wants to know exactly how they will be judged and on exactly what grounds. One result of the audit culture is the need to focus on the demonstrable outcomes of any activity, and to express those outcomes in clear, unambiguous language.

These developments have had enormous effects on the work of educational programmes, and indeed on institutions more generally. Patton (1999) suggests that the requirement of the audit society to demonstrate performance in terms of outcomes has brought about a crisis for many organisations:

> *In my judgement, the challenge of using evaluation in appropriate and meaningful ways represents . . . a crisis in institutional arrangements. How evaluations are used affects the spending of billions of dollars to fight problems of poverty, disease, ignorance, joblessness, mental anguish, crime, hunger, and inequality. How are programmes that combat these societal ills to be judged? How does one distinguish effective from ineffective programmes? (p. 4)*

The aim of this book is not to discuss processes of evaluation and accountability in adult literacy education, though they have changed the field considerably over the last few years (St.Clair and Belzer, 2007). The increased audit demands in literacy education are relevant to this book's central question about the lifelong effects of literacy learning in two ways. Firstly, accountability frameworks have helped to clarify the claims that are made for the effects of literacy learning and to provide data on those claims. For example, the large scale analyses of household data that are now available are primarily inspired by the need to provide evidence that literacy makes a difference. These data sets can contribute directly to our understanding of the question. Secondly, the way audit demands are framed can help us to understand the shortcomings of any particular approach to understanding the effects of literacy, leading to a more sophisticated reading of the data available to us.

In this chapter I discuss the process of evaluating outcomes from different perspectives in some detail. This is simply because so much of the evidence on the effects of literacy is derived from evaluation procedures or accountability mechanisms and it is crucial to approach them from an informed viewpoint. When we try to understand what a particular form of learning has to offer it is useful to start by considering how we can frame the outcomes and how they can then be linked back to the learning itself. Unfortunately, this is not nearly as easy as it sounds like it should be.

47

The evaluation problem

One of most difficult challenges in understanding the effects of literacy learning can be summarised as 'the evaluation problem' (Styles, 2009). In the clearest case of this problem, there are three initial assumptions:

1. There is a specific population of individuals at whom the intervention is aimed.
2. Any improvements in the educational outcomes of the target individuals as a result of the intervention are measurable.
3. The evaluation needs to discern the effect of the intervention on the outcome measure of interest. (Styles, 2009, p.85)

So the aim of evaluation is to capture the effect of the intervention within the intended population. This seems extremely clear. However, to be really accurate, it is important to be certain about what effects come from the intervention and what comes from something else completely outside the scope of the programme. For example, what if a Spanish speaking adult simultaneously starts attending a programme to learn English and starts a new job where all her colleagues speak only English? It would be surprising if her English did not improve quite dramatically, but would it be reasonable for the programme to claim the credit for that improvement? I would suggest not, but at the same time the programme may well have contributed something.

In a perfect world, the way to deal with this would be to clone the individual and have one clone just start the new job while the other attended the programme. Then the progress of the two could be compared and we could detect with some confidence the contributions of the programme, and those from general life experience. The unfortunate fact that we cannot clone people is what gives rise to the evaluation problem. It can be summarised as the impossibility of knowing what somebody would have learned if they had not attended the programme.

In economics this is known as the counter-factual, the 'what if?' situation. An example of this in practice is the idea of the opportunity cost of an activity, which looks at what a person gives up to do something rather than the cost of the activity itself. So if I give up a well-paid job to spend three years as an apprentice tree surgeon, the opportunity cost of that activity is three times my original salary minus whatever I make as an apprentice. In economic terms this kind of calculation can be tricky to get right even though the concept behind it is quite straightforward.

In other areas of life, including education, the counter-factual is far harder to understand. Yet it is crucial to comprehend it to some degree in order to appreciate the value of a programme, especially as the expectations for programmes to demonstrate their value grow. Suppose that a person has been in a literacy programme for a year and has developed certain skills over that time. The key evaluation question is whether that person could have developed more skills, or developed them more fully, in a different situation. Huge numbers of factors can play into this question. It is possible that they would have learned more by attending more hours per week, or by being involved in a family literacy programme. Perhaps an online course would have been better, if they had access to a computer and broadband, or they would have been happier in a group setting rather than with an individual tutor. There are endless sets of factors that have to be considered in assigning a value to the programme that learner experienced. And yet programmes are expected to demonstrate that their way of doing things is not only valuable, but more valuable than potential alternatives.

When the effects of literacy learning are examined, it is important to have a way to justify the conclusions drawn. There are many anecdotal stories about the benefits of literacy learning, and on a human level these are interesting and persuasive. They should not be dismissed lightly. However, they may not be entirely persuasive when trying to make the argument to a policymaker that funds should be allocated to adult literacy programmes. One of the most significant issues of the field is that so many of the tutors are either part-time or volunteer, and very often have little initial training or ongoing professional development. It may make more sense to have a group of full-time professional tutors instead, as they would be able to build up a strong set of professional skills. Making this argument would rely on a systematic demonstration that the more expensive full-time tutors would help literacy learners to learn more effectively, and that would involve going beyond anecdotes. The requirements are higher still when it comes to looking at the effects of literacy learning itself.

So what is needed is a way to link certain outcomes back to literacy learning in a credible and valid way. Very many effects are claimed for literacy learning and often they imply different ways of justifying the claim. Economic effects are quite different from the effects of literacy on self-

49

confidence or political engagement, for example, and the way they have to be framed varies significantly. There is no universal way of assessing the effects of literacy that will capture all the possible outcomes in a single measure or statement. Instead, there is a need to use methods that are appropriate for the specific effect to look at each possible set of outcomes.

There have been many different approaches to evaluation over the last several decades, and in this chapter there is no room to look at them all. What I have tried to do is to identify and examine the broad perspectives that seem to have had the most impact in education. These are quantitative approaches, based on statistical methods; qualitative approaches, often based on interviews and observations; and logic models. The last approach to evaluation is relatively new, but highly promising. Each of these approaches addresses the evaluation problem in a slightly different way, and is perhaps better suited to different effects. Before looking at them in more depth, however, it is useful to think about what we can say about cause and effect in educational programmes.

Correlation is not causation

One of the biggest challenges in working out the effects of any form of social or educational programme is the question of cause and effect. Unfortunately, this would also be one of the most useful things to be able to comment upon. It would help us to make lots of important policy and educational decisions if we could say with confidence that poor school performance, for example, was due to a single cause such as a poor breakfast. Sometimes the desirability of being able to attach a cause to something outweighs the caution that we should be bringing to these questions, and all too often, in the newspapers and beyond, spurious claims of causation are presented as fact. This is quite unhelpful, especially when it refers to relationships about which we simply cannot know enough to make clear causational claims.

The temptation to claim clear understanding of causation applies on both sides of social issues such as ill health or limited literacy; where they come from and to how we can best respond to them. A fairly common explanation that is given for an adult having limited literacy capabilities is that they grew up in a family without much knowledge of education and therefore lacked the confidence needed to learn in a classroom. This contains within it a very strong causational claim that the individual's limited literacy was caused directly by their lack of confidence and indirectly by their family circumstance. An educator who claims that since coming to adult learning classes the individual has grown in confidence and is beginning to expand their competence in literacy is also making a strong causational claim. While it would simplify programme planning a great deal if these claims were accurate, they are really not rigorous enough to base broad decisions on. While they are certainly observable facts that the person did grow up in such a family and has changed since coming to the programme, this does not tell us a great deal about the causes of each process.

Perhaps the biggest single mistake in trying to understand how social issues arise and how they can be addressed is to confuse correlation and causation. Correlation refers to the tendency of two things to vary together, such as ethnicity and school results. In the United States, a typical pattern is for African American and Hispanic students to do less well on standardised tests than White Non-Hispanic students, while Asian students do better than anybody else. There have been attempts to attribute this directly to ethnicity and claim causation by suggesting that people of different ethnicities have different IQs (Eysenck, 1971). This claim is not only misguided morally but also because the observation that children from different backgrounds may tend to score differently on IQ tests does not provide any information about the reason for those differences.

Correlations can arise from repeated observations of behaviour that can be analysed from a qualitative or quantitative perspective; in the case of statistics the most commonly used measure is the Pearson r. The existence of a correlation tells us nothing more than that two things vary together. We cannot tell if one influences the other, if there are other factors at play, or whether this relationship will exist in other circumstances. In the case of ethnicity and educational outcomes, this means that we have no way of knowing if ethnicity 'causes' school results, if factors such as racism or socioeconomic status are at play, or if the results would be the same in a country that was predominantly Asian. The value of correlations is that they are relatively easy to identify and are very useful as starting points for questions as long as we bear in mind that correlations are not answers in themselves (Chafetz, 2005). Correlations should inspire us to ask us what is going on rather than assume that the relationship gives us the answer.

Causation is a great deal more difficult to identify. Causational statements are not based on probability, but on a directly identifiable link, with a clearly identified direction of influence. They are most often related to specific physical events such as 'the wind caused my dinghy to move to the West,' and become much trickier when humans are involved. Often causation is supported by statistical analysis of links between factors, but this requires great care:

> *There is very little having to do with human existence that can be proved, and a great deal that can almost be proved. Those things that can be proved get their proofs from scientific examination and understanding of the mechanics involved, resulting in an experiment, the results of which remain constant no matter how many times the experiment is done. Statistics can provide proof only when everything being measured is accounted for. (Chafetz, 2005, p. 137)*

This is an extremely high bar to set. Crano and Brewer (2002) suggest that the main problem in assessing causes in social research is that almost everything has naturally occurring covariates. This basically means that it is incredibly hard to isolate one factor of interest. These covariates have three forms: there could be a hidden third factor, there could be multidimensional causation, or there could be confusion about which are the independent variables (the inputs) and which are the dependent variables (the outcomes).

Some researchers will use more sophisticated statistics to attempt to demonstrate causation, such as multiple linear regression. This is a way to find out which of the variables influences the other. Whereas correlation just shows that the factors are linked, these techniques can show which one needs to be changed to change the other, and also how much of the change in the second factor is due to the change in the first factor or even a group of factors. This adds the possibility of prediction to analysis. However, there is an important point to make here. Because it can be shown that a change in a particular factor predicts a change in another factor does not mean that the change in the first factor explains the change in the second. As Crano and Brewer (2002) explain:

> *If, as we hold, valid explanation requires a comprehensive theoretical understanding of the relationship among variables, then the failing to distinguish between prediction and explanation is a dangerous practice. (p. 137)*

In other words, statistics can help us to check out the relationships that we think might exist, but cannot create theory simply through manipulation of numbers. This is partly because, once again, finding a relationship does not tell us everything that is going on in any particular situation – in technical terms, it demonstrates covariance but does not explain it. For example, we could well prove statistically that very nearly 100 per cent of bananas are yellow when they are ripe. This is clearly a good strong correlation, but tells us almost nothing about why bananas are yellow.

This insight has led to the development of even more sophisticated statistical techniques, such as structural equation modelling, that start from a theoretical statement and rigorously test its powers of prediction. But again, this does not prove that the causation is 'true': 'the confirmation of a hypothesised structural equations model lends confidence in its validity and, in some cases, helps to render implausible some alternative explanations.' (Crano and Brewer, 2002, p. 141) This is a long way from a proof.

This discussion could lead to despair about the possibility of ever having a proven causation in literacy learning, and that is probably a healthy reaction. Despite the desire of policymakers, funders, managers and educators to know for certain what the outcomes of a given programme are, it is unlikely that we can ever find a way to demonstrate these relationships unproblematically. It is important to be extremely cautious about claims that causation has been demonstrated in any form of social research, however helpful it would be if this were the case. Instead, it is important that we think carefully about the way literacy plays out across people's lives in subtle and partial ways, asking what literacy learning is associated with. This may not be the sound bite that makes the case for greater funding (though it could potentially lead to it) but is necessary in the effort to build a more nuanced and more robust understanding of literacy's effects.

When looking at the evidence for the effects of literacy learning, it is important to bear in mind the cautionary notes sounded in this and the previous section. Different approaches to capturing outcomes try to deal with the evaluation problem and the elusive nature of causation in different ways, and it is interesting to see what these are.

Statistical approaches

For many researchers, the best way to deal with these two problems is through the application of statistics. In a perfect world for statisticians, the entire population would be split completely randomly into two groups, and one group would have the chance to learn literacy while the other would not. This randomised controlled trial method deals with the evaluation problem and issues around causation because all the imaginable factors that might impact on the results other than the factor being tested are balanced out between the two groups (Styles, 2009). However, depriving half of the world of literacy to prove how useful it is to the other half would not be very ethical – or very popular. Because of this, a different approach is usually taken, and there are very few randomised controlled trials in education.

Another way of looking at the effects of literacy learning would be to collect data on the lives of people who have gone through adult literacy programmes and compare them with another group. They could be compared with themselves before programme entry, for example. So income pre-entry could be compared with income after the programme. Or they could be compared with another group with a similar background who did not go through a programme. There are theoretical and practical reasons why this does not tend to work out well in practice. If we compare the learners to themselves pre-programme, then it is really difficult to work out what about the programme made the difference, or if both programme involvement and the change of income arose from a third factor. The individual could have been offered a better job on the condition that they enrolled in a literacy programme. The pragmatic reasons for this being a hard approach are the difficulty of following learners for long enough after they leave a programme to capture all the outcomes. In addition, it is quite challenging to find people who could be eligible for a programme but are choosing not to take it. Even if they could be found, the very fact they are not taking a programme makes them different from people who do, and makes it difficult to draw conclusions.

An approach that has drawn considerable interest in recent years is statistical analysis of large scale surveys, often longitudinal. There are two aspects to be considered in this type of work. The first is the source of data to be analysed. In recent years, particularly in the UK, high quality longitudinal data has become available in the form of cohort studies (see, for example, www.understandingsociety.org.uk). These studies follow one group of people over a number of years, looking for relationships between different factors. So, for example, level of education can be compared against income or health. Instead of random assignment to groups, as suggested above, the strategy in this case is to match people on all sorts of dimensions except the one of interest.

Data is now available to understand the lives of thousands of people over a number of decades, and to identify some fairly subtle patterns. A lot of the work by the Centre for Research on the Wider Benefits of Learning (see Feinstein, Budge, Vorhaus and Duckworth, 2008) is based on looking at these patterns and investigating the relationships between the variables. This allows us to identify some strong associations between specific factors and life outcomes.

Nonetheless, the cautions mentioned above have still to be recognised. As Miller and Salkind (2002) remind us during a discussion of path analysis (one of the most recent methodological developments):

> Extravagant hopes for causal explanations should not be entertained – at least not yet. The inability to deal with all variables in a social system, to measure and plot their exact interactions, makes the results in most problems only the first approximations to causality. (p. 398)

Path analysis requires a theoretical framework to be built in advance of it being tested on the real life survey data. The theory is built into a simplified path diagram that focuses on a number of key factors, and the numerical relationships between the factors calculated. At this point the true test of the model occurs – whether the calculated relationships are similar to those observed empirically. This approach to analysis offers an extremely powerful tool for testing an assumed causational relationship, since if the model's predictions and real life results are seriously out of kilter the theory is not supported. It is important to emphasise that this way of looking at data, like any other research method, does not generate causal laws. It allows for prediction but not explanation.

Despite these cautions, the utility of large scale survey research should not be underestimated. It allows sufficient manipulation of factors for researchers to be able to come close to comparing similar people with different literacy capabilities, and to begin to work out what the effects of literacy on their wider lives are. In summary, quantitative approaches are growing more sophisticated and as they do, they are able to point with more certainty to critical factors in people's lives. However it must be remembered that the power of these approaches still relies on a strong theoretical starting point to work from.

Naturalistic approaches

Many people working in education are sceptical about the ability of quantitative methods to help us to understand the subtle and often highly individual outcomes of learning. They are worried about the over-simplification involved in creating a statistical model of human behaviour, and concerned that many of the most important outcomes of education are not captured by existing quantitative evaluation models. For example, in the early years of the twenty-first century, when a new quantitative national accountability system was being introduced in the United States under the Workforce Investment Act (WIA), Bingman, Ebert and Bell (2000) argued strongly for the inclusion of learners' perspectives in understanding outcomes. They reported that:

> *Based on studies conducted in Tennessee in which adult learners reported a broader and more complex set of outcomes than the WIA core measures, this paper suggests that learners have a different perspective on performance than the authors of WIA and that their perspectives should be taken into account at the policy level as well as by local programmes. (p. 1)*

The authors go on to explain that while learners did talk about outcomes that would be captured by the WIA measures, such as employment, they also talked about outcomes to do with how they saw themselves and how they used literacy in everyday settings. The authors suggested that a broad range of measures should be adopted in order to capture the nuanced outcomes of literacy learning. In making this argument, the report fit well with a number of evaluation approaches claiming that understanding the outcomes of a given programme in any depth requires getting close to it and understanding the subtleties. In these approaches to evaluation, the aim is to treat the programme as 'naturally' as possible, observing it working in its context and not artificially re-designing it in order to test its effectiveness.

While there are many varieties of naturalistic approach to understanding educational outcomes, it is probably fair to say that two forms dominate. The first is objective testing, where the outcomes of the educational programme are set in advance, and then the actual measured outcomes are compared with the predicted outcomes (Shufflebeam and Shinkfield, 2007). So a literacy programme might predict that 70 per cent of its participants will grow in confidence during the programme, then ask the participants to find out if they believed they were more confident. As long as seven out of ten say yes, then this could be taken as evidence that the objective was met and, more importantly for the discussion in this book, it would be reasonable to state that the literacy learning could lead to an outcome of increased confidence. Of course there are significant issues with this type of evaluation, not least that it is very hard indeed to come up with a question about confidence that is not leading.

In some literacy education systems, participants can set their own objectives as part of the learning process. In Scotland, learners develop Individual Learning Plans, and their success is measured by whether they achieve the outcomes identified in the plans (St.Clair and Belzer, 2007). What tends to happen is that people naturally set widely divergent objectives for themselves, and it is very difficult to pull them together into coherent statements about what literacy learning is doing for people more generally. So while this approach is helpful in understanding what individuals want to learn and do learn, it is not very useful for understanding the wider effects of literacy learning.

Another approach that possibly offers some more confidence in claiming outcomes is the case study approach to evaluation, where:

> *the study looks at the programme in its geographical, cultural, organisational and historical contexts, closely examining its internal operations and how it uses inputs and processes to produce outcomes. It examines a wide range of intended and unexpected outcomes. (Shufflebeam and Shinkfield, 2007, p. 182)*

The advantages of this approach are that without a pre-determined set of objectives to 'look for' the evaluation may work better in identifying outcomes that were not explicitly built into the programme design, and may be more open to more complex sets of outcomes. Rather than restricting evaluation to a list of funded objectives, there is the opportunity to create a more inclusive model where both employment and increased confidence can be claimed as outcomes, along with whatever other values the participants identify. The findings really only apply to that specific context at that specific time, however.

The difficulty of applying the findings from one context to another is a very significant problem for understanding the effects of literacy learning using naturalistic methods. People who prefer statistical approaches can be dismissive of naturalistic approaches, saying that they are anecdotal and rely on stories rather than verifiable insights. While the last section demonstrates that causation is also tricky to demonstrate using statistics, it is the case that naturalistic approaches gather data primarily from people involved in any given programme and cannot compare their experiences with those of people outside the programme in the same way that a population survey allows. So naturalistic approaches are always limited in what they can say.

These limitations do not prevent naturalistic approaches, with their focus on understanding how people interpret the value of their experience, from being enormously valuable. The fine-grained details of how individuals think of themselves and their learning cannot be dismissed in the pursuit of an illusory general truth. Naturalistic approaches should be appreciated for what they have to offer our understanding of literacy, even though they must, as with statistical methods, be treated with some caution.

A theory-based approach to outcomes

This section looks at an approach to understanding effects that goes beyond the divide between statistical and interpretive approaches. It is called the theory-based approach to outcomes, or sometimes referred to as logic models. The central idea of this approach is that understanding the effects or outcomes of any programme begins with a theory of why, and how, the programme works. Then each component of the theory can be examined in its own right to give an overall picture of the effects. In an area such as literacy where building a conclusive causational case is difficult, a theoretical approach can help by breaking the claimed effects into manageable units. Instead of examining the claim that strengthened literacy capabilities automatically leads to a better paid job, a theory-based approach would allow each step of this linkage to be examined. We might, for example, look at the way skills are rewarded in the job market, and work back from that to look at what it means to be able to demonstrate literacy and numeracy skills at a given level.

Weiss (1995) suggests that evaluation based on analysis of programme theory serves four purposes, two of which are especially relevant here: 'it facilitates aggregation of evaluation results into a broader base of theoretical and programme knowledge' and 'evaluations that address the theoretical assumptions embedded in programmes may have more influence on both policy and popular opinion' (p. 69). In other words, theoretical approaches to evaluation help the results to have broader applicability, which is one of the ways evaluation findings will be used in this book. In addition, the examination of the theory behind programmes, according to Weiss, helps them to be useful and relevant to decision-makers, meaning that addressing the core ideas of literacy learning through evaluation can help to create a clear, convincing and realistic rationale for the field. Chen and Rossi (1989) state that in developing theory-based evaluation they wanted to 'encourage researchers, programme personnel, and social scientists generally to think through and identify the processes linking programme treatments and desired outcomes.' (p. 300)

The notion of theory-based approaches is not attractive to everyone, nor is it applicable to every case. While recognising that a number of critical questions can be addressed by theory-based evaluation, Shufflebeam and Shinkfield (2007) caution that:

> The nature of these questions suggests that the success of the theory-based approach is dependent upon a foundation of sound theory development and validation. This, of course, entails sound conceptualisation of at least a context-dependent theory, formulation and rigorous testing of hypotheses derived from the theory, development of guidelines for practical implementation of the theory based on extensive field trials, development of valid instruments for assessing key aspects of the theory, and independent assessment of the theory. (p. 187)

These are clearly fairly high demands for any area of education to meet, yet in literacy education these conditions are largely fulfilled. There is a theory of how literacy benefits people in a number of areas of their life. The testing of the hypotheses arising from that theory is what this book intends to pull together, based on extensive and varied field trials of literacy education in the form of thousands of active programmes worldwide, with access to a wide range of instruments for examining aspects of the endeavour. Finally, independent assessment of the theory is what we have been working towards over the last twenty years of existence within an audit society.

Theory-based models allow us to address some of the problems of evaluation and causation, as well as encouraging the combination of statistical and naturalistic approaches. It is useful to look at each of these in turn. The evaluation problem arises because people who get involved in a certain programme may be different from those who choose not to, making it difficult to discern what effects the programme itself is having. Theory-based approaches set this aside by laying out a clear and rigorous framework for what the programme should be able to do – a testable proposition. With issues of causation, theory-based approaches can help by breaking down the causation into steps that can more easily be tested for validity. That is not to say that causation can be proven, because it still remains beyond our ability to do so, but it does mean that the factors we believe are related are a lot closer together. Instead of leaping from literacy to income, we take a far smaller step from literacy capability to workplace competence with practical tasks and ask whether that theorised relationship is supported by evidence.

Because theory-based evaluation breaks the effects of an intervention into smaller steps, each of these steps can be assessed using different evidence appropriate to the claimed relationship. So it may make sense to use statistics to show that less confident learners tend to engage less with literacy and yet use naturalistic methods to provide evidence that literacy learning boosts confidence. Within a theory-based model of literacy learning, there is room for the best evidence to be applied to relationships, and this need not take any particular form.

The most common type of theory-based evaluation in current practice is probably the logic model (Kellogg Foundation, 2004). In this model, the resource put into a programme is conceptually separated from the activities of the programme. In turn, the outputs of the programme are considered apart from the outcomes and the impact. While this approach is obviously a bit artificial compared to the way real life programmes work, it is nonetheless quite a useful technique for working out what is actually going on in a programme. For our current discussion, the separation of outputs, outcomes and impacts is especially helpful. Outputs are what the literacy programme delivers, for example two classes of four hours each every week. Outcomes are what participants get out of the programme, in terms of capabilities, skills or attitudes. More confident letter writing would be an outcome, as would entering a college course. Impacts are the broader effects on the community or system arising from the programme, such as increased college attendance by historically marginalised groups.

As we move through the next few chapters, looking at how literacy learning plays out in various areas of life, an implicit logic model of how literacy works will be playing out. It is based on the capabilities approach described in the second chapter, and the idea that application of appropriate skills allows individuals to achieve their ends in a given situation.

Conclusion

In this chapter some of the issues and possibilities of evaluation have been explored at length because so much of the information we have about literacy learning comes from evaluations, and it is important to understand a little about how they work in order to assess the utility of the data they produce. I have looked at the evaluation problem, and discussed the impossibility of proving causation. This means that over the next few chapters any claims to have proven an effect or outcome of literacy learning will be treated with some caution. The best we can do, I suggest, is look as carefully as possible at some changes in people's lives that seem to be associated with literacy capabilities.

Yet that may be enough. If we can create a rigorous theory-based model and test the components of it with a fair degree of confidence, then it is possible to make claims for the effects of literacy learning in various domains. The rest of this book will be dedicated to exploring that idea in the light of the capabilities model described in Chapter Two.

Before we move on to look at the effects of literacy, however, we have another issue to work through. This is the way that literacy is measured. After all, if there is claim that more of some sort of literacy learning has beneficial outcomes, then it is essential that we can work out what type of literacy, and 'how much' we are talking about. The next chapter will look at this issue.

CHAPTER FOUR

Measuring matters

In order to link the outcomes and the process of literacy learning it is important to have some kind of measure of what people are actually learning. In theory, an argument could be made that any sort of involvement in literacy education at any age is going to be an advantage for individuals, and this is probably true. Developing a system that works well for learners and ensures that they get what they need is more demanding. We need to know what sorts of text engagement are valuable, and the depth of that engagement. Is it useful for people to be able to read Shakespearian English, and to write well-formulated essays, or do they gain almost as much by being able to read a popular newspaper? How do we tell the difference between these capabilities? How can educators tell how much somebody has learned by attending a given programme? What sorts of literacy capabilities are there across the population as a whole? In the current era particularly, where can public funds best be placed?

In order to discuss the effects of literacy learning in a systematic way there are two arguments that have to be taken into account. They are:

- that certain levels and forms of literacy capability bring benefits to an individual, and potentially to the society to which they belong; and
- that increased capabilities bring increased benefits to individuals and societies.

Laying out the arguments in this way raises all sorts of interesting questions. It is quite straightforward to come up with a range of hypotheses, such as that there are no benefits to types and levels of literacy capability 'below' a given level (taking us back to the functional literacy model) or that for literacy learning to be worthwhile it has to take people past a threshold. Unfortunately for literacy theorists and educators, it is not possible to answer these questions with any degree of certainty. Not only is it astonishingly difficult to isolate the effects of literacy from other factors, as discussed in Chapter Three, it is also necessary to pull together data from many individuals in many different contexts each of whom has different levels of literacy capability expressed in different ways.

In this chapter I will look in more depth at two ways to look at literacy capabilities. The first is individual, concerned with what capabilities specific people possess. Any measurement of literacy begins from this level, although the overall emphasis may be quite different. Any statement about literacy capability has to begin with the things that people can actually do. The second is population measures, where the aim is to find out what kind of capabilities exist in a large group of people and how they are distributed. This kind of measure allows literacy to be related to social factors such as class, income, gender, ethnicity and so on. The main focus of this section is the series of Organisation for Economic Cooperation and Development surveys that began with the International Adult Literacy Survey in the early 1990s, and continues today. At the end of the chapter, I will pull these two different approaches together and suggest what they can tell us about our central question – the effects of literacy learning.

Understanding the capabilities of individuals

Measurement of individual's literacy capabilities is perhaps the most intuitive way to think about assessing literacy. To a lay person it probably seems like a very straightforward task to come up with a way to find out what people can and cannot do with text. After all, school systems are based on the idea that people start by learning the easiest aspects of literacy and then move on to more challenging material. The same system (or a slight variation of it) should work for people throughout their lives, one might think. As with so much to do with literacy, the answers are not that simple. There is a range of ways of looking at individuals' capabilities, and each approach offers certain advantages and disadvantages. For the purposes of our discussion in this book, no one method tells us all that we need to know about literacy capabilities and further outcomes.

In the very broadest terms, people's capabilities can be measured in an entirely individual way or compared against a pre-determined standard. Each of these tells us something useful, but quite different from the other. In addition, each approach cannot really stand in for the other – it is important to know in advance what you are trying to find out.

Individualised approaches to assessing literacy are most often found in educational programmes, particularly where there is a commitment to learner-centeredness. Here learners are invited to identify their own objectives for learning and to reflect on these goals at a later date. These goals may be completely open, as in Scotland, or they may contribute to achievement within a qualification framework, as is the case in Ontario (St.Clair, 2009). It is also possible to include highly subjective measures within this approach, such as confidence or interest in reading and writing. Because these approaches are so individual and personal they can be extremely sensitive to people's contexts and learning needs, and they may also help build learner confidence and a feeling of self-determination. The aims of learning literacy are often left very open in this kind of approach – it really is up to the learner to work out what they need to know and how they will know they know it. Often the social practices theory of literacy is used as a theoretical framework for these approaches, and learners have an opportunity to comment on the value of what they have learned not only in terms of narrowly defined literacy capabilities, but also on the level of emotion and personal development.

These individualised approaches are, however, much less useful for building a broad picture of the effects of literacy. The precision that gives these approaches such educational value comes at the cost of the ability to summarise across groups of people. So we can say that a particular learner can now write a letter to the council complaining about inadequate heat, for example, but other learners are going to have other tasks they want to perform. The result is that often attempts to capture individualised literacy learning across a society ends up as a long list of things people can do that they could not before, usually with very little consistency. One person can now use commas, another knows how to read the paper, the third can understand their payslip. None of these outcomes are trivial, by any means, but the diversity makes it truly difficult to model what literacy capabilities do for people. There is a tendency to fall back into anecdote, something the adult literacy education sector is prone to do. While these anecdotes are powerful and important, they contribute only marginally to building an argument for literacy education that will grab the attention of policymakers and, more importantly, their budget.

Generally, comparing people's capabilities to pre-determined standards is a lot more common. These measures can still have instructional uses, but they also allow for some sort of broader comparison and link more directly into qualifications frameworks. An example of this approach on a practical level is the Certificate of General Educational Development (GED) in the United States and Canada. If you get a GED as an adult, then you are considered to have attained the same capabilities as somebody who went through the Grade 12 graduation process in high school. The GED has both a direct measurement function, as it implies that the person has mastered a certain range of capabilities, and a signalling function, as it tells others unambiguously (at least in theory) what that individual can do. Many formal qualifications can be seen as having a degree of literacy within them – a PhD, for example, shows that an individual can produce a significant manuscript within the tradition of academic literacy. It is reasonable to say that all qualifications have a dual role, in that they not only represent a particular set of capabilities in summary form, they also tell external parties that the holder of the qualification was interested in, and able to, actually get the qualification. It is not a simple matter to work out if employers, for example, select people because they have specific skills, or because they have a qualification that the employer sees as desirable. Certainly, the qualification requirements for the same jobs have increased significantly over the last few decades. Qualifications are generally not a very reliable way to understand literacy capabilities in operation.

There is a huge range of standardised tests that purport to measure individuals' literacy capabilities directly. They produce results in different forms, ranging from an exact score to a general level to a specific 'grade level equivalent' in the case of North American tests. In recent years England and Scotland have produced qualifications frameworks that span everything from well below secondary school level to doctorates (for the Scottish Framework see Scottish Qualifications Authority, undated). Literacy capabilities explicitly map onto these frameworks, and the frameworks in turn map onto employment sectors and educational programmes. This produces an allegedly seamless system of capability, education and employment.

There are a few problems with such measurement approaches to literacy, including the assumption that literacy capabilities lie along a single continuum from what a beginner needs to learn to fully-fledged competence. Perhaps the strongest objection to this assumption is that it does not seem to reflect what we know about how people develop or use literacy capabilities. While it may be possible to draw up a linear model of literacy learning based on schooling, that is because schools are designed to deliver a linear teaching model in a way that serves the greatest number of students as well as possible – it does not tell us a great deal about how literacy is acquired and used in wider settings.

There is discontinuity at the lower end of the literacy learning curve. In an alphabetic system, people learn the entire reading process (as described in Chapter One) and end up able to read only a few words. Certainly people who do not read can often recognise a few words, such as 'pull' and 'no exit', simply by exposure. But to move from letter recognition to meaning requires a huge number of mental operations to occur, and to occur quite rapidly. In other words, we have to bear in mind that by the time people can read anything, they have already mastered a substantial range of key concepts and abilities. The lower end of the learning curve is actually a huge step, and we can say surprisingly little about this step beyond the observation that some people have taken it and others have not.

A second issue is the problem of spiky profiles. People generally do not have equally well-developed literacy capabilities across the board. Generally this is taken to mean that components of literacy, such as their reading and their numeracy, are not equally strong (Green and Howard, 2007; Brewer *et al.*, 2006), but it could also be applied at a much more fundamental level. So even within their literacy abilities people will have some areas in which they are particularly good and others in which they struggle. One of the issues here is inter-textuality, in that texts tend to refer to each other and the more that you read in a particular area, the more you understand of the texts. People who like sports can make perfect sense of the commentary on football that I simply do not understand in any meaningful way. The idea of spiky profiles can be applied to any small component of literacy and to any user of literacy, meaning that linear measures have significant limits.

It is also worth mentioning the practice of comparing the literacy capabilities of adults to school attendance, whether this is done through grade equivalence or through 'years of schooling'. At the current time, we simply do not know how helpful this is, though evidence seems to suggest it is not a very accurate way to think about adult learning. As Verhoeven (1994) summarises, 'it is clear that such distinctions are not accurate and will provide little insight into the actual abilities and the educational needs of adults' (p. 5). Among the issues are that adults may not learn the same things at the same rate as children, that adults have substantial experience to bring to learning, and that grade levels, by definition, are tied to school-based forms of literacy. Measures of years of schooling and grade level equivalency seem to offer, at best, a narrow and problematic way to summarise literacy capabilities.

Individual measures do offer an enormously important strength in some cases – the ability to measure changes in literacy over time for the same person. It is becoming more common for people involved in literacy learning to have pre- and post-tests, meaning that it is possible to look at where they started and the distance travelled. What's interesting about this is that the actual way their development is measured is not necessarily important, depending on the purposes to which the results will be put. Sometimes, it will be enough to say that enhanced capabilities have been demonstrated.

If they are setting out to show change over time, measures do need to have certain characteristics. They need to be highly sensitive. It is important to be able to capture relatively small changes quite accurately, because it can take a long time to learn literacy abilities and it can be critical to represent small increments in capability. Measures should also be strongly focused on the specific elements of literacy that the individual is interested in learning. It is not important that measures are externally meaningful – if I am in a literacy education programme of some kind I may not need to be able to show anybody else what I am learning. It does matter exactly what is being learned when the aim is to show that a certain type of learning produces a specific result, but generally a more open approach is called for.

Any argument that changes in literacy capabilities produce benefits calls for a measure capable of capturing differences over time and separate from the formal schooling system. People may gain capabilities over time through their work or family life, or may lose capabilities as life changes (I used to understand trigonometry). Measuring these changes must logically always be based on the same person, requiring a longitudinal research design that is unfortunately very rare in literacy work. If it has been done, it is usually in the context of a specific programme, and relatively small scale (the exception to this, cohort studies, will be discussed in the following section).

It is interesting to consider whether the lack of precise information about the effects of changes in literacy capabilities is because there has been little call for such data and the increased interest in these matters is so recent, or whether there are underlying methodological challenges. My own suspicion is that there is a bit of both. Looking at changes in the capabilities of individuals and linking them to wider effects would require painstaking and well-designed long-term research in a form that has not been supported by funding organisations to date. It would require incredibly detailed information about a lot of people – both in literacy programmes and not – to give depth to the findings. There are certainly various projects that offer some aspects of this design, but none that bring all the elements together.

Given the challenges of measuring literacy meaningfully at the individual level, it is useful to consider if perhaps there is another way of doing it, using population measures of capabilities.

Literacy capabilities across a population

Over the last twenty years or so there has been increasing interest in looking at literacy capabilities within different countries. There seem to have been three main reasons for this. The first was the growing popularity of human capital theory as a way to think about the prerequisites of national prosperity. Human capital theory emphasises the importance of human skills and knowledge in the development of economies (Becker, 1975; Laroche, 1997), meaning that it is helpful to know what the levels and distribution of those skills is at any particular time. The second reason was growing interest within the Organisation for Economic Co-operation and Development in understanding the workings of skills, including literacy capabilities, within developed and developing economies (OECD, 2009). Finally, the 1980s and 1990s saw many concerns expressed about the quality of education systems, and assessing these allegedly universal skills appeared to offer a way to double check the effectiveness of education.

Measurements designed to provide a snapshot of skills across a large number of people need different characteristics than those for individual measurement. It is possible to use relatively insensitive measures that do not provide a great deal of detail. Taking the notion of functional literacy to its logical conclusion, in fact, it is quite possible to consider the desired capabilities as something people either have or do not have. This is what has happened in Scotland, where the economically desirable level of literacy has been set at Level 4 of the Scottish Credit and Qualifications Framework, and people falling below this level have been seen as 'having severe literacy and numeracy problems' (Scottish Government, 2007, Indicator). When looking at population measures it is not necessary to know everything about an individual's skills – often models can be used to link qualifications or specific tested results to broader capabilities. Finally, it is important for population measures to have to have some degree of compatibility if they are to allow for useful comparison, making standardisation common.

The interest in measuring literacy across populations came to a head in the early 1990s. There certainly had been attempts to achieve these measurements in the past, particularly in North America, but at this point key players came together to create and administer the International Adult Literacy Survey (IALS). The process and results of this survey, the later International Adult Literacy and Life Skills Survey and the forthcoming Programme for the International Assessment of Adult Competencies have dominated discussion about the effects of literacy on individuals' lives. There have been parallel developments in the international measurement of school-based competencies, the Programme for International Student Assessment and the Trends in International Mathematics and Science Survey, that have underlined the desirability and utility of large scale surveys such as these.

The IALS had two aims:

> *The first objective was to develop scales that would permit comparisons of the literacy performance of adults with a wide range of abilities. Then, if such an assessment could be created, the second goal was to describe and compare the demonstrated literacy skills of adults in different countries. This second objective presented the challenge of comparing literacy across cultures and across languages. (Kirsch and Murray, 1997, p.16)*

The IALS broke new ground in several directions at once. The instruments used were innovative, combining a great deal of background information with a highly sophisticated test design that could deliver assessment of literacy capabilities based on correct/incorrect answers to 22 questions. The test items themselves combined text with graphics, and emphasised particular sets of capabilities. The instruments were produced in various language versions, allowing the eventual involvement of some 22 countries in IALS. The scale for understanding literacy capabilities was newly developed, featuring five levels numbered from one to five, with five indicating more developed capabilities. None of these developments was without difficulty, and none went unchallenged in the professional literature on literacy.

The definition of literacy used for IALS was 'using printed and written information to function in society, to achieve one's goals, and to develop one's knowledge and potential' (Kirsch and Murray, 1997, p.17). It is worth noting that this is an incredibly broad set of factors to be claiming to measure with any precision. While definitions of literacy have been becoming broader, due to deeper understanding of the complexities and overlaps of the key ideas, it does not necessarily follow that defined measures have to broaden. In some ways, a case can be made for more precision in measurement as a strategy to deal with increased complexity of definition. In the case of IALS, the broad definition of literacy was broken down into three domains: prose literacy, using information form texts; document literacy, using information from forms, graphics and other non-continuous text; and quantitative literacy, using arithmetical operations on numbers embedded in text. It should be noted that this last domain is not numeracy, in the sense of conducting different levels of mathematics, but a measure of the ability to find and use numbers in a simple way within text documents.

Each person surveyed answered a number of questions with a difficulty level expressed as a score from 0–500 in each of the domains. Their final level on each domain was the point at which they had an 80 per cent chance of responding correctly. As the difficulty increased above this point their chance of an incorrect answer would go up. So a person could have a final score of 226 in prose literacy, 318 in document literacy and 410 in quantitative literacy. Each of these scores would represent a specific level, say level one, level three and level four respectively (this would be a highly unusual set of results as generally people had very similar scores on all three scales in IALS).

The test items themselves were based upon theoretical work on literacy test design conducted by one of the lead researchers. The general model for the tests was that an individual was presented with a piece of writing (the test document) and asked to answer a question concerning the content. The answers could be a few words needing to be written into the answer page, a number to be entered in a blank space on a form, or simply circling a piece of information on the test document. The research suggested that salience, defined as 'the ability to find and extract sufficient information from among highly relevant information in the stimulus material' (Kirsch and Guthrie, 1980, p. 91), was the most important single predictor of the difficulty of a test item. The authors went on to identify four further variables that predict difficulty: the degree to which the order of information presentation in the test document matched the order in which it was requested in the question; the sheer amount of information in the test document; whether words and typography matched between the question and the test document; and the total number of information categories the respondent had to work with. This led to a fairly sophisticated model of test item development that has continued to influence design strongly to this day.

In order to ensure some degree of brevity to the survey, the design of the items in the IALS reflected an approach called 'Item Response Theory' (IRT). The general idea of IRT is that tests do not check directly for a specific trait such as literacy capability, but instead the choice of answer (the item response) provides nuanced information about that trait. Twenty-two items provides a huge range of different answer patterns each of which can be linked quantitatively to the underlying trait. This test design is probabilistic, meaning that for a population estimate of a given trait, testing more people is better as it makes it more likely that errors will cancel out.

IRT relies on a number of assumptions being true (Brannick, undated; Partchev, 2004). The first main assumption is that one trait explains all the given variations in responses. In the case of IALS, that means accepting that each domain represents a real and undifferentiated capability. The second main assumption is that answers to test items are linked to the trait by a uniform relationship that stays constant in different circumstances. This means that a given response indicates the same literacy capability in different languages, different countries and for people with diverse life experience. The designers of the IALS test comment on this exact issue:

> To the extent that these assumptions are untrue — that is, the extent that real linguistic differences exist amongst countries or that the measurement protocol does not discriminate comparably across populations — the interpretation of international differences must be undertaken with care. (Kirsch and Murray, 1997, p. 22).

This issue is raised but not fully put to rest in the IALS documentation. One commentator upon the use of IRT in literacy testing has very clear views. Maclean (1987) believes that language use is fundamentally multidimensional and that the notion of a single underlying trait is simply unsupported. He suggests that human interaction with language is 'located in multidimensional space far away from the black hole of trait theory' (p. 3). The question of whether it makes sense to conceive of a single underlying trait remains a challenging and unresolved philosophical challenge in literacy survey design.

One problem for the test designers is that there is no agreed upon international scale by which literacy is measured and, indeed, no internationally agreed definition. So there is no solid starting point for the measures to work against, and the IALS procedure has to try to create one for itself as it goes along. The danger here is falling into circular logic, where the average literacy score on the three scales is taken as what should be the average because there is no external referent to compare against. The findings of the survey end up as completely descriptive and not necessarily directly helpful to policy. So if Ireland has an average of 242 for prose literacy and Scotland has an average of 238 it is not really clear what this says about, for example, their ability to be economically competitive. Further, both averages fall within the range designated as Level 2 on the five level scale, nearer the bottom than the top. It is not clear whether this is a problem or not.

What the IALS can comment upon quite powerfully is the distribution of individuals among the five literacy levels in each country. This was where IALS began to run into a great deal of trouble. In Scotland, one of the most developed economies in the world, and the home of free universal education for 140 years, 55 per cent of respondents were in the bottom two levels for prose literacy (Scottish Executive, 2001). In the United States, 47 per cent of the population was in these levels for prose, and 43 per cent in Canada. The highest scoring country was Sweden, with only 28 per cent at Level One or Two (Binkley, Matheson and Williams, 1997). The significance of these outcomes is that Level Three was identified as the functional level for a modern economy. In other words, the best scoring country appeared to have over a quarter of its population not functionally literate, and a relatively high scoring country seemed to have about half its population unable to function.

There were three possible responses to this situation. One was to state that the tests were clearly not valid, and to withdraw. This was the route chosen by France. A second response was to suggest that anything showing that half of the people in developed countries (no developing countries were included in the first round) were functionally illiterate was clearly flawed, and to ignore it. A third response was to take it at face value and panic, which is what a number of Western governments did. An example of this mode of response is the development of the hugely expensive and complex 'Skills for Life' programme in England, which set out to standardise and professionalise adult literacy education. The results have been mixed.

From the perspective of this book, the key question is what we can learn from the IALS and IALLS data. What we have is a set of static data concerning literacy capabilities measured using sophisticated but narrow methods. Even though the tools were designed to reflect real-life tasks, they were still pen and paper tests administered by survey staff in people's homes, and cannot be considered authentic assessments in the sense of fully representing real-life contexts. There are a number of concerned statistical commentaries on IALS and IALLS (cf. Henningsen, undated; Blum, Goldstein and Guérin-Pace, 2001) and others that deal with the literacy assumptions of the items (Hamilton and Barton, 2000). It seems reasonable to comment that the IALS is generally considered to be undertheorised in terms of the meaning and application of key constructs.

However, the value of the surveys may come from a slightly less ambitious desire than comparing literacy skills across countries. The survey collected an enormous amount of background data on respondents (roughly 600 data points per person) and a lot of that information has remained unanalysed. If we accept that the IALS instrument measured something broadly related to literacy, albeit primarily school-like literacy and the ability to take tests (Hamilton and Barton, 2000), it is possible to examine the distribution of that factor across different social groups within a given country. The earliest stages of that work seem to confirm that the distribution of literacy capabilities closely mirrors the distribution of other social capabilities. For example, in Scotland, higher scores were linked with better education, higher social class, better pay, less deprived area and younger respondents (Scottish Executive, 2001) and similar patterns played out in other countries. This should not be a surprise to anybody familiar with patterns of literacy capability. What is striking, however, is the degree to which these patterns were consistent and very significant. IALS shows us that we live in a world where literacy capabilities are distributed in a grossly uneven fashion that reflects other forms of inequity very closely.

The IALS findings will arise in a number of the chapters as we move through the effects of literacy. It can usefully show associations between social factors, but it is important to bear in mind that it is a limited approach. It does not tell us what people need to know to have a full range of literacy capabilities, or how they are affected by change over time. IALS is a snapshot, and currently not a fully developed one.

Following from the IALS research, the English National Research and Development Centre in Adult Literacy and Numeracy (NRDC) and the Centre for Research on the Wider Benefits of Learning have completed a number of projects using data derived from the UK cohort studies. These studies take advantage of existing educational and other information collected at regular intervals on over 17,000 people born in a particular week in a given year (1958 or 1970). These data sets offer an opportunity for powerful longitudinal analysis of key areas of interest. Up until 2004, the basic skills literacy and numeracy assessments built into the cohort studies was quite rudimentary, and only reached about 10 per cent of respondents. In the 2004 round, NRDC had the opportunity to create a new instrument based on the English Skills for Life framework and to include it in the survey for the entire 1970 cohort (Parsons, Bynner and Foudouli, 2005).

The group of 34-year-olds were asked about literacy capabilities in three ways. In the core questionnaire they were asked if they experienced any difficulties. There was then a set of multiple choice questions on literacy and numeracy, followed by a set of open response questions on literacy and numeracy. The average time taken for the entire literacy and numeracy test was around 29 and a half minutes (Parsons, Bynner and Foudouli, 2005). An adaptive design was chosen for the computer administered survey, so that people who did well on the first few questions were subsequently faced with more difficult questions. Results were then mapped against the core curriculum levels of the Skills for Life framework.

Since it has only been conducted once, this project cannot be considered truly longitudinal, though it has the potential to be administered again. At that point it will be the detailed, large scale longitudinal survey that would tell us so much about literacy capabilities. As it stands, it tells us very similar things to the IALS, albeit with the outputs expressed in a different form.

Is it measurable – does it matter?

The majority of the discussion in this chapter is perhaps a little pessimistic, reflecting the indeterminacy theory of educational measurement: the more detailed the measurements, the harder it is to pull them together or generalise from them. When we are trying to assess what people learn, we can choose either to be precise, which implies highly individualised methods of capturing learning, or to use a general measure, which gives up precision in favour of consistency. The only way to get around this dilemma would be to put enormous resources into a highly specific research project following many people for a long time, and even that would need to be placed at some point along the continuum.

So what can we say about measuring literacy capabilities? I think we can clearly identify some errors to avoid. It seems important to bear in mind that any measurement is more indicative than definitive. If literacy capabilities are not a single linear trait then it is imperative to be really cautious about measurements that imply that it is. Similarly, any measurement that seems to privilege one type of literacy, such as the type learned in school, will tend to present an incomplete picture. Literacy capabilities are likely to be highly individual and eclectic.

We also need to be very careful about arguments that a given level of literacy capability leads – almost automatically – to economic or personal success. Even if, as the IALS results suggest, the majority of people in Scotland are below a functional level of literacy, they are still functioning very well. The same applies to every other society. Irrespective of what abstract measurements show, as long as there is some degree of match between what people can do and what they have to do in their lives, then they are functionally literate. It is worth noting that over 90 per cent of people surveyed in the IALS were satisfied with their literacy capabilities – surely a finding that undermines claims of a literacy crisis.

There is a strong tendency to spurious precision in discussions of literacy. Because a test is designed to be highly precise, producing a result something like 'this person has grade 3.7 literacy,' does not mean that the finding is valid. Validity in data comes from understanding the trait to be measured extremely well, and then working outwards from there to build a construct (a testable factor) to use in understanding how much of the trait there is. In educational testing, there is a tendency to work with constructs that are capable of precise measurement even if they are not fully theorised. The example of race and intelligence discussed in Chapter Three is an example of this. Instruments for measuring IQ can deliver great precision, but without a really clear idea of what we mean by IQ and what it indicates, we are very likely to go down the wrong path in our analysis. This is not meant to dismiss the imagination and skill that goes into designing instruments for assessing literacy, but simply to sound a note of caution in the application of the findings.

What testing gives us, finally, is an indication of tendencies regarding the outcomes of literacy learning. It points towards some important connections and relationships, but can never directly answer questions around how much of a particular literacy capability will produce a certain outcome. It can tell us a great deal about the direction of the relationships so that we can rule out the possibility that increased literacy capability leads to decreased income (as well-educated people flock towards working for charities). Yet we cannot say with certainty that a person who has a test score of x needs to get to y, at which point a whole range of benefits will become available. This kind of claim, whatever its source, needs to be treated with scepticism.

The next few chapters of the book bring together evidence on the outcomes of literacy capabilities in some key areas. My approach to evidence is to treat it as a range of valuable clues regarding literacy, and to treat the specifics of the evidence in each case in its own right. So throughout this discussion, whenever I introduce a piece of evidence about literacy I will also lay out how reliable I think that evidence is, and what sort of claims can be based upon it.

It would be good to think that the problem is not having enough evidence to make causational arguments and that shortcoming will be addressed over time, but I do not believe that is the case. I believe that educational research will always have to deal with partial, indicative evidence, simply because of the nature of education as a social endeavour. There will always be a need to pull together a patchwork of diverse evidence to understand the process and effects of educational efforts. The key to this approach is creating an evidence-based model of how the educational process is working (St.Clair, 2005), which is quite different from taking the results of research as 'real'.

Conclusion

In this chapter I have looked at the ways in which literacy can be measured, and suggested that there is a fundamental tension between precision and breadth in the knowledge we can have of educational processes. To some extent this could be resolved, at least for England, if the cohort studies were to be repeated. But it is important to note that here, once again, the notion of literacy is somewhat restricted to de-contextualised skills.

76

It provides important information, but a multiple choice assessment on a computer screen is different from standing in a shop choosing between differently priced items, or budgeting limited funds for a household.

In each of the areas to be examined in the following chapters I will be pulling together diverse sources of evidence to be able to say something about the way literacy capabilities play out. The lack of definitive, large-scale evidence need not be a problem as long as we are prepared to accept that the information we have available to us to examine the claims in each area will be diverse, incompatible, sometimes contradictory and always patchwork. Nowhere is this more true than in the psychological effects of literacy – how does reading and writing change our thinking? The next chapter looks at some of the key ideas.

PART TWO

REVIEWING THE EVIDENCE

CHAPTER FIVE

The literate mind

An interesting place to start our discussion of the impacts of literacy is by looking at the way reading and writing changes thinking. For a long time it was taken for granted that it simply did. This was partly borne of the classical suspicion of written, permanent language, as summarised by Plato: 'No man of intelligence will venture to express his philosophical views in language, especially not in language that is unchangeable, which is true of that which is set down in written characters' (Plato, 360 BCE). Here Plato was expressing his concern that the apparent permanence of writing could trick humans into believing that their thinking has permanent value – a folly to Plato given the ambiguity and imprecision of written language. Over two thousand years later this argument strikes us, perhaps, as a bit odd. Often when we want to express something clearly we will choose to write it down (as in a contract or will) rather than speak it. Is that because we have been seduced by literacy, have our minds been changed by the use of texts, or is writing simply a handy tool for remembering things? That is the kind of question I will discuss in this chapter.

In the spirit of Chapters Three and Four, it is important to identify a logical model for what we are looking for when we refer to the psychological effects of literacy. The most basic hypothesis here is that literacy capabilities transform the way people think. Learning to apply the appropriate skills in specific contexts actually changes the way people conceive the world and themselves. It seems to me that there are two ways this could happen. Perhaps the structures learned through engagement with text generalise across all of our thinking, so that we look for and reinforce linear understanding of the world. Or alternatively, the content that we can access through written language changes what we have to work with. In other words, literacy changes either the way we think, what we think with, or both.

In terms of assessing this hypothesis, we need to assemble a range of evidence. It is helpful to begin with the possibility that the development of literacy transforms society. This well-established and deeply controversial issue reflects the psycho-social dimension of literacy and serves as a backdrop for later sections. Next it is important to look for evidence that literacy capabilities change cognition. Related to this, there is a need to examine the emotional impact of literacy capability, including whether literacy affects self-efficacy. Convincing evidence of any of these impacts suggests that literacy capabilities do have psychological impact, but it does not necessarily tell us if this impact is desirable or the degree of change involved. The conclusion of the chapter presents a summation of what we know about the psychological implications of reading and writing – which are more subtle and yet more far-reaching than we might anticipate.

Psycho-social effects

As mentioned in the introduction, the fact that human brains have evolved to be able to use written language is fascinating. Human brains have not changed very much over at least a couple of hundred thousand years, so it follows that we have had the ability to use symbols to represent language, at least in latent form, for a very long time. If using symbols to represent language were a directly evolved ability, it would have to have evolved a long time before that ability was used to any degree. This is an interesting but unlikely proposition – humans did not evolve other forms of tool use and then wait for several millennia before using a stone axe, for example. This simple observation suggests that there is something irreducibly social and cultural about literacy. The ability to work with written language flowered when the social conditions were right, using capacities developed for other functions.

The known history of literacy is quite patchy, and the related notions of 'literacy' and 'being literate' seem never to have had a stable meaning. I do not intend to review the same historical discussions that others have already explored so well (cf. Graff, 1987, 1995; Mace, 2001), but there are a number of key points that underline the interesting twists and turns of literacy. Graff (1987) lays out four central insights early in his discussion of literacy in the West. First, he points out that the development of literacy is surprisingly recent (roughly four to five thousand years ago). Second, there is very little evidence about historical literacy, even in later periods. Third, literacy has generally been restricted to a few individuals within a society and has not approached universality until very recent times. Finally, the relationships between oral and written cultures are complex. Taken together, these points suggest that there is no clear cut-off between 'pre-literate' societies and 'modern' societies that use text as an everyday communication tool. What we see instead is rapid and relatively inconsistent development of different technologies for reading and writing in different places at different times. This makes assessment of the effects of literacy at the psycho-social level more complex than might otherwise be the case, as we do not have 'before' and 'after' literacy examples to compare.

It is interesting to ask what happened around five thousand years ago to bring this latent ability of humans into fruition. Up until that point, of course, humans had used symbols such as cave paintings and pictographs to communicate meaning, though this use was usually representational (with a picture of a deer for a deer) and eclectic. This representational approach remains influential in logographic written languages such as Chinese and Japanese. Literacy researchers broadly agree that in the West it was the Sumerians who began to use written language systematically, with a degree of standardisation of script and meaning. Marxists and capitalists alike will be gratified to learn that the motives for the standardisation of Sumerian were most likely related to the needs of state organisation and commerce across a large territory. A standard written language allows for a valuable characteristic difficult to achieve in spoken language: permanence. Writing can transcend time and space in a way speech cannot.

Sumerian writing was syllabic rather than representational, and seems to have been the first to have symbols linked to the sounds of speech rather than whole words or the meanings of speech (Graff, 1987). The written symbols would correspond with a syllable such as 'cot'. While logographic systems basically require a different symbol for every word, leading to thousands of different symbols (for more discussion on this point see Henderson, 1982), syllabic systems can use a smaller set of symbols combined in different ways. One advantage of this smaller set of symbols is the increased ease and speed of learning the written form of a language (Graff, 1987; Henderson, 1982). It is perhaps important to underline that the main advantage of changing to a syllabic alphabet was likely to have been teaching efficiency rather than the ability to express more profound or more abstract ideas, as the vast and beautiful literature of logographic culture shows. The educational influence on language began early indeed.

The Sumerian writing system was developed further in the Mediterranean region, and the system used in English and similar languages today came into being about 2,500 years ago in Greece. This was the fully phonetic alphabet, with letters for the individual components of spoken language. So instead of having the two symbols (for 'apple fruit') used in Chinese writing, or the equivalent syllable symbols used in Samaria, the group of letters 'apple' could be used. This was yet more efficient in terms of learning and the streamlined symbol set, with a small group of letters capable of producing an almost infinite set of words (and therefore, representing almost infinite ideas). The general idea that written language evolved from logographics (with no relation between symbol and pronunciation and lots of symbols) through syllabics to alphabetics (with strong relationships between symbols and pronunciation and small numbers of symbols) was unchallenged in psychology and linguistics for a long time. The view that written language became more sophisticated and expressive along the way has only been debunked in recent years by writers looking more deeply at the structures of language (Strauss and Altwerger, 2007).

The key question here is what we can learn from changing social forms and their use of written language, particularly the extent to which literacy affected the form of society. The traditional view, still in vogue until the late 1960s, was that literacy and civilisation were linked in a relatively unproblematic way (cf. Goody and Watt, 1968). Put simply, the idea was that literacy, particularly in its more 'advanced' alphabetic forms, allowed members of a society to perform key tasks essential to a modern democratic society, such as recording laws and judgements, ownership of property, the development of modern science, and so on. More significantly still, the argument implied that access to written resources allowed particular logical forms, such as the syllogism, to be developed. This strong form of the literacy thesis holds that the distribution of literacy within society moves from an elite to everybody through an inevitable progression, breaking down oppression and the dominance of traditional 'myths' as it does so. For the commentators of the 1960s, writing as inheritors of the Victorian tradition of social improvement, literacy was the key driver behind the development of primitive societies into contemporary democracies.

This section will focus on one claim of this thesis – that literacy drives social form. This argument has been challenged extensively over the last forty years, both on a theoretical and empirical basis. It assumes that societies share a desire for rational organisation and that in the co-evolution of society and written language 'everything depends on textual precision versus the laxness of utterance' (Collins and Blot, 2003, p. 31). The general idea of the strong thesis has underpinned a great deal of international policy – its vestiges can be found, for example, in the UNESCO commitment to education as a route out of poverty and oppressive social structure, as discussed more fully in Chapter Eight.

Since this type of view has been challenged so much, even without considering the problems inherent to any distinction between 'primitive' and 'developed' societies, a modified 'weak' literacy thesis has been proposed. The weak thesis is well expressed by Olson:

> . . . we must not allow our new understanding of literacy to eclipse the intricacy of oral language and oral tradition. Literacy is a resource that is particularly important to some forms of discourse, to solving a certain range of problems and to functioning in certain social institutions. But literacy does not exhaust the range of valued forms of discourse and valued forms of rationality. (1989, p. 13)

Here Olsen is emphasising that the lines between written and spoken language are not as clear as they were once assumed to be, and that the societal advantages of literacy are not as clear as they might have been. Yet he is still claiming the centrality of literacy as a social resource. Perhaps one way to understand this claim is to reduce it to a relatively pragmatic level, and ask what written language actually allows people to do that spoken language does not.

Within a society, written language has two significant differences from the spoken word. The first is that, as mentioned above, written language is relatively permanent. This means that it can be archived and referred back to almost indefinitely. One implication is that the text gains authority within such a society, and becomes more important than spoken language. A tragic example of this in recent history is the relationship between settlers and indigenous people in North America. The Native Americans expected the Europeans to honour their word; the Europeans did not necessarily believe there was anything to honour until it was written down. Time and again Europeans exploited this difference to gain ownership of land and restriction of the original inhabitants.

The archive function is more complex than it seems at first. Archiving means more than simple storage, it also means that it is possible to create a hierarchy of knowledge, with the big ideas pulled apart from the details. Winchester (1985) argues that written language allows the mind to be free from minutiae while considering the structure of an argument, it allows the simultaneous consideration of a wide range of ideas, and allows arguments to continue for tens or hundreds of pages (or indeed books).

The second difference is that written language transcends time and space. There is a need to be cautious with this claim, as a lot of this same function is now fulfilled by telephones and other extensions of the spoken word. For the vast majority of human cultural history, transmitting human language over distances meant that it had to be translated into symbolic form and then reconstituted by the receiver. To this day, the authoritative versions of communications continue to be written, and the widespread adoption of e-mail and texting as informal communication methods has brought back the written word into the everyday sphere. Texts are powerful.

One way to look at the social effects of literacy is to ask, as Winchester (1985) does, whether developed societies could continue in anything like their present form if literacy vanished overnight. And the answer appears to be that they could not. This seems to support some version of the thesis that literacy affects society, but literacy appears to be reduced to the level of any other social tool, such as mass transportation or a power utility, to which the same argument could be applied.

Based on the balance of evidence, which is necessarily fairly limited in scope and depth, it seems reasonable to conclude that literacy, as a component of shared culture, does have an impact upon that culture. It is far from clear what that impact is. At a minimum, the ability to archive human thought for transmission through space and time would make some things possible that would not be feasible without written language. At this level of significance, literacy can be seen primarily as a tool, serving purposes that pre-existed it – the thoughts were already there, writing and reading just provide a means to record them. At a maximum, the compilation of human knowledge and thought over millennia transforms the meaning of being human, at least for those humans participating in the creation or application of the compilation. In this view, the writing of human experience allows it to be challenged, reflected upon and – perhaps ironically – re-written. Literacy is not a supplement to human thought, but a basis and formative structure for that thought.

Most likely, the answer lies between the two, with literacy indeed offering a tool, but one without an implicit teleology or any tendency to privilege a particular direction of social change. It may well be that reading and writing allow reflection on texts and potential modification, but that has not been the case with Confucian texts in China, where precision of reproduction is paramount. It may be that alphabetical script forms are easier to learn and allow greater freedom of expression, though that was not the case for the Soviet Union. There seems to be little evidence that the development of literacy drives or dominates social development. Finally, I suspect that literacy changes society to the degree that the society in question is amenable to change. It does not transform social circumstance, but it does provide a set of resources able to be applied by those who would. A society with a universal approach to literacy does offer a unique psycho-social environment for the expression of literacy capabilities. The institutions of such a society will be set up to expect and exploit the use of written language, making it a real disadvantage not to be able to participate. Whether or not the actual exercise of literacy capabilities affects the way people think, the mismatch between a person's capabilities and what is the expected norm for a given society will surely affect their perception of themselves.

Literacy and cognition

If we accept that having literacy as part of a culture does affect the psycho-social milieu to some extent, it raises the question of whether literacy capabilities change the psychological makeup of individuals. This is not the perspective discussed in chapter one, where we looked at the psychological processes involved in the use of written language. Here we are asking what processes are supported by written language. Does being able to read and write change the way in which we see the world?

We might anticipate some key changes based on our discussion of the psycho-social context. It would make sense to theorise that there might be changes in memory, and these could take two forms. It is possible that literacy erodes long-term memory, as people are able to use written language archives instead of having to remember things themselves. At the same time, there could be evidence that short-term memory improves due to the need to retain recently read text as a context for new reading. In addition, it would make sense to imagine that the linear and hierarchical nature of text processing might encourage thinking to take on that form (as in Goody's argument about syllogisms). The final proposition is that the ability to reflect on language use would lead to a more critical or even sceptical view of the use of language. Each of these possible effects follows logically from the characteristics identified in earlier stages of our discussion.

There is no reason to believe that any of these cognitive changes, if evidence could be found for them, would necessarily be a good thing. If we reject the strong literacy thesis, as I have suggested that we must, then this entails rejecting the idea that any of these changes would lead to 'better' thinking. It might allow people to think about things differently, and that might lead in some circumstances to increased capability, but we must always retain some degree of caution about claims that being able to do or think something leads automatically to pre-specified and valuable outcomes.

One difficulty in looking at these issues is that most of the research evidence available to us concerns children learning to read. This introduces two complications. The first is that children are generally learning literacy capabilities in school. This means that what they are learning is academic, but more seriously, also means that the cognitive effects of literacy and learning are tangled up together. If there were an increase in critical language use, for example, it would be extremely difficult to know if this came from interaction with written language or with the experience of being in school. The second complication is that children, by definition, are getting older and developing. Again, any cognitive effects have to be separated from the process of maturation that children are going through – perhaps development of critical thought is simply an inevitable component of getting older. The second of these issues is potentially addressed by doing research with adults, but the first would require research on people who were teaching themselves to read and write, and even then the division would not be clear.

The most influential attempt to disentangle these issues was Scribner and Cole's (1981) work in West Africa. A group of people called the Vai demonstrate interesting patterns of written language use. There are three written languages used by the Vai: English, taught in school; Vai, learned from others in the community; and Arabic, often learned in a Qura'nic form, memorised by rote. Different people in the community have different capabilities, but there are a number of people who can work in only one of the written languages. In theory, this means that it should be possible to compare people with Vai literacy and no schooling to people with English literacy, which always involves schooling. Another comparison group is Vai who are literate in none of these languages. The study was ambitious in its scope, and was conducted over several years using substantial survey instruments and psychological testing.

The results of the study turned out to be quite surprising, not least to the authors. The first was that literacy made much more sense when considered as a set of socially specific practices rather than isolated skills. They define practice as 'a recurrent, goal-directed sequence of activities using a particular technology and particular systems of knowledge' (Scribner and Cole, 1981, p. 236). Based on this, they argue that 'literacy is a set of socially organised practices which make use of a symbol system and a technology for producing and disseminating it' (p. 236). This is one of the first times that the notion of literacy as social practice is mentioned, and certainly influenced the broader acceptance of literacy as an activity embedded in people's lives.

The second finding is really a cluster of insights. In summary, the ability of a person to do well with a test that reflects a particular cognitive ability that could be theoretically associated with literacy is related to the extent to which they have been in a situation calling upon that specific ability – whether it was related to literacy or not. In other words, if you have a job that requires abstract classification of items (one of the classic areas that the strong literacy thesis claims for written language) then you will be good at that classification whether you can read and write or not. As Scribner and Cole put it:

> Our results are in direct conflict with persistent claims that 'deep differences' divide literate and non-literate populations . . . On no task – logic, abstraction, memory, communication – did we find all non-literates performing at lower levels than all literates. (1981, p. 251)

This does not mean that literacy is associated with no cognitive effect whatsoever. They add 'we can and do claim that literacy promotes skills among the Vai, but we cannot and do not claim that literacy is a necessary and sufficient condition for any of the skills we assessed' (pp. 258–259). The skills tended to cut across all the variations of literacy among the Vai, driven more by experience and practice than anything else. The cognitive effects of literacy came about because certain skills were applied mean-ingfully and frequently in the practices of literacy, rather than from the literacy capabilities themselves. This is a subtle point, but a crucial one. It suggests that literacy only changes thinking to the extent that it calls for rehearsal of thinking strategies common to all humans, and that these strategies could potentially be developed in other contexts that call for the same practices. So playing poker, which involves multiple levels of sorting, might teach abstract classification as well as using written language.

There was one set of skills that Scribner and Cole identified as strongly linked to schooling – the ability to talk about things. These skills included exposition, logical tasks, and memory of a list of names, but even here experience and age were far stronger factors. These are the com-municative strategies that are explicitly modelled by teachers for years, so it would perhaps be surprising if people attending school did not pick them up to some degree.

If we accept Scribner and Cole (1981) at face value – and it is cer-tainly a very well-designed and nicely executed study – then the case would appear to be closed on the idea that literacy enhances thinking skills. Indeed, even though the literature available for discussion of these issues is limited, there is a fair degree of support for the view that literacy does not substantially change cognition. It is informative to work through the different areas and see what the evidence suggests.

The effect of literacy capability on long-term memory appears to be extremely limited. Long-term memory is generally seen as possessing very little volatility and not really open to a great deal of change. As Flower and Hayes explain: 'unlike short-term memory, which is our active processing capacity or conscious attention, long-term memory is a relatively stable entity and has its own internal organisation of information' (2004, p. 47). So fears that use of written language would erode the ability to remem-ber as everything became transferred to a textual archive have little basis in the way long-term memory works.

There do seem to be some links between reading ability in children and short-term memory, but the evidence is quite confused. One per-spective that fits quite well with current thinking is that the capacity of working memory is relatively fixed, but that individuals can become more fluent at certain activities, providing them with more cognitive headroom. When I started to learn to drive, it took my complete concentration to change gear, never mind trying to miss the stable block (Luckily for me I was learning on a farm. And yes, I did hit the stable.). Many years later

I can have a conversation, listen to music and drink coffee while driving. This is the notion of automaticity mentioned in Chapter One. The relevance to reading is that the factor that determines whether a person's working memory is up to the task of reading a given text is the degree to which they are practiced at the putting together that type of text (Byrd and Gholson, 1985).

A later analysis suggests that 'many of the cognitive differences observed between readers of differing skill may in fact be consequences of *differential practice* that in itself resulted from early differences in the *speed* of initial reading acquisition' (Cunningham and Stanovich, 1998, p. 1). The more practice in reading, the more automatic and swifter text processing becomes, the more processing space is left for understanding the message of the text. So there is little evidence of reading affecting short-term memory beyond helping it to become more efficient, at reading. These arguments fit well with Scribner and Cole.

The possibility that reading and writing enhance linear, classically logical thought is, again, difficult to test. There is very little evidence around this proposition, and what does exist is tied up with schooling and maturation effects. There is a view that writing involves the ability to express ideas more clearly in words because in writing 'cohesion is lexicalised' (Tannen, 1985). This means that the only tool available to communicate meaning is the arrangement of words. For literacy to have an impact on the thoughts underlying speech, it would be necessary to show that spoken language did not have the imperative for lexicalisation. This proves to be extremely difficult to do – it seems that both oral and written language use highly contextualised lexicalisation structures (Tannen, 1985). There can be little support for the idea that literacy makes a difference in an area with no clear difference between spoken and written language.

Finally, there is the hypothesis that literacy may help people to be more critical of language use through the development of meta-linguistic skills. There is some evidence that exposure to written language does indeed enhance language use, primarily through exposure to vocabulary. Written language exposes the reader to a far wider range of less usual words (Cunningham and Stanovich, 1998). In addition, and reflecting earlier points about practice in reading enhancing reading, good readers tend to read a great deal more than struggling readers. Children who score at the 90th percentile for reading spend about 21 minutes a day reading outside school, covering about 1.8 million words a year in non-school reading. Those at the 10th percentile spend 0.1 minutes a day for 8,000 words a year. The average (at the 50th percentile) is 4.6 minutes a day for 282,000 out-of-school words (Cunningham and Stanovish, 1998). While it is not really clear whether better readers read more because it is easier for them or it is easier because they read more, reading volume does appear to go along with reading ability as captured by test scores. The development of vocabulary involved in this cycle can be considered a meta-linguistic skill.

The contribution of this kind of meta-linguistic skill and other forms of meta-cognition to task performance is challenged, however. Byrd and Gholson (1985) found that there was little relationship between meta-cognition and reading task performance, and concluded that meta-linguistic abilities really did not make that much difference. It seems most likely that, as with other aspects of literacy capability, critical engagement with texts comes about through practice in critical engagement with texts. Literacy capabilities lead to meta-linguistic skills to the extent that a given context calls for the rehearsal of those skills, rather than there being an automatic flowering of these skills as people learn to read and write.

Overall, and perhaps rather surprisingly given the intuitive attraction of the literacy thesis, there is very little evidence that literacy capabilities necessarily lead to changes in individuals' cognitive structure. There does seem to be a flow between contextual demands, rehearsal of the skills needed to meet those demands, and improved performance on tasks associated with those skills, but that framework is more about general cognition than about literacy capabilities specifically. If there seems to be little evidence that literacy capabilities necessarily affect cognition, there is the question of whether there are other forms of psychological impact. In the next section we turn to affective matters – emotions and self-efficacy.

Literacy and self-perception

It is a very common claim that literacy learning can make a difference to the way people see themselves. This would fit with the idea of literacy capabilities, as increasing capability to achieve intended ends can be expected to increase the belief in one's own ability. So the central question is whether a change in literacy capability produces a positive change in self-perception. As one of the findings derived from a series of large-scale studies, Feinstein *et al.* (2008) underline the importance of self-perception to individuals:

> *Positive self-concept promotes beneficial health behaviours and protects mental health. If an individual has high regard for themselves generally, and of their abilities in particular, they will consider themselves capable, be more inclined to persevere in the face of adversity, and take care of themselves not only in the here and now, but also in the future (p. 22).*

This suggests that any positive changes in self-perception would potentially be extremely important and valuable outcomes of literacy learning, and this is reflected in the frequency of claims that there are connections between literacy and the way people see themselves. In the literature available to us, the claims fall into three categories. The first is that literacy leads to increased confidence, the second is that it leads to enhanced self-esteem, and the third is that it affects the sense of self-efficacy. Many different terms are used for quite similar constructs throughout the literature, and these terms are not always used consistently, so my approach here is to tie the evidence either to:

1. confidence, meaning an emotional state based on the belief that an individual can achieve what they set out to achieve;
2. self-esteem, meaning that the person values themselves; or
3. self-efficacy, the belief that the individual can set their own goals and control the process of getting to them.

These factors are closely related but do represent distinctive components of self-perception. I have laid them out in this manner to show the movement from a more emotional concern with confidence to a more active concern with self-efficacy and getting things done.

There is a significant body of work in the literature of adult literacy claiming that literacy learning enhances the confidence of learners. This is quite often framed within the claim that bad experiences of schooling have reduced the confidence of learners in educational settings, because of openly malicious teachers or unsupportive environments more generally. Another version of this claim begins with the premise that growing up in a household where there are low levels of engagement with education can lead to a lack of the cultural capital (the 'know-how') necessary to navigate the educational system, and therefore to a feeling of uncertainty. Explanations such as these make sense on an intuitive level.

A typical study is the examination, by focused interviews, of the experiences of 30 adult learners at one further education college in England. The study found that 93 per cent of learners identified increased confidence as a key indicator of their own success in the programme (Eldred, 2002). The next most cited indicators, at 30 per cent, were improvement in reading and writing at work, using the telephone, and the difference in skills being noticed by family or friends. This suggests that confidence is an extremely important outcome, and this degree of recognition of confidence is not unusual. McGivney (2002), one of the most accomplished people working in the field of learner outcomes, argues that 'soft' outcomes are the most important to learners and that confidence is the most important of these. She cites Reisenberger and Sanders (1997): 'confidence should not be dismissed as a nebulous by-product of a good learning experience but should be seen as an important outcome of adult learning which tutors should plan for and encourage' (p. 25).

A recent longitudinal study of adult literacy learners in Scotland underlines the importance of confidence as an outcome. Maclachlan, Tett and Hall (2009) state that 'there appears . . . to be a marked correlation between engagement in learning and increased confidence' (p. 339). Interestingly, the activities where that confidence was evident were not necessarily related directly to text literacy, but to communication more broadly.

The next area to discuss is self-esteem, which can be considered perhaps as the way confidence is reflected within the learners' views of themselves. Again there is a wide range of evidence put forward for the notion that literacy learning has a positive impact. One of the clearest explanations, and one that seems very close to the notions implied by literacy capabilities, is provided by Fingeret and Drennon (1997):

> *As students' abilities to engage in literacy practices develop, their image of themselves may move closer to their ideal and self-esteem may increase. In addition, increased self-esteem may be fostered through experiencing themselves successfully relating well to others, including college-educated volunteers and staff members; helping others, as seen in their interaction with groups; and writing pieces that others find worthy of publishing. (p. 84)*

The link that Fingeret and Drennon are implying here is that learners come to value themselves more as they experience success in and around interactions with text. This is supported by the results of a large-scale longitudinal study in England, which compared learners and non-learners. The study used a standard self-esteem scale and showed significantly higher self-esteem for learners, though the statistical significance of this result varied over the course of the study (Metcalf and Meadows, 2009). The same scale was used a number of years earlier in a US study, and again showed that literacy learning was associated with higher self-esteem scores (Bingman, Ebert and Bell, 2000).

It seems reasonable to conclude that there is an association between self-esteem and literacy learning, especially if increased social interaction is taken into account as an indicator of self-esteem. Fingeret and Drennon (1997) propose that limited literacy capabilities may be associated with a degree of shame, and that as literacy improves this burden of shame is lifted. While this proposal is perhaps beyond the data they provide, it does have a degree of plausibility in a society where strong literacy capabilities are taken as the norm.

Finally, we can move further into the active realm by looking at self-efficacy. Here our interest is whether expanded literacy capabilities make people more likely to believe that they can set and attain their own goals. Again the evidence for a connection between learning and self-efficacy is strong. McGivney (2002) points out that increases in learner self-esteem and self-efficacy were held to be the most important benefits by further education practitioners, and that increased confidence supports improvements in self-reliance and self-perception. Bingman, Ebert and Bell (2000) specifically identify enhanced self-efficacy as a learning outcome claimed by eight out of the ten learners they followed.

There is evidence from large-scale surveys to support the importance of self-efficacy. In Comings' (2009) description of a major study of persistence among adult literacy learners, the programme's ability to support increased self-efficacy is identified as one of the keys to keeping learners engaged. Other studies, while using different language, tend to support the notion that the belief in one's ability to set and attain goals is enhanced by literacy learning (Maclachlan, Tett and Hall, 2009; Feinstein et al., 2008). It does seem that there is evidence for a connection between literacy learning and belief in the ability to attain goals, though it is perhaps less extensive than the support for the link between literacy learning and confidence or self-esteem.

Overall, there is some evidence that engagement in literacy learning leads to affective benefits in terms of the way learners see themselves, as we might predict from the capabilities model. The findings around confidence, self-esteem and self-efficacy are mutually consistent, and suggest that there is a relationship between these factors and literacy learning. For those who are interested in the development of literacy capabilities as a way to increase human potential, this looks like good news.

Unfortunately, there is a catch. A lot of the evidence for this discussion is derived from qualitative programme evaluations, where learners are interviewed about their experience. This offers the opportunity for learners to present their own perspective on the impact of their learning, but does also raise questions regarding the way they were asked and the expectations they may have picked up from programme instructors. It is not clear what the long-term meaning of these findings is, as Beder pointed out at the end of an extensive survey of evidence on impact:

> *Of all the evidence presented in this study, the evidence that adult literacy education produces gains in positive self-image (and similar constructs such as self-confidence and self-esteem) is the strongest . . . the question is not whether learners' self-image improves with participation, but whether improved self-image is a lasting effect that promotes impact in the human capital domain and reduces social dependence. On the one hand, it could be that reported gains in self-image are no more than the short-term elation people normally experience when they have completed difficult and protracted tasks. On the other, the effects might be lasting. Although . . . the relationship between enhanced self-image and the attainment of other benefits needs to be established. (Beder, 1999, p. 78)*

Another significant issue arises because of the tie with programmes. Most of this data looks at literacy learning, conflating two elements: a change in literacy capabilities and the experience of being in an educational programme. In other words, how can we be sure that the literacy capabilities have anything at all to do with the affective changes? Perhaps learning car mechanics, or Sanskrit, or dog grooming would bring about similar changes?

This is an especially important point given the IALS finding that in Scotland 93 per cent of people were quite satisfied with their literacy capabilities irrespective of the level they tested at, a consistent finding across the nations surveyed. In addition, 84 per cent of those at the lowest level rated their reading skills as excellent or good (Scottish Executive, 2001b). This finding cannot be dismissed as simply people not knowing what they do not know. Henningsen (2006) identifies this assumption as a major shortcoming of the IALS survey, and suggests it is less patronising and makes more sense to accept that most people think their skills are quite adequate. The issue for affective outcomes is that if most people are happy with their capabilities and think they are already quite good, it seems to reduce the room for improvement through strengthening of those skills.

One possible further argument for the impact of literacy is that when people are asked about how things have changed since being involved in the programme they often frame their answers regarding confidence, self-esteem and self-efficacy in direct reference to increased literacy capabilities. These are two examples taken from research referred to in this section:

> Four times and I finally, finally done it [passed the GED]. And it was all kinds of certificates. I got them all on my wall, you know, and I keep looking at them and think, 'Well, I did that.' [Suzanne] (Bingman, Ebert and Bell, 2000, p. 12)

> It has helped me to use the computer and I need it for work. I can also inter-act with friends better because of the computer, because I know what they are talking about. (Maclachlan, Tett and Hall, 2009, p. 341)

In each case, the speaker is linking changes in self-concept directly to lit-eracy capabilities, specifically to things they formerly could not do but now can. This suggests that for the learners, skills and affect run together in a mutually reinforcing way.

One way to make sense of these different perspectives is to suggest that the appropriate application of skills in specific situations tends to sup-port confidence, self-esteem and self-efficacy, and the failure to do so diminishes these affective factors. Faced with such a situation, the indi-vidual has two choices. One would be to increase the potential for the appropriate application of skills by increasing their repertoire, the other would be to avoid those situations in the future. It could be that the high levels of satisfaction with literacy capabilities demonstrated in the IALS comes from people's ability to avoid circumstances where they would be dissatisfied.

In the end, there is no way to separate the influence of changes in literacy capabilities from the influence of the educational process in changing self-perception. What we can say with some confidence, however, is that literacy learning as a holistic process can very reasonably claim a positive significant effect on the way individuals see themselves, and that learners ascribe this to an increase in capabilities.

Conclusion

The conclusion to be drawn from this discussion is a great deal more subtle than might have been hoped. There seems to be little evidence that literacy changes the psycho-social environment of a society to any substantial degree, and certainly not in any predictable direction. Literacy does not lead to democracy, or modern science, or any other outcome automatically. For individuals, learning literacy does not seem to have a direct or powerful effect on thinking, beyond enhancing those cognitive skills that are practiced during reading and writing. There does seem to be some evidence that literacy capabilities can support confidence, self-esteem and self-efficacy, but even here there is a problem separating the influence of literacy from the influence of education.

Hidden within these rather cautious findings, however, is a strong and positive message. If the literate mind is not that different from the mind of people with less developed literacy capabilities, it means that anybody, potentially starting at any point in their life, has the potential to expand their literacy skills. Within our increasingly logocentric global society, there is evidence that literacy capabilities do provide resources that can be put to positive ends, but there is no magic property of literacy here. What these findings suggest is that almost anybody, in the right circumstances, has the potential to gain access to a valuable set of capabilities, and that they will potentially become more positive in the way they see themselves as they do so. Society, skills and self-perception are not shaped by literacy, but each of these can call upon literacy to extend its force and its reach.

CHAPTER SIX

Economic effects

In this chapter we are going to discuss one of the dominant ideas about literacy capabilities in current discussions, the notion that literacy capabilities are linked to income. Just as with the psychological impact, the argument is made on two levels. There are claims that literacy is directly related to income for individuals, with the implicit corollary that increased capabilities leads to increased personal income. There is also a claim that a nation with higher literacy capabilities among its population will be more productive and have a greater Gross National Product. This argument is certainly used in reference to the developed economies, but perhaps even more insidiously with the developing economies of the Global South. The way to get out of poverty – for nations or individuals – is learning, and learning literacy in particular.

It should be clear by now that these claims cannot be accepted without a great deal of caution. They are too reminiscent of the autonomous view of literacy (Street, 1984), where literacy can change the nature of a society on its own, or the strong literacy thesis discussed in the last chapter. These sorts of statements lead to important questions about whether literacy is really that powerful as an economic driver. The first section of the chapter looks at the relationship between literacy capabilities and individual income in a very straightforward way, asking what evidence exists for any kind of connection between these two factors, and later sections look at the broader socioeconomic effects.

The connection between literacy and income

There is a lot of data showing that lower scores on literacy tests tend to be associated with lower incomes, lower status employment and a range of other challenges. Even though occasionally the heads of massive corporations or well-respected creators come forward and identify themselves as people with limited literacy capabilities, that is not the norm. Most people with few qualifications and a restricted range of capabilities tend not to be making very much money (Scottish Executive, 2001). In this section I will look at the evidence lying behind this connection, and look at some other aspects of the economic associations of literacy, such as data suggesting that people with limited literacy capabilities tend to use more social supports and rely on social services more.

Perhaps the best place to start is with the substantial body of work that has recently been conducted as part of the IALS projects. Part of the impetus for the IALS surveys in the first place was a desire to understand more about the economic significance of literacy for individuals and for national economies. The approach adopted in the survey was to have an extensive background questionnaire, which provided a range of information about the life and experience of the person being surveyed. This background information could then be linked to the person's literacy score, and connections with employment history, income and so on could be analysed.

The final report for the IALS survey (Organisation for Economic Co-operation and Development, 2000) presents data for the 22 countries involved in the surveys to that date. The findings are robust and, in many ways, extremely convincing. They show that workforce participation varies between those with lower literacy test scores (Levels 1 and 2) and those with higher scores (Levels 3, 4 and 5). The difference is far from consistent across the 22 countries, varying from around five per cent in Switzerland to around 30 per cent in the Netherlands, but there is always a difference. There are also indications that literacy scores are related to the type of job people have, with managers tending to have higher scores on the prose scale and technicians doing well on the quantitative scale. These results support the idea that employment level and employment type are linked to literacy scores.

The report also makes the point that there is a degree of 'looseness' between people's measured literacy skills and the education level they have attained – people with strong qualifications may have lower scores on actual skills tests, and vice versa. One recurrent theme of much of the discussion around literacy levels is how the levels map across to qualifications. We will return to this question, but for now it is sufficient to note that there is a fair amount of overlap between the two concepts in discussions around literacy even though the exact relationship between tested skills and qualification levels is not clear.

Countries involved in the IALS often conducted additional research on the economics of literacy using their national statistical organisations and local databases. These analyses tried to pin down the income implications of literacy capabilities directly. In the Netherlands, Groot and Massed van der Brink (2006) estimate that the income difference between somebody with lower secondary education and a similar person with higher education appears to be around 39 per cent. They say:

> *Of the low literate persons, five per cent has no income of his or her own and more than 70 per cent does not have a remunerated job. Another 18 per cent belongs to the 20 per cent of people with lowest income. And, of the low literate persons, only two per cent belongs to the 20 per cent with the highest income. (p. 7)*

Of the most literate group, 3.5 per cent have no personal income, and only 18.3 per cent have no income from paid employment. Groot and Massed van der Brink (2006), based on their own previous work, suggest that each extra year of education realises about 3700–4800 Euros per year of additional income. Even though the authors move backwards between skills and education, the argument for the economic value of capabilities is strong.

The same type of argument regarding the value of additional education is common in other countries. In the United States, Kirsch, Braun, Yamamoto and Sum (2007) suggest that: 'The expected lifetime earnings of males with a bachelor's degree in 1979 was 51 per cent higher than their peers with only a high school diploma. By 2004, however, this difference had widened to 96 per cent' (p. 4). The authors go on to predict dire consequences for the United States due to the continuing disparity in skills and rates of degree completion among different groups, which are likely to entrench current social divisions.

While slightly less alarmist in tone, Hankivsky (2008) makes a very similar argument regarding the cost of people dropping out of high school in Canada. She analyses both social and individual costs, and predicts that over the course of a lifetime somebody who does not complete high school will earn about $104,000 less than a comparable person who did graduate from high school. It seems that there is a consistent and compelling body of evidence to support a case for a connection between even those levels of education that are common and lifetime earnings – in other words, you do not need to be a doctor or a lawyer to start seeing real economic returns to education.

An Australian study backs this up. Here the researchers compared three different ways of measuring the benefit of staying on at secondary school an extra year, in response to new legislation raising the leaving age an extra year (Leigh and Ryan, 2005). The conclusion was that even allowing for inflation and other variables, and assuming that no extra qualifications were obtained during that year, people stood to make about three times more during their lifetime than the lost income from that year. And that assumes, of course, that people leaving school would be moving immediately into paid employment.

Probably the most advanced work on relationships between literacy scores and a host of social variables, including income and employment status, has been conducted in the UK over the last ten years. The UK, while taking part in the initial round of IALS in 1996, chose not to take part in the second round a few years later. The two sources of data for the highly sophisticated analyses conducted recently have been cohort studies, where all the people born in one week of a given year are surveyed repeatedly, and a new survey instrument designed to reflect the definition of basic skills driving the English Skills for Life system. The following discussion is informed entirely by work conducted in England, but is probably broadly consistent with the situation in the other three nations of the UK even though they have their own education systems and approaches to literacy.

It is necessary to acknowledge that the UK has a different approach to qualifications than most other countries. It is very highly qualification driven, and the variety of qualifications at different levels is daunting. There is also a historical acceptance that many people in the UK will not achieve advanced qualifications – the UK has remained a highly stratified society with different expectations for people from different backgrounds. As Reder and Bynner (2009) argue 'in countries such as England, the problem [of differentiation in the society] is compounded through an educational system that implicitly accepts that a substantial proportion of children will 'fail'' (p. 5). Overall, the effect of this situation is to make the linkages between educational attainment and literacy capabilities even less clear than in other national systems.

Nonetheless, the UK has produced some sophisticated analyses. One interesting study looks at the advantages to marginal learners of staying on in education, meaning that individuals on the cusp of leaving at the end of compulsory schooling decide to stick with it (Dearden, McGranahan and Sianesi, 2004). This is roughly equivalent to the education and skills levels posited as a key change in literacy capabilities – Level 2 to Level 3 in IALS terms. The researchers looked at evidence from the 1970 Birth Cohort Study when the people involved were in their late 20s, and found that the return to men for staying on was 11 per cent, and for women it was 18 per cent. This is not the same as the return to everybody if all stayed on, but it does mean for people who are right at the boundary between continuing and leaving, continuing education is the rational choice. A second range of studies using data from the same cohort at the age of 34 showed around a 10 per cent return on tested literacy and numeracy skills (Vignoles, de Coulon and Marcenaro-Gutierrez, 2008).

This is confirmed by another piece of research from roughly the same period, but this time using the Skills for Life survey dataset. Again, researchers were able to quantify the benefits of increased literacy and numeracy capabilities, conceptualised as higher scores on the tests used (Grinyer, 2005). In this analysis moving up one literacy level, from Entry 3 to Level 1 (Level 1 being roughly equivalent to average results on the examinations taken at the age of 15 in English schools) brought a return of 12 per cent extra income, with more for women. For numeracy, the same step brought 6 per cent more income, and high levels of numeracy, unlike high levels of literacy, brought a premium of 19 per cent. These results support some of the analyses based on the IALS. Across most UK-based studies there are clear indications that the returns to numeracy skills are both clearer and more substantial than those to literacy skills.

An important step forward in this type of analysis is increasing interest in conceptualising the issues in terms of trajectories. It is becoming more credible to view people's life-courses as being strongly influenced in the early stages, which sets a direction for them to follow throughout their schooling and employment. As Bynner and Parsons (2009) put it in a study of the 1970 cohort:

> *Through the wide range of data in all the domains of childhood and teenage and adult life, we can also extend analysis to the part the basic skills play in*

life-course construction as the critical mediators of the conditions of early life on subsequent pathways into and through adulthood (p. 32)

There is a huge range of factors that are relevant to literacy scores. Even though the scores for literacy and related skills are based on different instruments for people of different ages, the pattern of scores – who does well, who does less well – has remained constant for these individuals from the age of five. Some of the factors related to literacy scores at age 34 are low birthweight, whether parents had extended education, social class of father's employment, growing up in an over-crowded home, parental expectations for school-leaving, parental interest in education, and living on a council estate as a child (Bynner and Parsons, 2009). Taken at face value, this study suggests that a great deal of individuals' futures is determined through accident of birth, leading to a rather bleak view.

At this point it may be helpful to introduce an alternative perspective. As mentioned earlier, France pulled out of the IALS and conducted its own survey. Even though the proportion of the population identified as having potential issues with literacy was far smaller in the French survey, there was still a strong link between literacy scores and employment status. The French estimate is that around 8 per cent of employed people have limited literacy capabilities versus 15 per cent of unemployed people (Agence Nationale contre l'illitrisme, undated). One marker of the distinction between the French approach and the general OECD/IALS way of looking at literacy is summarised in the comment that:

Most illiterates are not marginal people. Over half of them work at a job . . . these men and women have succeeded in building up their skills without recourse to the written word and most of them have a job and make consider-able efforts every day. This is why we must stop defining those facing illiteracy only by what they do not know, but also accept to recognise them for what they do know how to do. (p. 8)

This seems like a salutary reminder that while their are clear statistical connections regarding limited literacy capabilities and limited income are clear, this is not the whole story. There are three important points that even the most sophisticated of these survey instruments has not completely cleared up. The first is the vexed issue of causality, as I mentioned in chapter three. These studies do make a convincing case that limited literacy capabilities are linked in general terms to less income, and that seems like an intuitive finding. But it is not clear whether limited literacy is the cause for low status low pay jobs or the result of these jobs. We do not know how much two women who came out of school on the same day with the same qualifications would differ twenty years later if they had different jobs. Perhaps one became a librarian and worked with text all the time, while the other provided care for elderly parents and worked as a book-keeper for local small businesses. It would hardly be surprising to see some divergence here. I am certain that my numerical skills would be far weaker than my cousins the aero-space engineers, and far stronger than those of my lawyer cousin.

The second issue is the reliance on scores on literacy tests as an indicator of real world skills. I do not want to go on about this at length here. Perhaps it is enough to point out that sitting a test for literacy skills, whether at home using paper and pencil as was done in IALS, or on a laptop, as in the Skills for Life survey, is not a totally valid indicator of applying appropriate skills in specific situations. This is a significant issue for any form of skills testing, and there are so many confounding factors that could come into play that it is very easy to devalue the surveys. This would be a shame, because they probably do tell us something extremely valuable, though not with the precision that is claimed for them.

The third issue is what Silles (2007) calls 'the sheepskin effect.' Simply put, this means that even if two qualifications take equally long to get, say a degree in economics and an electrical apprenticeship, the higher status certificate brings more rewards. This is a real challenge to models that use years of schooling as a way to understand the value of education and skills. It seems that qualifications are not only about skills, but act as signals to employers about other traits they might find desirable. While in the 1970s the sociology of education would perhaps have claimed that the entire value of qualifications was telling employers that this person would be a docile and obedient employee, it is likely that both the content and form of certification matters. One recent study tries to pull apart the cognitive and non-cognitive traits represented by qualifications, and suggests that they are probably fairly equally valuable (Pasche, 2008).

The problem here is that as soon as you start to examine the way literacy capabilities shape income, you run into issues of certification quite quickly. It means that it is really difficult to compare like with like, because an IALS Level 3 performance in an individual with a degree simply does not mean the same thing in the labour market as identical performance from somebody who dropped out in grade 11. Attempts to isolate literacy skills, creating a sort of 'new autonomous model' of literacy, can very easily appear naive in the face of the economic and social experiences of life.

We have not yet addressed whether a change in literacy capabilities will lead to a change in financial status, and in order to understand that we have to look at the way literacy levels affect the economic situation of that whole population. As with so many other aspects of literacy, the individual economic effects, both positive and negative, are modified by the context.

National prosperity and literacy

One of the factors behind the increased interest in basic skills over the last two decades has been a concern that limited literacy and numeracy capabilities among the general population reduce a nation's ability to respond to the newly globalised market. This is summarised in the following quote:

> *The origins of this concern [with basic skills] lie in the technological transformation and globalising pressures, which have been a dominant feature of their economies since the 1970s . . . Such poor skills may not only be a challenge for the individual in functioning effectively in adult life but are also seen as constituting a major economic cost in terms of lost productivity and international competitiveness. (Reder and Bynner, 2009, p. 1)*

Sometimes the descriptions of the situation have become quite hysterical – this is consistent with a history of crisis mentality in adult literacy education (Quigley, 1997), but may not reflect the most considered position:

> *. . . a rising chorus of national and international studies that have singled out some pervasive and unhealthy trends in the Canadian economy. Specifically, Canada's preparedness to compete in the increasingly competitive, knowledge-based global marketplace is in jeopardy . . . it seems clear that this downslide is rooted in a chronic national blind spot – a lack of awareness that investing in the human capacity of Canada's workforce is paramount to success (Bailey, 2007, p. 4)*

The argument behind this view of basic skills is a simple one. If we now live in an era of an essentially unified worldwide market where manufacturing plants, financial services and corporate head offices can be situated anywhere, then businesses need some kind of incentive to base themselves in a particular part of the world. Access to markets is no longer a strong enough factor due to the cheapness of transportation, and underbidding on labour will never be an option for the Western economies given the low wage rates in countries like Vietnam. However, the argument goes, it may be possible to create, attract and sustain trade by offering a high skills environment, where companies will pay a little more to their workforce because they know they can expect high productivity and high standards from them. This is seen to be guaranteed by education.

This picture is a modification of a human capital argument. In the 1960s economists were struggling to understand the extraordinary recovery of economies such as West Germany, which had been almost wiped out by World War II reparations and heavy bombing of production sites. Yet twenty years later, they were incredibly healthy and strong, and economies such as Japan were even expanding into new markets and winning a reputation for high quality. These developments suggested that economies did not thrive by physical plant alone, and that there were other factors at play. A loose alliance of economists began to model a factor they called 'human capital' as a way to summarise the education and experience that workers bring to economic processes (Becker, 1975).

Conceptualising these traits in this way allows the knowledge of humans to be analysed just like any other form of capital, based on an assumption that humans make rational investment decisions. It is possible to calculate the cost of investment in human capital (including opportunity cost, the loss of other opportunities implied by investment in one area) and calculate return on investment. In the original version of the theory researchers were interested in macro-level human capital, or the distribution of knowledge within and between economies. Over the last four decades, the theory has been applied increasingly frequently to micro-economics, the study of individual behaviour. While that shift is highly attractive to policymakers seeking to understand the operation of the economy on a human level, there is still some way to go in ascertaining whether it really is a good model of human behaviour— for example, while on average a population of people may make rational decisions, it is less clear that individuals necessarily do.

The corollary of the human capital approach is the effort to explain less desirable outcomes. Negative economic and human effects such as high health care costs or involvement in crime can be quantified as much as the positive ones can be, and then connections can be made between investment in human capital and the returns on this investment both in terms of positive economic impact and avoidance of negative economic impact. Health and family impacts of literacy will be discussed in subsequent chapters, but mostly they follow the same line of argument as economic advantage, so if that should prove to be credible then some of the reductions in negative impact can also be accepted.

Literacy has become a key concern in this kind of argument, with statements something like 'increasing the skills of the population of the UK by one level would increase GDP by x percentage points' being fairly common. This is, of course, a causational statement, and needs to be treated with our customary caution. However, there is a wide range of evidence, based on a human capital approach, that skills and economic growth are associated very strongly. The question remains open regarding exactly what kind of human capital is associated with what kind of growth. Blundell, Dearden, Meghir and Sianesi (1999) state:

> *Two major strands of thought have emerged. The first one sees human capital just as an ordinary input in production: the level of output depends on the level of human capital. This implies that the growth rate of output depends on the rate at which countries accumulate human capital over time. The other idea views human capital as the primary source of innovation, increasing individuals' capacity both to produce technical change and to adapt to it. Education levels (human capital stocks) are thus linked to productivity growth, and the returns to human capital accumulation are justified by the separate and crucial role human capital plays (p. 16)*

What the authors are suggesting is that either *quantity* of human capital matters, and it is not too important what form it takes, or *quality* is all important, because human capital works in a different way from economic capital. In a simplified sense, the question boils down to whether a country is better having 100 per cent of the population at secondary education level, or 30 per cent of the population with doctorates and everybody else with primary education. This is a political question to some degree, since there are important value questions lying behind any strategy selected. The question is whether it is better to educate a few people more highly, leading to an elite, or to aim for equity at the potential cost of limited economic return.

108

The claim that literacy education, among other forms, is the key to prosperity is not limited to the developed economies. The UNESCO Education for All (2008) programme promotes basic education for every human as a right and an expectation – and an important contributor to a range of desirable outcomes including poverty alleviation. The countries with the lowest levels of educational participation are often dealing with the highest levels of deprivation, and the opposite is also true. The richer the country you are born into, the more likely you are to get advanced education. But it does not follow that investing scarce resources into education at the expense of other social programmes leads to economic success. Wolf (2002) discusses a range of evidence showing that both strengthening economies (such as the erstwhile Asian Tigers) and weakening economies cannot be linked to educational investment. And students in the countries that were wildly successful in the 1980s and 1990s did not score any more highly on standardised testing than the Western countries – until they were successful. At that point they had money to invest in schooling and simultaneously their performance began to improve markedly.

Broad evidence suggests that different types of education appear to be more or less educationally significant in different types of economy. For developing economies, the widest possible participation in primary and secondary education is related to economic growth, whereas for OECD (developed) economies tertiary education is the more important factor. Cross-country studies show that the initial average level of schooling is strongly correlated with growth (Blundell, Dearden, Meghir and Sianesi, 1999), so the higher level of education everybody can reach in the first place, the better it is for the entire society. The answer to the question above, about whether quality or quantity matters, appears to be that both are associated with high-income, high-growth economies. The available data seem to suggest that the optimal situation would be a well-educated general populace with some highly educated specialists.

As with the discussion of the psychological impacts of literacy, it is very difficult to tease apart the economic impacts of literacy from those of education more generally. One way to do this would be to look at countries with literacy capabilities measured through IALS and compare the predictions of GDP based on those figures with the predictions based on schooling. Coulombe, Tremblay and Marchand (2004) did exactly this, and found that literacy skills were a better predictor of economic conditions than more traditional measures. This work implies that it is not just education that matters – it is exercise of skills in the workplace and home lives of the population. Wolf (2002) supports this conclusion, based on British data from IALS, and makes an interesting argument that in developed economies it looks as if higher levels of education are more significant than they really are simply because people with better literacy skills stay on at school and move into tertiary education. So individuals with strong skills show up as highly educated, making it look like it is the education that matters when perhaps the most important consideration is the skills. Taking these arguments together suggests that perhaps developing and OECD economies are not really that different after all; the acquisition and application of literacy capabilities is a central economic factor.

There is still an issue with causation here, which I think it important to address. Blundell, Dearden, Meghir and Sianesi (1999), discussing attempts to understand the value that education adds to an economy, state:

> *The problem with these studies is that there are considerable difficulties in the definition, measurement and comparison of skills and competencies. There are also problems establishing the direction of causality: does more education lead to higher growth or can richer countries afford to spend more on education?*
> *(p. 16)*

While these problems are significant, on balance there is clear empirical evidence that literacy capabilities within a society do play a part in economic development. Equally, economic development both demands those capabilities and pays for their acquisition. Education is hardly a luxury, but it is expensive, and it requires a fairly well developed infrastructure to deliver effectively on anything like a universal level. It is difficult for a society that does not have resources to create a schooling system. Once it is created, and is delivering literacy capabilities to the population, the school system is in itself an economic driver and a consumer of its own products. The historical pattern of clever schoolchildren going on to become school teachers is an ancient and honourable one (Wolf, 2002). Overall, economic development and literacy capabilities are strongly tied together.

That does not mean that literacy is a magic bullet. Literacy alone cannot drive economic success and neither should literacy capabilities be identified as the cause of economic difficulties. The significant factor is the fit between the capabilities available to the population and what is required within the economy. This suggests there is a need to do better than the broad generalisations that opened this section, with their assertions that limited capabilities have a direct – and dire – costs for the economy. The level of skills needed to be successful and productive in employment are not identical. Rather there is a distribution of required capabilities across different sectors of the economy. It certainly could be that the distribution of capabilities might not match the requirements at certain times, but that would seem to be a natural consequence of rapidly changing economies and a heavily front-loaded education system where people are expected to be able to work for up to fifty years using literacy capabilities they learned in their teens.

If we accept that strong economies and strong capabilities go together, then it makes sense to ensure that those capabilities are strengthened and maintained whenever possible. This brings us to a slightly different question – can strengthened literacy capabilities change the economic situation of individuals?

Better capabilities and income

The balance of evidence suggests that levels of education do affect individual income, with the costs of each year of schooling past compulsory school leaving age associated with clear returns. In addition, there is good evidence that literacy capabilities are strongly related to the economic performance of a country. In general terms, there are convincing reasons to believe that literacy capabilities are a good thing economically. It is not yet clear, however, whether literacy education for adults is a good investment *purely* on an economic level. The question is the extent to which the individual's long-term trajectory determines economic outcome, and the ability of individuals to change the direction of this trajectory once established. As Johnston (2004) cautions:

> It is one thing, therefore, to say that an increase in literacy skills would be beneficial for individuals (or for firms or for the economy), but quite another to say whether this can actually be achieved, what it would take to accomplish it, and how much it would cost. This is not to suggest that adult literacy programmes are ineffective, just that there is little effectiveness information in the literature and what little exists is inconclusive. (p. 45)

In almost all cases, the economic rewards for any education take the form of increased work income, so the place to begin is how the labour market works, and what it rewards. Wolf (2002) suggests that there has been a polarisation in the Western labour market between jobs that need high level training (including university degrees), and jobs that really require fairly limited skills. The pay associated with these jobs tends to reflect the skills demanded in the position, so economic impact for an individual means that they have to be able to move upwards in the employment structure. This means either a move from unemployment to employment or a move from a lowly paid job to a better paid one.

The challenge is working out how this upwards movement happens. Individuals need to be able to signal that they have increased literacy capabilities, and most employers would not be interested in looking at 'before and after' test results to check that the individual's capabilities were strong. Within the current economic system, the key to this signalling is qualifications, in the sense of formal certification. The IALS evidence that actual tested skills may be a better indicator of productivity is intriguing, but the real world tests that people tend to care about are qualifications. Some jobs also require other indicators of human capital such as experience and on-the-job training, but qualifications are almost a universal requirement.

We have already seen that it is difficult to know whether employers reward qualifications for the actual content of the learning or other factors associated with the qualification, such as behaviour or even willingness to learn. To some extent it does not really matter, because of the way qualifications are used as a filter. Even with the strongest pragmatic skills, it would be impossible for somebody to become a bus driver without the appropriate license. Over the last few decades the extent of, and necessity for, qualifications has expanded enormously. The European Union, and the UK in particular, seem to have led the world in the assumption that qualifications can ensure competency. There are many misgivings about this assumption (Han, 2008), especially the notion that complex human behaviour can be reduced to tests. The significance of formal qualifications, however, is unlikely to reduce in the near future.

What this suggests is that the direct economic impact of enhanced literacy capabilities is likely to come through a qualification that signals those skills to the labour market. This argument is not without challenges – economic research indicates that returns to getting a high school equivalency qualification in the United States may be as low as zero (Heckman and LaFontaine, 2006) or as high as 19 per cent (Tyler, Murnane and Willett, 2000). Overall, however, the mechanism for these signals to operate and the evidence for each step are convincing. These findings suggest

112

that the European Union, with their complicated sets of gradually stepped qualifications, may be on the right track compared to jurisdictions with larger gaps between education levels. The smaller steps mean that learners get more frequent opportunities to demonstrate their progress, with the potential economic benefits this entails. In effect, it lowers the threshold for economic returns to become visible.

There are also indirect economic impacts. One way for this to operate is for enhanced literacy capabilities to allow the individual to enter further study. If this was full-time study there would be an initial dip in earnings, followed by a substantial increase. Another indirect impact would be a promotion that happened some time after the individual strengthened their capabilities. Perhaps a person who was at home providing childcare for some time was able to strengthen their capabilities and enter the workforce at a higher level when their children entered school. In each of these cases it would take longitudinal research designs to capture fully the individual impacts of increased capability. Recent research based on the English Skills for Life study shows exactly these delays at work – there is evidence that the economic benefits may not become evident until three years after a literacy or numeracy course is completed (Grinyer, 2005).

Two further factors play into the individual economic returns. The first is whether there is a demand for the newly acquired capabilities in the labour market. If I learned to read ancient Greek it would demonstrably strengthen my literacy capabilities, but it seems unlikely that this would directly result in a better job. The second is whether people are prepared to act as rational actors and maximise their personal return. If they are not, then the wage premium for stronger capabilities will not be realised. If I learn my Greek, perhaps I could make a little bit more money as a Professor of Classics at Harvard. Unless I am willing to move to Boston this benefit will remain unrealised. Once again the positive impacts of literacy are highly contextualised, and do not flow automatically. In economic terms, there needs to be a match of supply and demand.

The importance of the learner's role in applying skills is underlined by discussions of progression and achievement. Learners often refer to an economic impact directly related to what they are learning, through new employment, their existing employment, alternative income generation or simple savings in living costs (McGivney, 2002). Once people have stronger literacy capabilities they express them in various ways, and some of those uses have economic implications.

There has been a tendency in recent policy to suggest that perhaps literacy education should be targeted at those who are close to a particular threshold, like IALS Level 3. The thinking is that if Level 3 is the point at which returns to capabilities kick in, then the people who are closest to this point (and therefore cheaper to lift to it) should be the priority – it is an easier 'win' both for the people themselves and the broader economy. This logic does not work perfectly, partly because the nature and level of a universal threshold is very difficult to establish. In addition, one highly sophisticated study looked at what the effect of literacy and numeracy courses would be on those who choose not to take them despite relatively weaker capabilities. The study found that the returns would actually be far higher for the people who did not attend the courses (who tended to have weaker skills) than they were for those who did (with stronger skills) (Grinyer, 2005). In summary, it makes little sense to assume that resources should be dedicated to people with any particular range of capability, since advantage can accrue across the board.

In this section I have tried to be as rigorous as possible about the effects of strengthening literacy capabilities on individual incomes, and the broader economic benefits generally follow. Again the central message is that we cannot assume that there will automatically be benefits to individuals, but we can say that strengthened capabilities, particularly when signalled by qualifications, increase the range of economic options open to people.

Conclusion

The economic return to literacy is one of the most difficult and complex areas of analysis, and in this chapter I have attempted to capture the primary perspectives and arguments. There are many hundreds of studies that could have been cited, but they tend to support one side or another of the various issues without laying any to rest. There is no conclusive evidence one way or another for many of these questions. The answer you get depends on the way that researchers frame the issue and what perspective they want to promote.

What we do know is that stronger literacy capabilities are strongly associated with higher personal income and the related social benefits. The other side of this relationship is that it would be difficult for people to secure higher personal income without appropriate literacy capabilities. Literacy and numeracy capabilities are fundamental resources, and

Oxford Brookes University
Harcourt Hill Campus

Customer ID: ******85971

Title: Why literacy matters :
understanding the effects of literacy
education for a
ID: 0092960806
Due: 05 February 2015

Total items: 1
09/01/2015 15:11
Checked out: 2
Overdue: 0

Thank you for using the
3M SelfCheck™ System.

strengthening those resources may or may not have economic implications for individuals. What is certain is that without the opportunity to strengthen capabilities no potential for economic benefit exists. In a world that rewards literacy capabilities, it is essential for all to have access to those capabilities.

Some of the conclusions in this chapter are slightly surprising to me. The arguments for credentialing, for example, are stronger than I expected and also more complicated. I also think that the balance of evidence for the general economic benefits of literacy learning is more conclusive. There is still no causational argument or automatic link between literacy learning and economic benefit, but there are such overwhelming logical and evidence-based arguments for seeing them as closely related that it would be irresponsible to deny the connection.

CHAPTER SEVEN

Literacy and health

The relationship between literacy capabilities and health is one of the most interesting and potentially important areas to discuss. In recent years the relationship has often been captured in the phrase 'health literacy,' though there are very many versions of what this means. There is an important difference between developed and developing nations, primarily because the infrastructure within which health literacy functions is so different. In France, for example, health literacy may focus on doctor-patient information exchange or nutritional choices whereas in other parts of the world they key concern may be practices of household hygiene.

One of the challenges of understanding the ways literacy and health are linked is working out how exactly the links might function – in other words building a model that can be examined. While there is considerable evidence of some degree of correlation between higher levels of literacy and better health, the picture is not entirely clear. This is to be expected in some ways, as so many external and unpredictable factors other than literacy capability have an impact on the health of individuals. In the first section of the chapter I discuss a influential framework for health literacy and health outcomes, which contains within it a number of possible pathways of influence. A lot of the literature on health literacy has been created within the broad area of medical sciences, and takes the view that a key function of literacy is accurate and efficient distribution of the available medical information. As we shall see, however, the evidence seems to support a more complex picture of the interactions of literacy and health.

As we work through the arguments and the evidence the picture that emerges is one of multiple connections between health and literacy rather than one clear incontrovertible link. It seems that these connections perhaps provides more insights into the conditions facing people with lower literacy capabilities and less about the way that texts support a healthy life.

Data on health and literacy

There is a wide variety of information, largely from surveys and life-course work, showing a relatively convincing connection between education and health (Lundborg, 2008). There is far less evidence about the relationship between literacy capabilities and health outcomes – that is, whether a person with little schooling but strong text capabilities would experience positive health effects. Part of the reason is that it would be incredibly hard to set up research around such a question. However, there is a reasonable amount of available data that bears on the issue indirectly, and it seems reasonable to state that people who have higher literacy capabilities also tend to have higher levels of health and healthy behaviour.

One of the strongest pieces of research supporting this claim was conducted in the UK, based on the 1970 cohort study. Bynner *et al.* (2001) were primarily concerned with the economic effects of strengthened literacy capabilities, but they did also look at selected non-economic outcomes. Their findings were interesting, as they show a considerable difference between the effects of numeracy and literacy as measured using a specially developed test. The data shows that at people with strong numeracy skills (by which they meant above Level 1, or around general school leaving level) at the age of 33 have a six to nine per cent lower probability of long-term health problems. This is a very significant connection. Literacy skills do not show the same pattern; they are not related to long-term health. Both physical and mental health are affected here as well, with stronger numeracy skills associated with a lower likelihood of depression. These results are fascinating, and raise all sorts of questions about why numeracy would be associated with better health. One tentative suggestion might be that the common factor is employment, since stronger numeracy capabilities are associated with employment. However, stronger literacy capabilities are also associated with employment but do not seem as important to health outcomes as numeracy.

A second report from a related group of researchers, using biograph-ical methods and published around the same time (Schuller *et al.*, 2002), found little evidence of education, defined more broadly, directly affect-ing health. However:

> *More commonly reported was the preventative effect, where respondents talked about how education had helped them avoid, minimise or address depression. This outcome is a major component of what we have termed the sustaining effect of education. Much of it relates to benefits that stop short of the medical, but that have significant implications for the interrelationships between educa-tion, health and community policies (p. vi)*

This suggests that even though education such as literacy learning may help to keep people well, especially in terms of mental health, it might not help unwell people to get better. This is quite an important difference, and once more blurs the line between the benefits of literacy capabilities and those of being involved in learning generally.

A year later another configuration of related researchers working in the same area looked at the UK National Child Development Study (Feinstein *et al.*, 2003). They examined four questions: 'whether smokers gave up smoking; whether those depressed at 33 recovered from depres-sion; whether those not depressed at 33 were less likely to become depressed; and whether or not people increased their level of exercise. [They] also considered the change in units of alcohol drunk and in life sat-isfaction' (p. iv). The answers showed some positive effects of learning, such as around 27 per cent of people involved in a few courses giving up smoking compared to around 24 per cent of non-learners, but there were also strong indications that people who do a lot of learning also smoke and drink a lot.

A 2008 summary report on the personal benefits of learning identi-fied by the Centre for the Wider Benefits of Learning's cohort studies (Feinstein *et al.*, 2008) was extremely positive about the connections between education and health. It suggested that 'people with better qual-ifications are more likely to have healthy lifestyles, to be fitter and slimmer' (p.10). They argue that involvement in adult learning could prevent over 100 cancers per 100,000 women, improve mental health and longevity, and affect general health positively. Once again, these results are not specif-ically about literacy and health, but do include literacy learning as one of the forms of education considered.

In the United States, data from the International Adult Literacy Survey have been used to illuminate the connections between literacy and health. Rudd, Kirsch and Yamamoto (2004) created a 'Health Activities Literacy Scale' (HALS) (p. 2) composed of 191 items from the literacy surveys that could be defined as relevant to health-related demands. There were five categories of these demands: health protection, health promotion, disease prevention, health care and maintenance, and systems navigation (referring to the ability to work with healthcare systems). Each of these was then linked to specific literacy capabilities examined by the IALS and the earlier National Adult Literacy Survey. The general form of the argument underpinning this approach is that if a person cannot read graphs in daily life, then they cannot read them in a health-related situation. One concern with this approach, however, is that people who score more highly across the tests in general literacy are very likely to score more highly on this sub-set of items, and that it may not differentiate attributes specifically related to health outcomes clearly enough.

The findings of the study were that people's score on the health-related items was related to their education level, ethnicity, country of birth and age. Well-educated, white, US-born young people would be at the top of each of these scales. Wealth also mattered, with working adults with income from savings or dividends scoring well, and retired people scoring lowest. Reading engagement and civic engagement were also associated with a higher HALS score. As with the surveys generally, it is important to bear in mind that these relationships do not necessarily show a causational relationship, and that other mechanisms may be at work. At the same time, it seems unsurprising that the same characteristics of individuals emerge consistently as being associated with higher literacy scores.

If we wish to look more closely at whether having a level of education generally makes a difference in health, one interesting approach is to look at twins, where childhood environment, family background and similar factors will be identical. Lundborg (2008) conducted research on American data looking at the relationship between health and education in twins. He used level of education attained as the main measure rather than years of schooling, and compared across to self-assessed health and the number of chronic conditions, as well as a range of broader factors such as lifestyle, exercise and smoking.

The results suggest a causal effect running from education to health. Higher educational levels are shown to be positively related to self-reported health, but negatively related to the number of chronic conditions . . . My results do not provide any evidence that the education/health gradient works through important lifestyle factors, such as smoking and overweight, or factors such as job risks and health insurance coverage. (p. 21)

In other words, the data seems to demonstrate that education does make a significant difference, and not because it makes people less likely to engage in potentially unhealthy behaviour. As income is controlled for in the study, it is also possible to rule out the possibility that more highly educated people are better paid and able to afford better food, housing or medical care. As the twins in the study were American, it seems particularly interesting that the health outcomes still followed the education level whether or not individuals had health insurance, and therefore could experience quite different levels of care.

A few years before the idea became quite so popular Nutbeam (1999) offered a framework for health literacy, which he saw as a necessary part of health promotion more broadly. Nutbeam suggested that there was three broad types of health literacy. The first is functional, covering the ability to read and understand information provided in a health context. The second is interactive, meaning the person can interpret and act independently on information received. The third is critical, and involves empowerment of the individual towards action around the social and economic factors affecting health. Even though Nutbeam's work has been influential on adult literacy educators who have come to look at health literacy, it seems to have less purchase on health professionals. For most of the writers on health literacy who come from a health background the major concern is the first of Nutbeam's categories – can individuals read and follow instructions correctly? There is a tendency in these perspectives to overlook the difference between understanding advice and complying with it.

Health literacy links health outcomes directly to literacy capabilities. One Australian study (Hartley and Horne, 2006) emphasises the importance of health concerns in understanding the benefits of literacy learning, and suggests that both surveys and small scale studies can help to provide evidence. The authors suggest that there is a need for work to raise the profile of literacy as a contributing factor to health, and agree with Shohet's (2004) argument that in many ways literacy and health concerns are parallel. They suggest that health outcomes may be a key argument for investment in literacy education. In many ways, this reflects general discussion about health literacy, but shares with other views a lack of clarity about what is meant by health literacy.

There seems to be an important difference between health literacy and literacy capabilities in a more general sense. Health literacy is not just about understanding a message, it must also be put it into practice to have any meaningful effect. Kerka (2003) discusses a number of dimensions that may make a difference to the way health information is used. She begins with the need for people to understand the communications about health, and points out that developing plain language communication is a more complicated aim than it seems. There is a danger of over-simplification or, conversely, of text that is seen as plain language by the health professional appearing complex to the patient. Even if the goal of plain language is achieved, Kerka suggests that social and cultural factors need to be considered. For example, different ethnic groups may view different sources of information as the most credible, or may take different stances on health as an individual or collective issue. Finally, there is the question of whether people will actually act on the new knowledge they possess after engaging with health-related material. It is far from clear what is the relationship between understanding the message of a text and making sustainable steps towards healthier behaviours, and what sort of factors might mediate that relationship.

There have been a number of specific health literacy tests developed to try to isolate the characteristics of literacy most applicable to a healthcare context, and some of these are extremely concise. Perhaps the best known – in the United States at least – is the 'Rapid Estimate of Adult Literacy in Medicine' (REALM) (Davis et al., 1993). The word recognition test takes one to two minutes to administer, and the results correlate well with several other more complex and time-consuming tests of literacy capability. While this may help health professionals to tailor their services appropriately, it does not address the social or cultural complexities of health perceptions or the questions about putting new knowledge into practice. The emphasis on word recognition rather than word comprehension may be problematic as well, since recognising the word 'arthritis' is quite different from understanding the complexities of osteoarthritis versus the other forms. The notion of the quick test of language is strongly lodged within the functional view of health literacy.

Nonetheless, if the limitations of these tests are recognised, they can contribute to more informed understanding of the connections between literacy and health. DeWalt et al. (2004) conducted a systematic review of the available evidence on the connections between literacy and health. The review examined 44 research studies using standardised tests as the measure of literacy and relating those measures to health outcomes. The reported findings included a connection between stronger reading ability and greater knowledge of health services and health outcomes. People who tested lower for literacy capabilities tended to use less preventative medicine (such as influenza inoculations) and also tended to have more periods of hospitalisation. One study showed that higher literacy was associated with better compliance with medication; another showed the opposite. There were some cross-generational effects, such as the finding that the higher the reading level of the parents of a diabetic child the better the control of the child's blood sugar levels. Supporting the studies from the UK mentioned earlier, there was some evidence that people with lower literacy skills were more likely to suffer from depression. In one study this relationship disappeared when controls for demographics, social support and so on were put in place. In their summary, the authors or the review suggest that there is reasonable evidence for the belief that:

> reading ability is related to knowledge about health and health care, hospitalisation, global measures of health, and some chronic diseases. People who read at lower levels are generally 1.5 to 3 times more likely to have an adverse outcome as people who read at higher levels. We found less information on the relationship between literacy and health care costs and the role of literacy in mediating disparities in health outcomes according to race, ethnicity, culture or age. (p. 1236)

Based on what we know, it seems likely that in developed economies there is some sort of relationship between engagement with text and health status. However, there are several aspects of this relationship about which it is important to be cautious. It is not clear how much the relationship is mediated by social factors such as class, education level or income. There is evidence on both sides of this particular issue. It is also not clear what we mean by health literacy. If we adopt the functional approach and say that it is the ability to read and understand instructions, it seems straightforward that this will affect the ability to follow instructions. If a more complex definition is adopted, one that includes the ability and the right of individuals to make their own decisions about treatment options and 'compliance' then literacy becomes more complicated. It could well be that stronger literacy capabilities allow better understanding of instructions, but equally allows the individual to get hold of alternative information that suggests they should not follow the instructions. Showing that there is some sort of relationship between literacy and health is important. In itself, though, it does not help us to understand health as an outcome of literacy learning.

Connections between literacy and health

If the connection between literacy capabilities and health outcomes seems credible, it is important to understand exactly how this connection might work. From the previous section it is possible to come up with a number of possible mechanisms. There are not necessarily mutually exclusive, but emphasising one pathway will de-emphasise the others and change the way we think about the possible health outcomes of literacy. It is important to acknowledge that at the present time there is not really enough clear data to suggest that one of these mechanisms is definitely correct or to rule out any others, but nonetheless I think it is quite useful to consider them.

Perhaps the most obvious possibility is that people with strong literacy capabilities can simply read instructions better when they go to see a doctor or other health professional. It could be that they are better able to comprehend instructions such as '3 times a day for 6 days' or 'Avoid salty food with this medication.' This is a strongly functional approach to understanding the connection, and relies on a number of assumptions. The first is that general literacy capabilities transfer seamlessly to health-related contexts, about which there is very little evidence. Rudd, Kirsch and Yamamoto's (2004) analysis of HALS makes this assumption, in contrast to Kerka's (2003) argument that there is a special interpretive frame for health-related information. At this point there is no way to know the extent to which health literacy is simply 'general' literacy applied in a health-centred context or whether it has a more specialised set of abilities contained within it. Two further assumptions, briefly alluded to earlier, are that people follow instructions when they can understand them and that following instructions will lead to positive health outcomes.

A second explanation for the link between literacy and health is that people who have stronger literacy capabilities tend to make healthier lifestyle choices, such as taking exercise and not smoking. The research from the Netherlands discussed earlier (Lundborg, 2008) suggests that this may not be the case, since educational level was found to influence health outcomes separately from lifestyle factors. However, this explanation cannot be ruled out on the basis of one study, and it would fit with Nutbeam's (1999) concept of interactive health literacy. This explanation suggests that stronger literacy makes it more likely that people will manage their own health more effectively.

This explanation can help to shed some light on the finding in the UK surveys that numeracy skills affect health outcomes more than literacy skills. Reyna and Brainerd (2007) look at research on the ability of individuals to assess risk and understand ratios, which they argue are key components of making informed health decisions. They illustrate this with some straightforward examples of odds and percentage questions around disease prevalence and chances of infection. This would explain the results of the UK survey as arising because people with lower numeracy skills find it harder to make the right health choices in the face of quantitative information. The generally accepted definition of health literacy in the United States reflects this type of thinking:

> *The degree to which individuals have the capacity to obtain, process, and understand basic health information and services need to make appropriate health decisions (Institute of Medicine, 2004, as cited in Kutner et al. 2006, p. iii)*

The third, and final, explanation for the link between literacy and health is that people with stronger literacy capabilities, including numeracy, are able to manage any health conditions they experience more effectively. This may or may not mean that they do so more effectively – several of these studies use self reporting, and it could be that more active management of conditions makes people feel better without changing the underlying condition. The scenario here would be that if somebody with strong capabilities fell ill, they could research the condition and learn a great deal more about it than somebody with less developed capabilities. There has been more interest in the idea of the patient as active participants in health decision-making over the last few years, and less expectation that patients will simply do as they are told by the professionals. In this context, an individual with access to a wide range of information is likely to be better placed to work alongside the members of the healthcare team. It is quite possible that the arguments above about the importance of numeracy would still apply, since decisions will have to be informed by quantitative data. An example might be the decision to choose chemotherapy or radiation treatment, where the patient needs to weigh the likelihood or remission against the difficulty of the treatment.

Each of these possible pathways between literacy and health seems logical and fits with the available data. In my view, all three probably represent part of the truth, alongside many other potential pathways. In other words, stronger literacy capabilities play out in all interactions around health, whether to do with lifestyle choices or with interactions with healthcare professionals. The data tends to show slightly weaker connections than might be expected simply because the effects are not causational. People with stronger capabilities do not necessarily behave in healthier ways (I'm thinking here of many professors who smoke, for example) but strong literacy capabilities may make it just a bit easier to learn about healthy choices when you want to make them, explaining the correlation.

The data discussed in this chapter does not fully rule out the possibility of there being underlying factors explaining both higher literacy scores and more positive health outcomes (Reyna and Brainerd, 2007). A lot of the reviewed research tries to control for factors like social background or employment status by comparing people with similar background but different literacy scores. What cannot be controlled for, however, is the possibility that literacy scores themselves represent some underlying factor that affects health but is not directly related to engagement with texts. As an example, perhaps people who are healthier and more positive about their general life conditions simply do better on tests – this would lead to results that show literacy as a protective factor against depression. As with many of the factors that make a difference in health studies, literacy is extremely difficult to isolate and analyse. It is probably naive to expect that this will be possible in the near future.

There clearly is some connection between literacy and health, even though its form is not clear. One way to clarify the connection a little may be to look at developing countries, where health literacy is also being recognised as an important issue. What sort of effects do programmes that focus on expanding health literacy have on health outcomes in these contexts?

Developing countries

The first thing that has to be stated when looking at literacy and health in developing economies is that there is an enormously strong assumption that the two are connected. It is hard to find unambiguous evidence that this really is the case. The difficulty of tracking down clear data means that it is not possible to say whether literacy capabilities have no effect in these contexts or that the effects of literacy are very profound indeed, affecting a wide range of conditions that support health outcomes. The 'Education for All' strategy (UNESCO, 2008), one of the key drivers of educational policy in developing countries, views literacy as a fundamental building block for more equitable and healthier societies.

There is little doubt that poverty, limited literacy capabilities and very significant population health issues generally occur in the same places at the same time. At the time of writing – and for several previous decades – the parts of the world suffering most keenly from these three afflictions are in the Global South, particularly sub-Saharan Africa, the most environmentally vulnerable parts of South Asia, and South America. Ghana, for example, has an average gross national income per capita of $270 (well under a dollar a day), can provide only 60 per cent of its population with access to primary schooling, and has an estimated adult illiteracy rate of around 26 per cent overall and 34 per cent for females (Aoki, 2005). The definitions of 'primary schooling' and 'literacy versus illiteracy' would not be obvious to a Western observer. Primary schooling continues to a very basic level, and can include older children and young adults. Literacy is considered as the ability to read very basic texts. These conditions are not unusual in the developing world, and it seems sadly predictable that people in situations with such overlapping aspects of economic and educational deprivation face enormous health issues.

There is evidence that literacy education can make a difference to people's lives in developing economies. A functional literacy programme in Ghana was found to lead to a wide range of outcomes, including a more positive attitude to education, better support for children's learning and increased awareness of health options (Aoki, 2005). Many of these benefits may arise from involvement in an educational programme rather than from literacy capability itself, but they are still important to acknowledge.

One of the surprising recommendations of the review of the Ghanaian programme was that literacy education should be un-politicised. Though the author makes a good case for this in terms of increased programme stability and effectiveness, it may simply not be possible to achieve this in the light of the intersections between poverty, disease, limited literacy capabilities and characteristics such as identity. Given these entanglements, any literacy education programme, irrespective of audience, location and purpose, will have political dimensions to it. Perhaps the clearest example is gender. Throughout the developing world one consistent factor is that females have less access to education and have less developed literacy capabilities than males. This is not a coincidence but rather the product of many years of prioritisation of male education, often because men were expected to be more economically productive than women. Whatever the rationale, the notion that is acceptable for boys and girls to have differential access to knowledge and capabilities is a cultural and political norm in many developing economies – as indeed it was in the West until very recently.

The reduced emphasis often placed on education for girls and women is especially ironic given the enormous degree of leverage that education for females can often have on the direction of national economic development. One of the most obvious pathways is the ability of mothers to care for their children, and 'women's formal education is associated with the survival and health of their children in many contemporary societies' (Schnell-Anzola, Rowe and LeVine, 2005, p. 19). One study conducted in a barrio of Caracas, Venezuela, attempted to unravel the influence of maternal education on children's health and to understand more about the exact operation of this link. The researchers cite studies from Morocco, South Africa and Guatemala showing the strength of the relationship (Schnell-Anzola, Rowe and LeVine, 2005) and suggest that there seems to be a connection between women's schooling and demographic outcomes, but that this connection comes by way of literacy and access to health information.

The study measured the actual current literacy skills of the women involved as well as looking at level of formal schooling, and came up with some interesting findings. Women tended to retain their literacy capabilities quite well from their initial schooling, so the importance of what is learned as a child should not be overlooked. But formal education alone was not a very useful predictor of the way in which they dealt with health related information as adults. The women's actual literacy skills – albeit conceived in an academic way – provided more powerful insights into their ability to understand and produce the types of communication required in health contexts. In statistical terms, about 18 per cent of the variance in health-related behaviours could be explained by literacy skills. In educational research, this is a convincing result, especially as the researchers' caution means that they have gone to some lengths to ensure it is a highly conservative estimate.

The Schnell-Anzola, Rowe and LeVine (2005) study is an important attempt to understand the ways in which greater literacy capabilities leads to fewer, healthier children and lower infant mortality in developing economies. The authors argue that literacy capabilities allow individuals to use the discourse that predominates in official organisations concerned with health. The women are able to understand health promotion messages better and explain health conditions more clearly because of their literacy capabilities. The study differentiates between the ability to use language in a school-like way and the extent of broader literacy capability, and finds that the broad use of literacy matters. This fits well with the model presented in chapter two, with the implication that broad literacy abilities provide a pool of practices upon that can be drawn upon as needed for a given context.

One study (Berhane, Högberg, Byass and Wall, 2002) attempted to separate out the effects of various factors on the death rate among adults in Ethiopia in the late 1980s and early 1990s. They found that gender (being female made a person less likely to die during this time) and literacy were the most significant factors predicting survival. People who were considered not to be literate were around two and a half times more likely to die over the period than people of the same age in the same situation who were not. The authors do not offer an explanation for the difference beyond suggesting that 'women's education is considered to be one of the strongest determinants of health, since educated women are more likely to break cultural norms and taboos that are detrimental to their health' (p. 718). They go on to support women's literacy education as a way to enhance survival.

Perhaps the best way to conceive of literacy and health in developing countries is to view them as factors that must be grown in parallel, even though this would involve enormous political and economic commitment. The existing research points to a number of factors that strongly influence the ways literacy contributes to health outcomes. The first is gender discrimination as discussed earlier. The relationship between women's education and reduced family size is well-documented, and the World Bank (1993) has identified educational access for girls and women as one of the most basic ways to improve health in developing countries. The situation is improving, according to UNESCO's annual reports, but there is still a considerable way to go. It is perhaps worth commenting on the use of family size as a health outcome in developing countries. The measure is not intended to imply that fewer sub-Saharan Africans would mean fewer poverty-related problems. Rather, the number of children ever born to a woman is a good indicator of the circumstances in which children grow up. As their lives become less perilous due to economic or health circumstances, including starvation and war, a higher proportion of children live to become healthy adults, and the need to have many children to secure the family becomes less pressing. So a situation where women can choose to have fewer children is likely to be a healthier one for all members of a community – and women's health literacy is a key component.

> [Save the Children] has identified the adult female literacy rate (the percentage of women over the age of 15 years who can read and write) as one of the 10 key indicators to assess women's well-being. It is estimated that two-thirds of the world's 960 million illiterate adults are women . . . A mother's level of education correlates closely with a child's risk of dying before age two years . . . Educated women are more likely to postpone marriage and childbirth, give better health care to their families, and send their children to school and contribute to overall economic growth. (Kickbusch, 2001, p. 291)

A second factor affecting the links between health and literacy is the availability of literacy education in a language relevant to the lives of the community. A considerable proportion of the world's poor are rural and are members of minorities even within nations that are themselves minorities in global terms. Developing nations often have one official language (possibly that of a colonising nation, with all the complexities that implies) and many local languages. It is quite possible for teachers 'posted' to rural areas to know only the official language and be unable to communicate with the parents of the children in the schools. Not only does this lead to dissatisfied parents and teachers, it also results in low levels of parental involvement and high teacher turnover (Pansiri, 2008). The relationship between instructors and learners is a key component in educational process, and this issue needs to be addressed if literacy education is not going to simply reproduce colonialism on a more local scale.

A final factor to consider is the credibility of the information that can be obtained by people with health literacy capabilities, and whether the community will believe 'the official line.' There may be cultural conflict between traditional practices and practices that reduce the spread of disease, for example, and different cultural groups will find different sources of information convincing (Kerka, 2003). For example, in many cultures a health message for teenagers from an elder may carry more weight than the same message from a young person, but in Westernised societies the reverse might be true due to the power of peer communication. There is also a political dimension to this factor. While in the West people generally expect government health messages such as 'eat more vegetables' to be well-meaning and relatively benign (despite well-known examples of misleading messages) this is not true of developing countries. Often the population's experience of government has not given them grounds to trust official communications. Wong (1999) describes the early years of HIV infection in China, and the huge degree of scepticism greeting the attempts at public health education. After decades of being deliberately misled by the government, people found it far easier to believe that HIV-AIDS was the latest attempt to control their behaviour than a new health threat.

The balance of evidence supports the importance of literacy education as a key contribution to health in the developing world, both in terms of its direct contribution to communication of health education and because of the side effects that come simply from being educated. The arguments are related to the second type of connection discussed in the last section, and the assumption that people with stronger literacy capabilities can make decisions that are more likely to lead to healthy outcomes for themselves and their children. While the arguments are powerful, however, it is critical to acknowledge that health literacy is not just about individual choices – it has to be part of a network of supports available to people living in poverty. Health literacy is both an individual and a social phenomenon.

Conclusion

The discussion of literacy and health outcomes remains unfinished because there is a great deal still to learn. It seems that stronger literacy capabilities can enhance the health knowledge of individuals, but the process of using health information as a resource for action, and how this translates into behaviour, is not clear. Perhaps the best way to summarise what we know so far about these connections is that literacy capabilities strengthen the ability of the individual to act autonomously around health issues. This could range from the ability to understand public health messages and choose how to act in response to them through to the ability to gain knowledge of a specific condition and actively participate in the management of treatment. In the end the subtle difference between health literacy and literacy applied to health are less important than the ability to obtain and assess information upon which to base actions.

The available research clearly and consistently shows that literacy capabilities are related to health. The obverse of this relationship is that lack of literacy capabilities reduces the ability of individuals and communities to make decisions around behaviour and healthcare. A second layer of this relationship is that literacy capabilities, especially for women, can be an indicator of a reasonable level of economic and personal security. From the perspective of health, literacy capabilities must be seen as intrinsic components of social justice. Failure to provide people with the literacy capabilities needed for engagement with health issues is not neglect; it is a form of violence against them and their children. To deny somebody the tools they need to attain a healthier life is to deny them life.

Health literacy is predicated on capabilities. For positive health outcomes, people have to have the skills available to them, but the situation in which to exercise them also has to exist. Just as the economic effects of literacy rely on both the availability of skills and the opportunity for people to profit by them, health literacy is a system of supply and demand. People have to have opportunities and motivation to make choices that are likely to promote health. The needs may be clear in the developing world, where billions of people still struggle for clean water and sufficient nutrients, but they are also pressing in the industrialised world. While I referred earlier to the example of professors who choose to smoke, there is unequivocal evidence that more educated people do live longer and have healthier lives with fewer hospital visits or chronic conditions. While literacy is perhaps not the whole story, it is a key link between knowledge, behaviour and the ability to thrive.

CHAPTER EIGHT

Family values

The central issue for this chapter is the intergenerational transmission of literacy capabilities, and specifically whether increased capabilities in children can be reasonably claimed as an outcome of adult literacy education. There are two separate questions that have to be teased apart here. The first is whether parental literacy engagement has a clear effect on children's literacy engagement; that is how sure we can be that children's capabilities are directly affected by those of the parents (I'm using parent here to include any adults who take on that role whether they are grandparents, older siblings or other caregivers). The second question is whether a change in parental capabilities, such as through a literacy programme, will have any effect on children's capabilities. It could be, for example, that parental literacy capabilities have a very significant effect indeed upon children's capabilities yet *changes* in parental capability are not passed on. Throughout this chapter I will try to keep these two questions as separate as possible, though inevitably some of the data has been created in circumstances that make this impossible.

The question of intergenerational transmission of educational outcomes such as literacy capabilities touches on an enormous body of work in sociology that sets out to understand how privilege and deprivation of various sorts are passed down in families. I am not going to spend a great deal of time on the literature around education as a process that reproduces privilege and deprivation, largely because there is insufficient space to do it any justice. For those unfamiliar with reproduction theory the central concern is how class, gender and ethnicity combine to ensure, for example, that 'working class children get working class jobs' (Willis, 1977).

The idea that education can be a conservative force helping to keep people in their place is a backdrop to this discussion.

Conventional wisdom holds that family context has a very strong influence on the educational attainment of children, and it would be reasonable to expect this influence to apply to literacy capabilities as well. But as we have seen in other areas, assumptions that seem quite reasonable may prove upon closer examination to have very little substance and it is important to consider the evidence. As with other areas, this is not entirely straightforward.

The first concern is the degree to which the dominance of school-centred literacy within research into family literacy clarifies or obscures the key issues. It may well be that young people growing up in families with little value attached to formal education do develop limited academic literacy capabilities; however, they may have very well developed skills in other areas. An example might be a couple of children growing up in a middle class family that adheres to progressive ideas about child development and sees schooling as inherently oppressive. The children will be provided with lots of resources such as books, art materials and interesting experiences, but may not be encouraged to adopt school-centred ways of reading and writing. Even though these children are likely not to score very highly on a test based on school-centred capabilities, they may well be able to develop and apply capabilities when necessary throughout their lives. It seems important to distinguish between school-based literacy and the abilities that can be developed in other settings through other forms of literacy – it could be that they are equally important in responding to future demand for capabilities. Research, especially in family literacy, often assumes that transmission of school-centred literacy is the most important consideration, but we do not know enough to be certain that this is the case beyond the direct immediate application in school.

When looking at literacy and the family it is useful to distinguish between incidental and intentional support for children's learning. An example of *incidental* support is where a parent has very strong literacy capabilities and provides the child with an environment rich in texts of many types, and some general support to engage with them. The home can be considered to have a literate culture. *Intentional* support refers to situations where the adults set out to provide their children with support in their education. In incidental support the literacy capabilities may or may not match those required by the school; in intentional support it rarely does not. It is quite possible for both types of support to be available in one family. A child could get specific support for learning school literacies in English, for example, but also be exposed to a very rich incidental literacy environment in another language. The issue of intentional or incidental transmission of literacy capabilities turns out to be quite important in understanding literacy within families.

The potential for parents to use their literacy skills to supporting their children's learning has become quite a commonly cited justification for adult literacy programmes. This is a problem. On the one hand, of course, educators welcome any rationale that supports their work, but on the other, it can imply that the adults have had their chance and deserve to access education only if they apply it to their children. This seems like a dangerous route to go down, not least because of the implications for adults without children, or whose children are older. So exploring the family significance of literacy should not be see as a substitute for understanding adult literacy education in its own right. While the family elements of literacy are important, they are not everything.

In the next section I look at how literacy plays out in families, hopefully moving beyond the simple notion that stronger parental literacy capabilities directly enhance children's learning in school. What I would like to suggest in this chapter is that literacy capabilities are a cultural resource for the family and that resource can take many forms and have many different effects. Above all, I want to avoid any insinuation that parents are failing their children if they do not intentionally support their school-based literacy skills – a criticism implied by a great deal of the current writing on family literacy issues.

Parents' and children's literacy capabilities

There are a lot of strong statements concerning the ways in which parents' literacy capabilities affect those of children, and they very often promote the view that the relationship is both well understood and linear. In other words, there is an implicit assumption that the stronger the capabilities of the older generation, the stronger those of the younger generation will be. In this section I will have a look at that evidence, and then in the next section examine the possible explanations and mechanisms.

Brooks *et al.* (2008) suggest that the original interest in the inter-generational aspects of literacy learning came from longitudinal cohort studies such as the National Child Development Study (NCDS) in the UK. The

Adult Literacy and Basic Skills Unit commissioned a study of the data available from the NCDS, and 'the study found that children of parents who reported having literacy difficulties were around twice as likely as others to be in the lowest quartile nationally on reading test scores' (Brooks *et al.*, 2007, p. 18). This type of finding has been repeated with a fair degree of consistency.

One good example of cohort-based approaches to these questions is Parsons and Bynner's (2007) comprehensive analysis of the experiences of people with less developed literacy capabilities over their lifecourse. They take the view that literacy capabilities build up over time, and consider it important to look at the trajectory people follow through education, work and personal lives. Applying this perspective to the 1970 British Cohort Study, they look at the characteristics of people who test at the three lower levels of literacy and numeracy skills placement according to the English 'Skills for Life' framework. The highest level examined, Level 1, is equivalent to pass grades on the GCSE examinations taken by 15-year-olds or around Grade 9 in North American terms.

Parsons and Bynner (2007) found some surprisingly clear evidence of connections between family circumstances and literacy levels. The literacy skills of the cohort members (who were 34 years old at the time of the study) were related to the size of the family they grew up in, whether their mother had been a teenage mother and whether their parents had qualifications (particularly post-secondary for their mother). In their own family lives, people testing lower tended to have experienced more homelessness, were more likely to be single parents, more likely to have larger families themselves and to have children who did not view reading as pleasurable. One intriguing aspect of analysing a cohort study is that it is possible to look at data from earlier years and relate it directly to the outcomes for the same people. So it is possible to say confidently that for this group the socio-economic status of the family the year they were born, whether their parents owned their own house as the cohort members grew up, whether they were read to when they were five, what their parents' aspirations for them were when they were ten and their attitude to reading at 16 are all related to their current tested literacy and numeracy capabilities. At this point, however, we are well beyond exploration of inter-generational literacy (as a set of practices around text) and into social analysis – a point I will return to.

Feinstein *et al.* (2008) summarise the body of work around cohort studies:

> *Parental education and engagement in their child's development have a huge influence on children's educational progress and life chances. It is not a simple, straightforward connection, but recent research into young children's 'school readiness' and vocabulary development shows that, on average, the children of parents with no qualifications are already up to a year behind the sons and daughters of graduates by the age of three. (p. 11)*

Other studies reinforce the notion that there is some intergenerational effect. Lynch (2009) looks at the print literacy engagement of alleged low literacy families with low levels of income. Even though her intention is to show how complex the uses of literacy really are, she begins with a rapid overview of the literature that seems to promote the idea of a direct relationship between parents' and children's capabilities. She mentions a range of previous research supporting a link between parental literacy engagement and:

> *development and economic indicators, children's effective participation in school, health, and participation in school and community life . . . whether parents and siblings engaged in frequent reading and writing for personal purposes was connected to children's vocabulary development . . . parents' discussion of schoolwork and their provision of reading materials continue to support older children's reading achievement (p. 510).*

Emerging from the research is a picture that does not clarify the role of literacy as a stand-alone factor in the development of children's capabilities so much as it points to the way literacy capabilities are embedded within a web of advantage and disadvantage. In this case literacy capabilities may well be related to life circumstances, but there is little to suggest they are a predominant factor in the way that so much family literacy writing invites us to believe. For example, it seems unlikely that literacy capabilities act as a prophylactic against teenage pregnancy – the implication of the connection drawn in Parsons and Bynner's (2007) analysis above. An alternative way to view all this evidence is that some people live with limited resources, and that one set of those resources is literacy capabilities. Here we are starting to approach the ideas of reproduction theory, as mentioned in the introduction, and the claim that privilege and disadvantage are transmitted between generations by social artefacts such as education. So what is passed from the parental generation to the children is not specifically a lower engagement with literacy but a whole range of social disadvantage.

The social practices view of literacy would challenge this perspective, arguing that any family context has a range of literacy resources within it. This brings us back to the second issue mentioned briefly at the beginning of this chapter: throughout all of this work literacy is conceived and analysed purely in school-centred terms. There is very little consideration given to more eclectic or local forms of literacy practice. While it is true that school-centred literacy may be the form that leads most directly to economic advantage (in a meritocratic society) and that this form of literacy is not evenly distributed among families, the studies tend to completely ignore other forms of literacy practices either as inputs or outputs. Often they do not take any literacy capabilities into account if they are in languages other than the official language of the country where the study is situated – this is, of course, a huge problem in the United States, where Spanish is the home language of an increasing number of citizens.

If we adopt a more cautious approach to the idea that literacy is simply transmitted between generations, important questions start to arise. Parsons and Bynner (2007) point out that in order to even begin to understand the intergenerational factors we need to know the proportion of children with poor literacy capabilities who have parents in the same position. They cite work by Hannon (1999) showing that the vast majority of children with poor literacy skills do not have parents with poor literacy skills, and point out that there is not yet a clear theory as to why parent's literacy capabilities would manifest in their children's performance in such a direct way. After all, the number of parents lacking the literacy capabilities needed to support pre-school literacy and numeracy must surely be limited. What remain unknown, and are surely critical to understand, are the pathways that such intergenerational effects might follow – both in families with strong capabilities and those who engage far less with school-centred literacy.

Different pathways

There are a number of different ways to understand the transmission of literacy activities within a family. For the present discussion these can be summarised as two broad approaches. The first approach suggests that literacy capabilities are transmitted fairly directly and unproblematically within a family in a range of incidental ways. It suggests that literacy engagement is an aspect of family culture, and that some families have a culture more likely to lead to effective learning of school-like literacy practices for all the members of the family. This 'cultural osmosis' argument lies behind the notion that better educated mothers can lead to better attaining children irrespective of the mothers' efforts to teach their children school-based literacy in any explicit way. For the child, simply growing up in an educated culture will tend to support good engagement with literacy.

Cultural models focus on values and activities within the home, and the ways they play out in children's literacy use. One of the most influential studies on this area was completed by Denny Taylor. In 'Family Literacy' (Taylor, 1983) she looks at the transmission of literacy-related behaviours in six families with school and pre-school age children. The author is very open about the limitations of the study – 'all are white middle-class, living within a fifty mile radius of New York City' (p. 1). Taylor concludes that:

> *Growing up in an environment where literacy is the only option, they learned of reading as one way of listening, and of writing as one way of talking. Literacy gave the children both status and identity as it became the medium of shared experience; it facilitated the temporal integration of their social histories as the highly valued artefacts of family life became the prized commodity of the schools. (p. 87)*

In other words, there is continuity between the significance attached to literacy in home and in school – both places and times see it as highly important. Taylor continued with a radical further comment:

> *Considering literacy in this cultural context emphasises the need for educators to question seriously whether the present adult literacy programmes and parent education programmes tend to be too literally literate. It is entirely possible that the undue emphasis on specific didactic encounters might unwittingly undermine the opportunity for reading and writing to become socially significant in the lives of both adults and children, and therefore an integral facet of family life. (p. 88)*

Here Taylor seems to be suggesting that it can actually be harmful to attempt to teach literacy within the home and that transmission of literacy behaviours must be part of everyday behaviour. If this view were taken at face value, it would seem to suggest that there are few options for direct intervention in the intergenerational transmission of less-developed or alternative literacy capabilities. There would need to be a re-orientation of entire family cultures towards school literacy and away from the other types of literacy likely to be present in the home.

It was not Taylor's intention to perpetuate a deficit view of 'failing families,' but if the implications of the cultural view are thought through in a literal way they seem quite pessimistic. If literacy capabilities are cultural, and transmitted through the milieu of the family, it follows that children with limited capabilities must be growing up in a family that lacks some sort of resources. It also makes it difficult to imagine what can be done to ameliorate this situation. In the end, it seems to offer a very limited range of options to family members who want to support their children. One of the limits is due to the dominance of school-centred literacy in discussions around family literacy processes, with the associated tendency to de-value alternative forms. The logical implication is that supporting the school-centred literacy of children would require re-orientating the entire family literacy culture towards this particular form of literacy, which seems like an enormous and intractable task.

If literacy capabilities fit entirely with the culture model, then it is hard to see how families' engagement with literacy can be strengthened except through long-term investment in supporting parental literacy capabilities. This can easily treat the family as a black box that turns specific inputs into desired outputs. In addition, this would be a difficult model to put into practice because there are so many unknowns. At the simplest level, how much would it be necessary to spend on parental education to increase children's capabilities by what amount? However, approaching literacy in the family through the lens of cultural osmosis does provide little reason to intervene directly in intergenerational processes, unlike the alternative approach.

The second view suggests that the effort parents intentionally put into supporting the children to learn literacy and numeracy, including explicit drills and other activities is the dominant factor in intergenerational transmission of capabilities. I will call this the 'deliberate support' approach. Here the necessary strategies to support the child are learnable, and do not rely on the parent's own literacy capabilities.

The deliberate support perspective, by holding that parental efforts to teach literacy are the key to 'success,' places the outcomes for children more firmly at the feet of parents. There is a clear assumption that parents can take certain steps to ensure that children engage well with school-based literacy whatever their background. This separates the literacy capabilities of parents and children in an interesting way – it seems to assume that these two sets of practices are only loosely articulated.

Christian *et al.* (1998) use structural equation modelling to show that the level of support for literacy capabilities within the family is a strong predictor of children's academic skills on entering kindergarten. One striking aspect of this study is that maternal education (and therefore the literate culture referred to earlier) is a surprisingly limited factor. Mothers who had low education levels but who worked to support their children's learning of literacy and related academic skills ended up with children who had more highly developed skills than those mothers who were highly educated but spent less time supporting their children. This is a challenging result with complex implications, as it suggests that parents can take action and improve the lot of their children even if their own education is not extensive. There is further research supporting this conclusion. Phillips and Lonigan (2009), for example, conduct a cluster analysis that once again shows that supporting children's literacy learning can be effective whatever the parental educational levels. De Haan (2008) analyses a similar body of data to the cohort studies (the Wisconsin Longitudinal Study) using a relatively new statistical technique more powerful than correlation, and comes up with an even more radical finding – that parental education may well have no effect at all on children's educational attainment. It seems to suggest that we need to move beyond simplistic models of direct intergenerational transmission and move towards a more nuanced model involving both social structures and the actions of individuals.

One study (Park, 2008) looked at the results from the Progress in International Reading Literacy Study (PIRLS) in an attempt to understand how early home literacy activities (such as explicit displays of reading by parents, reading to children, etc.) affected children's capabilities in 25 countries. The conclusion of this study was that parents' education, number of books in the home and early home literacy activities do make a difference in all the countries, but that this varies according to the economic characteristics of the country in question – which in turn affects the form of schooling available to children. There are two interesting aspects to this study. The first is the acknowledgement of how much economic structures and related context affect literacy outcomes.

The second is more complex. The findings point to the significance of parents in children's literacy development, but go further. They seem to confirm that home literacy environment mediates parental education – in other words a parent with less education (and potentially less developed literacy) can make an enormously important difference. As the author expresses it:

> *The results suggest that, despite some correlations between parental education and home literacy environments, still a significant proportion of low-educated parents are engaged often with the child in literacy activities, have positive attitudes toward reading, and have a large number of books in the home. In other words, rather than simply reproducing educational differences among children from different socioeconomic origins, home literacy environments are important resources even for children from poor socioeconomic backgrounds to benefit from.* (p. 502)

So parental behaviours make a difference whatever the socioeconomic status and education level of the household. While this study, being based on PIRLS, still tends to privilege school literacy it is important to understanding family literacy because it shows that parents matter across a wide range of contexts.

One of the central aspects of deliberate support is 'reading readiness' (Leu and Kinzer, 1995). This claims that children go through a series of pre-literate stages that help them to bridge from spoken language to written language. Simple examples include children asking what words mean, or learning to hold a book the right way up. The role of parents and other carers is to pay attention to these behaviours and encourage them where possible. However, this approach also assumes that children learn text usage in a standard, linear process, and this is not necessarily the case (Walsh, 2007). Parents and carers do have potential advantages over schoolteachers when it comes to developing in-depth understanding of individual children and the way they think and learn, but parents and carers are unlikely to have years of preparation and experience in knowing what to do with these observations. So the argument that parents should support reading readiness is not as straightforward as it can sometimes sound.

While emphasising the importance of parental actions can offer the opportunity for parents to make a difference, it can also suggest that they are responsible when children do not come into school ready to read. This judgement is easier to make when the target is parents who are more marginalised from the education system. Despite the mantra that 'parents

141

are a child's first teacher' many parents believe it is the job of teachers to teach reading and writing, and this can have a deeply entrenched basis within a specific culture (Ko and Chan, 2009). In addition, many parents may well have their hands full just keeping a roof over the children's heads and food in their stomachs. To criticise these parents for not paying attention to pre-literate behaviours as a teacher would seems unrealistic, to say the least.

It would be extremely interesting to know more about the operation of literacy capabilities within families, and we are lucky to have an opportunity to gain some insight. Over the last twenty years family literacy programmes have grown up in many countries, and the evaluative and research work done in these programmes can provide invaluable insights into the way that the literacy capabilities of family members interact.

Learning from family literacy

There does seem to be evidence to support some connection between parental practices and children's school-centred literacy. In looking at the outcomes of literacy learning, however, we need to understand the connection in more depth. In particular, we need to ask whether changes in the capabilities of adults tend to support greater changes in the capabilities of children than would be expected simply from their maturation. Associated issues include how long it takes for adult learning to influence children's learning, what sort of changes in children's capabilities can be expected to come from what sort of changes in adult capabilities, and if there is a threshold that adults have to cross to contribute to children's learning. There is also the question discussed in the last section of whether adults themselves need to have strengthened capabilities or simply be educated in how to support the literacy learning of children.

A great deal of the information available about these questions comes from the United States because of the high level of interest in family literacy programmes there over the last two decades. Family literacy programmes are designed to strengthen the capabilities of both children and adults together, based on the conviction that intergenerational intervention will both enhance the capabilities of each generation and assist parents with supporting literacy development in their children. The basic concept is one of synergy; the notion that by working on a family system as broadly as possible the benefits will be greater than working on any or all of the components in isolation. This idea caught on in the early 1990s and led to the funding of Even Start programmes across the US.

Even Start is the largest commitment of resources to family literacy that has occurred anywhere in the world. The funding levels typically ran between $200 and $250 million per year for over a decade (which sounds like a lot until you calculate it is $4–5 million per state and well under $1 per person per year). Nonetheless, Even Start worked with tens of thousands of families in thousands of programmes, and had a great deal of research conducted on it over the years.

The Even Start model involved four components. Adult literacy education was a key part of the programme, and the idea was that parents (very usually mothers) would work on their skills in an adult-only classroom. At the same time, their children, from birth to eight years of age, would be getting a chance to participate in early literacy activities in another room. The third component was parent and child time, where the generations would be brought together to practice games and other strategies for supporting children's literacy. Finally, adults would also participate in parenting education. The components were given different weights in different programmes, and it is worth noting that the federal legislation supporting Even Start (latterly the No Child Left Behind Act of 2001) did not offer a clear definition of what the services should look like in practice.

The target group for Even Start was the people in the community who were most in need. This simple formulation could be widely interpreted, and led to some complications. For example, if the people most in need were Spanish speakers, was the adult education in Even Start meant to teach English, or could the programme be delivered in Spanish? This would, of course, raise complications in places like Arizona, where children have to be educated in English by law. Even Start was also strongly gendered (Prins, Toso and Schafft, 2009). The classes happened during conventional school hours, so that fathers or mothers who had day jobs could not attend and only parents who did not work during the day could attend. In practice, this meant mothers in most cases, reinforcing the traditional notion that mothers should be responsible for the care of young children. Also, while attendance in Even Start was not meant to be obligatory, from my own experience I know that welfare workers would certainly make very strong recommendations that people receiving benefits should attend. So any conclusions drawn from Even Start data about the effects of parental literacy capabilities need to be treated with care.

Over the time Even Start was operating there were many evaluations of the programme. These were quite influential in the decisions about whether the programme should continue or not, and the level of funding it should receive. A number of different approaches to understanding the programme and its effects were taken. This is extremely useful for the question we are trying to address, as it allows different perspectives on the relationship between adult and child literacy to be explored. At the same time, the available evidence comes from evaluations of a programme rather than research studies, and although Even Start is based on the assumption that changes in adult capabilities lead to changes for children there are a lot of other factors that can get in the way. In order to look at our question responsibly, we need to be quite precise about the way we approach it.

A lot of the research on Even Start comments on the way the programme was administered rather than measuring the outcomes systematically. It quickly becomes clear that it is not really possible to make a direct comparison between people who attended a consistent Even Start programme and those who did not, useful though that would be. The programmes varied so much, and the attendance and starting point of participants was so diverse, that there really was no single standardised model. In addition, people who were not attending Even Start could still have registered themselves in a wide range of other programmes for themselves and their children. One example is Head Start, which while not offering adult education has been shown to increase children's literacy capabilities (Ludwig and Phillips, 2007). When trying to isolate the effects of Even Start it is only possible to look at specific aspects of the programme and work out what those tell us about the interaction of adult's and children's capabilities.

The central claim made by Even Start is that it is better to support the literacy of the whole family rather than only one generation. The studies suggest that there is very little evidence for any kind of synergy at work. National studies comparing Even Start participants with control groups who had a variety of educational involvements does not seem to show that having the components all in one place, and theoretically aligned around a shared curriculum and developmental process, made any difference. Influential national US studies showed that people involved in Even Start certainly did learn, but they did not learn any more than people who were not involved in Even Start (Riccuiti, St.Pierre, Lee, Parsad and Rimdzius, 2004). Research consistently suggests that the synergy argument has very little evidence to back it up.

Family literacy advocates have been understandably concerned by this outcome, and the Goodling Institute of Family Literacy criticised the studies on a number of levels, pointing out that the benefits might be longer term than assumed – in other words there could be a time lag between adult learning and children's effects (St.Pierre, Riccuiuti and Rimdzius, 2005). The original authors of the national study went back a year later to check for this possibility, and came to the same conclusions regarding the lack of synergy (Riccuiti, St.Pierre, Lee, Parsad and Rimdzius, 2004).

Another group of researchers responded to the criticism by developing an idealised model of family literacy designed to maximise the potential benefits, and then comparing its outcomes with regular Even Start (Judkins, St.Pierre, Gutmann, *et al.*, 2008). If the carefully developed model produced better results than the diverse delivery of normal Even Start programmes then there would be credibility to the claims that Even Start would be more effective if more tightly delivered. There were no significant differences in outcome from the previous research, so there is still little support for the idea of intergenerational synergy in learning.

Overall, the question of how adult's capabilities affect children's capabilities is still open. Is it enough for children to grow up in a household with strong literacy capabilities, or do adults have to do something specific with the children to increase the children's capabilities? If the second, can those activities be taught and practised, so that all parents can be advised on how to support their children's learning?

Sénéchal (2006), perhaps partly inspired by the controversy about Even Start, conducted a meta-analysis of evidence on the types of interventions that make a difference to children's capabilities. The author divided the studies into three different types. The first, called 'read to child' contained those studies examining the effects of parents reading to children. The second, called 'listen to child read' similarly contained studies where the child read out loud and the parent listened. Finally, the 'parents teach child literacy skills' contained research where the parents explicitly set out to teach children how to work with text. Sénéchal's conclusion was that reading to children had an almost negligible effect on the child's capabilities, whereas listening to the children had a moderate effect. The third category was shown to have a very significant effect indeed. Parents who spend time with their children implementing even a simple strategy for showing their children how text works tend to make a big difference to the capabilities of their children.

Looking across the evidence on Even Start seems to support the importance of parents explicitly working with their children, though not the idea that a unified cross-generational programme is necessarily better. This is potentially good news for advocates of family literacy programmes, but does suggest that adult literacy education will not have a meaningful impact on children's learning. Even Start, designed as a programme that includes an adult literacy component, does not seem to be well justified by the evidence. Firstly, there is no evidence that increased adult literacy capabilities affect children's learning and, secondly, there is evidence that parents of any education level can learn a set of strategies to support their children. These results do not suggest that parental education is irrelevant, but they do give good reason for doubt about claims that providing literacy education to adults will directly strengthen the capabilities of their children.

The evidence available from Even Start is most fairly viewed as suggesting that literacy within families relies on both the pathways we discussed in the previous section – home literacy cultural osmosis and deliberate support can both make a difference. As in many other cases with literacy learning, there is a tight interweaving of the different aspects of support and capability development. As individuals respond to their family and social culture it will profoundly affect their development of capabilities, and those capabilities will affect the people around them, including their children.

Conclusion

It is possible to draw some conclusions, albeit cautiously, about the way literacy works within families. First, it seems that there is fairly strong evidence that some families have strong literacy capabilities, and where these capabilities intersect with the valuable forms of literacy within a given society, this could be a great advantage. It is less clear what happens with families who have strong literacy capabilities of a different form – for example, families who read and write in Spanish when the local schools are English-only schooling. While there may well be an uneven distribution of school-centred literacies throughout the population, there are studies showing that even those families that would be considered to be at the low end of this distribution have active and rich interaction with

146

texts (Lynch, 2009). So children who are growing up in a household where conventional school-centred literacy capabilities are limited may still be able to call on a wide range of literacy resources to support their own learning.

In my view, the evidence suggests that both the 'culture' and the 'deliberate support' pathways affect the literacy capabilities of children very strongly, and that they overlap to some degree. So a highly literate household with a limited degree of explicit literacy instruction will support children's learning, as will a household with limited literacy capabilities but careful instruction and encouragement. A further implication of the research is that working with adult family members to increase their literacy capabilities is likely to have little effect on the capabilities of children. It is far more effective to teach adults who wish to support their children's learning the necessary strategies within the adult's existing capabilities than attempt to bolster those capabilities. This argument seems to hold whenever adults have some degree of literacy capabilities, and at whatever level. The evidence suggests that parents with very strong literacy capabilities who wish to support their children's learning could benefit from familiarity with teaching strategies as much as parents with limited capabilities.

However, it seems that children's learning is not a strong rationale for adult literacy education. While literacy capabilities may be passed on between generations to some degree, there is very little to show that changing the capabilities of the older generation will automatically leverage a change in the capabilities of the younger. The value of literacy education for adults needs to be understood in its own right, without assumptions being made about the transmission of these capabilities.

We can say with some confidence that we know something about supporting the literacy capabilities of children, and that the necessary strategies may be teachable to almost everybody. This provides a great opportunity to move beyond patronisation or a culture of blame where parents are held to account for not supporting their children appropriately. It suggests that there are strategic resources that can be used by any family to support their children, and that the key issue is making sure those resources are available. Family literacy is not, finally, about making up for the shortcomings of the parent's capabilities – it is about ensuring that all parents and carers are aware of the possibilities available to them.

CHAPTER NINE

Social and political impacts

In this chapter I look at the specific question of how literacy education for adults can affect the social and political engagement of individuals and communities. This is an area that is close to my own heart as I have always been intrigued and motivated by the possibility that the effects of literacy education can go beyond the personal to contribute in a meaningful way to social change. The idea has been around for an extremely long time, of course, with John Dewey commenting on the links between communication, education and society almost one hundred years ago:

> Not only is social life identical with communication, but all communication (and hence all genuine social life) is educative. To be a recipient of a communication is to have an enlarged and changed experience . . . To formulate [experience] requires getting outside of it, seeing it as another would see it considering what points of contact it has with the life of another so that it may be got into such a form that he (sic) can appreciate its meaning . . . It may fairly be said, therefore, that any social arrangement that remain vitally social, or vitally shared, is educative to those who participate in it. (1916, pp. 5–6)

For Dewey, the ideal of democratic society required the participation of all the members of that society in an informed and effective manner, so communication was a key concern. Thinking through Dewey's propositions a little, it seems that he would consider communicative ability and education to come together, so that learning literacy would not only be about the technical skills of reading and writing. The process of learning, for Dewey, would inspire reasonable and democratic thought, leading to strengthened collective participation in the management of society.

The basic claim underpinning this view – that the outcomes of learning include a social dimension – turns up in a variety of forms. Literacy learning, both for younger people and adults, has been especially strongly linked to the development of inclusive and equitable social structures. The broadest and most profound claims need to be treated with some caution. If one is not careful, the claims can start to sound once more like the 'autonomous model' of literacy (Street, 1984) discussed in Chapter Two. Literacy makes a difference to society according to this model, but through a one-way process, with the changing communicative technology driving development in trade, information exchange and collective decision-making. Literacy is almost seen as an entirely independent outside factor bearing on internal social processes.

The autonomous model of literacy contrasts with the ideological model of literacy, which suggests that literacy is embedded within social contexts and has value and meaning for people in those contexts (Street, 1984). Instead of a neutral tool, literacy is both a product of, and an initiating force for, social processes. If the ideological model is accepted, then literacy *per se* cannot bring about social transformation, as a lever balanced on some Archimedean point. It is an interesting observation that many progressive thinkers are highly sceptical about the autonomous model of literacy, emphasising the social significance of literacy capabilities, until it comes to the notion that literacy can bring about progressive social change. At that point, the ability of literacy capabilities to transcend social structure seems to become acceptable once more.

Graff (1995) makes an interesting argument about the politics of literacy. He points out that if literacy really did bring about social improvements in some simple and automatic way, then we would expect the countries with the strongest literacy capabilities to have the most equitable societies and those with less developed literacies to be far more inequitable and unstable. This is simply not the case – it is relatively easy to find examples that contradict this pattern, including many cases where the uses of literacy were blatantly oppressive. Literacy capabilities within a society are mediated by the wealth of that society, the schooling system, the language communities and other factors to such a degree that there is very little evidence of any direct link between education and democracy.

The general proposition that literacy capabilities directly lead to social improvement cannot be accepted at face value. Yet the idea that literacy capabilities are communicative tools and that these communicative tools can be used for positive social ends does deserve to be examined. This enquiry has to be a subtle one, however. As with the other effects examined in this discussion it will only show up in certain contexts and at particular times.

It is also important to acknowledge that the arguments around the social effects of literacy capabilities are complicated and highly rhetorical. They tend to make a case for the effects that should be there rather than demonstrate their existence. The first task in discussing these arguments is to try to break them down a little and clarify exactly what they are saying, and in order to do this the chapter is divided into three sections. The first is concerned with literacy as a tool for community development, and discusses evidence around the notion that enhanced literacy capabilities make for stronger, more autonomous communities. The second looks at arguments around literacy as a contributing factor to social capital – in other words, the ways literacy and numeracy capabilities enhance people's social networks and involvement in wider structures. The third section tackles the most radical political perspectives, which view literacy as a means of criticising and changing oppressive social structures.

Before looking at the specific arguments in more detail it is interesting to reflect on the reasons why literacy has come to be seen as such a social force. For most of the world's population, even a hundred years ago, the notion that reading and writing ability was essential to social change would probably have lacked much credibility. To take extreme examples, the Chinese and Russian Revolutions, as well as the American Revolution in the more distant past, were conducted by people with limited literacy capabilities. There was, in each case, a group of people with stronger literacy capabilities who were involved in leading the struggles, but they also tended to be the people who stood to benefit by a new regime. There seems little clear evidence that gains in literacy capability lead to political liberation on any broad scale.

It may be that the notion of literacy capabilities as resources offers some insights here. Simply put, it could be that the opportunity to learn and use literacies is one of the restricted resources that people want to redistribute when they engage in social transformation. Literacy capabilities are not essential to social change, but lack of them may motivate people to believe that such change is necessary. In other words, revolution is not because of literacy, but perhaps literacy is one of the benefits of revolution.

150

Looking at the way literacy has come to feature so prominently in discussions of community development provides a good starting point for understanding the potential of literacy as a personal and collective resource.

Developing the community

The idea that communities can be 'developed' has existed at least since the Industrial Revolution, which gave rise to number of utopian communities such as Robert Owen's development of the mills at New Lanark. Even in this early example, the principle that underpins all community development is clear – that people can deliberately and collectively design and build communities offering better living conditions than those they currently experience. Community development is interested in increasing the ability of people to control their own lives and their own living conditions. A related idea in education and development theory is citizenship, where the central notion is to support people's appreciation of agency and their ability to participate in collective decision-making processes. A broad ideal of community development and citizenship education is to have a society in which people have the knowledge, skills, experience and confidence to take shared control of their own lives.

Throughout the history of community development there have been controversies about definitions, even of fundamental terms like 'community' (St. Clair, 1998). As might be expected for an endeavour that has to be highly localised if it is to have any chance of succeeding, the form of the projects varies enormously, as do the methods and expected outcomes. Community development projects seem to be bound by a shared commitment to the potential of communities to determine their own destiny rather than any particular educational or social approach. This can be read as a sign of great creativity and vibrancy in the field, but also can make it hard to understand the processes and the potential of community development. One of the most significant contributors to the modern field argued over 40 years ago that:

> The fuzziness of definition is due less to disagreement on words and more to difference in programmes. The confusion of interpretations arises from the varieties of methods that have been found to work. These, in turn, are dependent both upon the populations involved and upon the backgrounds of the practitioners. The field then is defined by the active programmes that practitioners describe. (Biddle, 1966, p. 5)

Among the sorts of programmes that are included in community development are educational programmes for women, housing action groups, campaigns against domestic violence, community economic development, citizenship programmes, co-operatives, small loan funds and training to be entrepreneurial. Historically, some of the most respected adult education initiatives, such as the Antigonish Movement or the Highlander Folk School, have had a deep and abiding concern with community development. Literacy education tends to feature quite strongly in many varieties of community development, particularly in the developing world (Beder, 1997), and it might be useful to look at an example from Vietnam to illustrate the kind of programme that is considered contemporary community development.

The Action Aid Vietnam programme (AAV, 2008) was established in 2000, and has received consistent funding from Action Aid and the European Commission. The rural ethnic minority population in Vietnam does not display well-developed literacy capabilities, and children from these groups often drop out of school due to poverty and poorly equipped schools. The AAV programme targets women, children and ethnic minorities in order to change this situation, and has incorporated literacy education into its community development activities. This has the claimed benefits of reducing the barriers to education for the target groups and also making it easier for literacy educators to develop appropriate, localised curriculum and materials. The programme moves through three stages: literacy, advanced literacy and community development. It is interesting to look at some of the language around this progression, as it demonstrates the philosophical framework of the programme very effectively.

The programme curriculum is designed to ensure that learners move progressively from illiteracy to becoming literate, meaning that they have the range of skills considered necessary to function proficiently and effectively for individual and community development. To this end, the programme is comprised of different themes that are pertinent for community development, including health (nutrition and HIV/AIDS prevention), community development and gender inequity, environment, agriculture (animal and crop farming), business training (local budget analysis) and income generation (AAV, 2008, p. 4).

The aims of the programme include empowering the community with the relevant information, techniques and skills to deal with problems and to promote social networking and organisation. Over the years between 2000 and 2008 AAV served 12,000 learners and claimed to show significant effects. The lessons learned by the programmes over that time include the importance of involving stakeholders (including the government) and regular capacity-building and support to facilitators (AAV, 2008).

There are a number of striking aspects of this programme description, but two are particularly worthy of comment. The first is that calling this programme community development does seem questionable. The community would appear to have quite limited input into the programme, given that the same structure has been delivered to 12,000 people. This raises the interesting question of whether a commitment to a collective local process really defines community development. If having a bottom-up process was the key to community development, surely the resulting content would vary more widely across so many people in so many settings. It seems that this programme may be driven more by content than is explicitly acknowledged, and this will have a bearing on the ability of the programme to increase the autonomy of community members. A top-down framing of what *should* concern the community does not increase self-direction irrespective of how radical the content is claimed to be. I'll return to this point in the final section of the chapter.

A second aspect is the placement of literacy within the programme. Not only is literacy seen as essential to community development, the chronology of the programme assumes that literacy *precedes* the ability to develop autonomy and tackle community issues. This is a fascinating placement of literacy at the centre of community development, and a particularly clear example of an assumption that lies at the heart of many development programmes. The view that there is a strong causational link between literacy capabilities and the democratic empowerment of the population is heavily promoted – and surprisingly rarely examined – by some of the biggest international agencies around. As Winchester argued (1985, p. 46):

> *Perhaps the most striking feature of the UNESCO discussions on literacy . . . Is that it is remarkably little based on either experiment or historical precedent . . . Action seems as much based on self-evident axioms and hope as on anything else. UNESCO assumes that literacy is a good thing – more latterly functional literacy. Furthermore, in no clearly defined or understood way poverty, disease, and general backwardness are believed connected with illiteracy; progress, health and economic well-being are equally self-evidently connected with literacy.*

Little has changed over the 25 years since these comments were published other than the branding of UNESCO literacy campaigns as 'Education for All,' and such enormous claims for the effects of encoding and decoding marks on a page should arouse a degree of scepticism. Indeed, the unproblematic UNESCO promotion of links between literacy capabilities and various forms of social development has attracted some critical attention both from literacy researchers and from people involved in programmes in the global south.

Wickens and Sandlin (2007) argue in their critical analysis of UNESCO and World Bank literacy programmes that postcolonial and developing societies may have to accede to Westernised views of education and literacy in order to gain access to aid funding. This case, the authors suggest, shows very clearly that literacy capabilities and autonomy are not essentially linked. It is essential to understand the context of literacy education, and ask what purpose it is intended to serve, for whom, and how. It is useful to ask the same questions of all types of literacy education that claim to make a difference on a broad social level. Some authors who live in the countries that host development projects have been making the same sorts of arguments for some time, analysing the way that aid programmes may serve to sustain the status quo and distract people from the potential of social change rather than support the changes. There are a number of very strong voices in the developing countries calling for the implementation of real social justice values within literacy and other development programmes. In the case of sub-Saharan Africa, for example, Maruatona (2004, 2008) argues for the development of strong lifelong learning policies and emphasises the need for programmes to be de-centralised on many levels. Not only control of the programmes and the topics covered should be in the hands of local groups, but the language of tuition should also reflect local values and conditions. Planning needs to be based on 'principles of equity, redress, democracy, development and reconstruction, development and integration' (p. 751).

The key question for our discussion is how literacy capabilities actually strengthen communities. More often than not, it seems that any effect is due to the social meanings attached to literacy practices rather than any quality essential to reading and writing. In the Civil Rights Movements of the United States in the 1960s, literacy education was a key component of action for Black Americans, but this was not because literacy was seen as inherently good or productive – it was because voting laws required people to demonstrate literacy before they could be put on

154

voters' lists (Zinn, 1999). The importance of the social structures and values surrounding literacy capabilities should not be too surprising, of course, but it does underline the need for careful consideration to be given to the role that literacy plays in community development and citizenship education. Put crudely, do literacy capabilities supply a way of looking at the world that leads to a particular way of engaging with community, or do communities demand a set of literacy capabilities as a prerequisite for engagement?

The evidence seems to show that literacy capabilities may make community organisation and development easier, but they certainly do not guarantee any such outcome. In some cases they offer a really attractive incentive for people to become involved in community development programmes because the ability to read and write is seen as a hugely pragmatic benefit by potential participants, as I discuss more in the final section of the chapter. This does not mean that literacy should be dismissed as unimportant to community development – even if we accept the most conservative conclusion, that literacy capabilities are important because they allow different forms of social engagement, this is still a powerful argument in support of literacy learning. It is the same principle that argues for people to have access to further and higher education, or even universal schooling. The fact that the value of these activities may come from signalling ability rather than the direct application of the skills learned in the educational process does not diminish their importance, especially to people who are getting the chance to learn them for the first time.

Contributions to capital

One promising framework for understanding education and development is the notion of 'social capital.' The term was originally used by Bourdieu (1986) as a way to explain how social and economic forces help to create and maintain capitalist culture. At around the same time Coleman (1988) was developing an alternative view of social capital, with more emphasis on the idea of social capital as a social resource and less on social capital as a tool of social control. He argued that 'social capital is defined by its function. It is not a single entity but a variety of different entities, with two elements in common; they all consist of some aspect of social structures, and they facilitate certain actions of actors' (p. 98). Coleman identifies three aspects of social capital: obligations and expectations, information flow capability, and norms accompanied by sanctions.

Putnam's writing (1993) made a very significant contribution to popularising the concept of social capital. He explained the perceived loss of concern for others within American society using a model derived from a study of Italian local government, with social capital as the central factor. Social capital, in Putnam's view, is the 'features of social organisation such as networks, norms, and trust that facilitate coordination and cooperation for mutual benefit' (p.1). Putnam was particularly careful that his version of social capital should not be seen as a substitute for economic capital invested in social programmes. He argued in support of social spending, for example, that 'social capital is not a substitute for effective public policy but rather a prerequisite for it and, in part, a consequence of it' (p.5). He also pointed out that badly designed development programmes have often tended to support the individual at the cost of collective social capital. This is not helpful in Putnam's view – efforts to develop social capital do not replace good social programmes, they underpin them.

The idea of social capital appears to have great potential to explain some of the peculiarities of social programmes, such as when youth outreach works in one area and not another. Perhaps the area where youth outreach failed to work lacked a sufficiently rich network of social capital to make the programme effective. Social capital also appears to be an attractive focus for policy-making. Policymakers can aim to increase social capital and run very little risk of criticism – to be against any policy with this outcome is to be against people.

When social capital is used by writers, one of two approaches is generally used. One is to view it as a literal form of capital, and attempt to devise instruments to measure it in absolute and relative terms (Van Der Gaag and Snijders, 2003). Economists often take this perspective. The second approach is to view it as a metaphorical form of capital, and approach it through highly descriptive methods (Preece and Houghton, 2000). While this conceptual flexibility is appealing to theorists, it also indicates just how problematic the term can be. One of the most difficult issues is definition, or knowing what counts as social capital. For example, if I meet somebody during a literacy education course and they later help me to find a job, is this human or social capital? To function as a robust theory there needs to be a clear definition of social capital so that it is possible to judge when it is, and is not, present. A second issue is whether social capital is a thing or a process. Is it the possession of one individual or does it

arise from interactions between people? If it is embedded within relationships, social capital is significantly different from other types of capital,
which can be entirely controlled by one individual. If embedded in networks, social capital must always be acknowledged as a community-based
resource beyond the possession of any individual.

Social capital is often presented as an unproblematic good, as if it contained a positive moral imperative, but this can also be disputed. The
Mafia, for example, has superb social capital, but it is hard to argue that this
results in a universally desirable outcome. Another example is the relationship between drug dealers and their customers – a highly trusting
relationship of social capital, with desired outcomes being achieved, but
not good for the community on a wider level. Finally, and perhaps most
problematically, there is little clear knowledge of how individuals or communities get more social capital. There are suggestions that communities
need to build or re-build their social capital, but there are few concrete
suggestions for how to enhance it.

Nonetheless, if we accept that social capital is pointing at something
important, which on balance I believe it is, then it's important to think
about how literacy education could contribute usefully to its enrich-
ment. This has been explored in some depth by researchers, and a group
of the leading thinkers on this question are based in Australia. Over the
last ten years or so, these researchers have worked to define the relationship between literacy and social capital and put it into effect. Not
surprisingly, their conceptions of the relationship have changed over that
time. In one of the first papers on the topic, Falk (2000) argues that 'social
capital is about the behaviour of collectives that facilitate action' (p. 1).
In both this paper and another discussion paper the following year (Falk,
2001) the interaction of human capital and social capital are heavily
emphasised, and the author goes so far as to say that 'social capital
includes human capital in its resource base' (p. 9). This suggests that the
formal education and experience that people possess can be considered
as only one part of the collective social capital found within a community. This is a fascinating idea, even though it raises all sorts of challenging
theoretical points. For example, it could be used to argue that having
more people with higher education in a community will support more
cooperation and participation – perhaps not a very useful notion. Falk's
perspective does usefully point to a clear link between the educational
capacities of a community (including literacy) and the ability of that
community to come together and get things done. This is very close

to the key arguments of those who would incorporate literacy into community development.

After a number of research projects, the view of social capital and literacy amongst the Australian researchers changed in quite a significant way. Perhaps in response to pressures from the current policy obsession with quantification, the need to understand how social capital affects people's lives, or on the basis of their empirical research, by 2007 the team was stating that their work was 'based on the premise that social capital outcomes can be identified as a private good' (Balatti, Black and Falk, 2007, p. 246). This is a significant change from the idea that social capital is about collectives, and seems to place social capital far more closely alongside human capital as a source of individual advantage. In this view, literacy education allows people to build networks that will be helpful in achieving their personal goals. This is a long way from community development.

Social capital has also been explored in other parts of the world. One interesting example came out of a longitudinal study of adult literacy learners in Scotland (Tett and Maclachlan, 2007). The authors adopted a definition of social capital that reflected the work in Australia as well as some important contributions from the UK: 'the networks, together with shared norms, values, and social trust that facilitate co-ordination and co-operation for mutual benefit, within and between groups' (p. 151). Tett and Maclachlan tie social capital to identity, on the basis that both learning and social capital draw on networks beyond the individual, but they state that 'the precise nature of the interconnectedness of social capital and learner identity is not easily isolated from a range of other determinants of learning' (p. 153). Their analysis shows some benefits to literacy learners in terms of increased activity and some enhancement of the specific social skills that are called upon within literacy programmes, but does not conclusively show that literacy education directly affects individual or community autonomy.

In my own writing on the topic of social capital and literacy in US literacy programmes (St. Clair, 2008), I acknowledge the importance of relationships in learning, but also sound a cautionary note. I am simply not sure that social capital theory is well enough developed to function as an effective analytical tool. There are too many unanswered questions, such as whether it is better to conceptualise social capital as a collective or an individual attribute, and how to ensure that it does make a useful contribution to people's lives. In all of the work discussed here there is a common phenomenon – the way that social capital becomes increasingly difficult to conceptualise and analyse the closer one gets to it. My view is that social capital is an important and interesting idea but lacks the clear boundaries and the parsimony that would make it a strong social theory.

There are two links that would usefully strengthen ideas around social capital and literacy. The first is the way that literacy education contributes to social capital. It has been suggested that literacy learners engage with three networks when they enter a programme – the formal network of the class setting, the informal network with other learners, and the instructor-based network that can operate both formally and informally (Balatti, Black and Falk, 2007). However, the way these networks work and how sustainable social capital outcomes can be assured, still needs exploration. The second link is between the social capital effects of literacy education, if found, and the ability to achieve individual or collective ends. While social capital may tend to be present in communities with strong self-determination, it is not clear how that actually happens. In terms of our discussion of literacy capabilities and social change, however, the move towards social capital as an individual attribute really does reduce its value considerably as a way to conceive collective and social value.

Reading for radicals

When the literature on the social and political impacts of literacy education for adults is reviewed, it quickly becomes clear that the dominant view on these issues is a radical approach derived from the work of educational theorist Paulo Freire (1971, 2004). The huge influence Freire has had upon adult and informal education, including literacy education in the developed and developing world, is surprising in some ways. His perspective is explicitly aimed at social transformation, yet appears to have found some degree of support even among more conservative educators. Freire's contention that all education is political in one way or another has become a widely accepted truth even in an era of profound pragmatism. His writing, at least in English translation, is not an easy read, and is far more embedded in radical politics than education, and yet is widely quoted with approval. It seems there is something within his work that has wide appeal.

There certainly is not enough space in this chapter to describe Freire's approach to literacy education in any depth at all, and there are huge numbers of existing resources that tackle this. Nonetheless, a few outline points might be helpful. Paulo Freire was a Brazilian adult educator of the post-war period, and took the view that literacy was essential to the liberation and empowerment of oppressed people. His work combines elements of Liberation Theology and Marxism, and is highly theorised within the European critical tradition. It also draws on the writings of various revolutionary figures of the twentieth century (Facundo, 1984). Freire appears to have had a complex relationship with ideas of revolution – he was born bourgeois, experienced poverty, created a literacy approach that was designed to support radical change, and drew extensively upon establishment resources in doing so. Certainly many readers of the 1970s, after his work was first translated into English, thrust a revolutionary mantle upon him, and he was not always too emphatic in rejecting it (Jackson, 2007).

In pragmatic terms, Freire's work is a clever combination of elements, which I can describe only very briefly here. He relies on groups of learners to identify themes of interest, based on various stimuli such as photographs. These generative themes are then explored using a combination of oral and written language. At the same time, people are taught letters and syllables that they can use to read and write about the themes. When the process is effective, it allows people to identify aspects of their lives that they would like to change while developing the literacy capabilities that will allow them to do so (Freire, 1971). Three of the key ideas of Freire's approach are dialogue (between learners and between learners and tutors), praxis (action informed by values), and education based in the lived experience of learners (Smith, 2002).

Freire's work has attracted criticism as well as positive attention. Again, there is not enough space to explore these critiques in depth, but it is important to recognise them. One aspect of Freire's work that is perhaps less well known to those who have not read the original texts is his degree of mysticism. He appears to believe in a transcendental humanism, somewhat ironically for a writer using Marx so broadly, and can be read as naive about human agency in the face of oppressive structures (Facundo, 1984). A second issue is his division of the world into 'oppressed' and 'oppressors' in a rather unhelpful way – most social theorists, even of Freire's time – would recognise a more nuanced complex of positionality. He also does not deal well with issues of gender – his voice is very masculine, and can be seen to place women as slightly different men rather than as people facing their own distinctive struggles (Jackson, 2007). Freire's agenda is very much a modernising one, and in its service he

160

allows particular themes to be more valuable than others irrespective of the putative bottom-up process. As Taylor argues, 'Albeit benign, Freire's approach differs only in degree, but not in kind, from the system which he so eloquently criticizes' (1993, p. 148). Finally, it is difficult to deny the degree to which Freire is influenced by the autonomous view of literacy, and the notion that literacy capabilities profoundly affect the world (Smith, 2002).

A fair view of Freire, I believe, is that he achieved an enormous amount in terms of opening up discussions about what education for adults and children can achieve, and what it should aim to achieve. He based this work on an eclectic social perspective, and was very much a man (sic) of his time. Yet he did move conversations about literacy and education forward and provide an inspiring vision of possibility. The outcome of literacy education, for Freire, is collective 'conscientization:' awareness of oppressive structures and the ability to address them. My central interest in this section is specifically whether this claim can be justified by people's experience.

Freire's approach to literacy education underpins the REFLECT programme, created originally by Action Aid International and which has been developed and applied in more than seventy (mainly developing) countries (Oxenham, 2004). There have been many strong analyses of the REFLECT programme (e.g. Greany, 2008; Tagoe, 2008; Fiedrich and Jellema, 2003; Cottingham, Metcalf and Phnuyal, 1998), and similar issues seem to be common to many of them. The first is the tension between the modernisation agenda of REFLECT and the frequently traditional belief systems of the participants. Here participatory principles can be difficult to sustain. If the individuals in the programme believe that illnesses are caused by spirits, then they are unlikely to identify hygienic household practices as a priority area for learning. Skilled facilitation is necessary to provide learners a chance to understand Western approaches to such issues without undermining the historical and potentially invaluable perspectives the learners bring to the programme. Unfortunately, all too often the modernisation agenda drives the process and leads to a devaluation of the knowledge held by the people the programme is meant to serve (Fiedrich and Jellema, 2003).

One particularly difficult example of this is gender. For many radical educators, gender relations in developing countries can be very problematic, and they would hope that women might gain the insights and power necessary to renegotiate the terms of their broad set of relationships, including marriages where appropriate, to make them more equitable. But what if the participants use their newly developed literacy skills to be more effective in traditional roles rather than challenge those roles? In this case, REFLECT may well have reinforced and extended inequitable structures (Greany, 2008). The way such issues are dealt with by the facilitator can affect the outcome profoundly (Cottingham, Metcalf and Phnuyal, 1998) although this observation does in itself challenge the claim to learner-centredness.

The second issue that arises is the collectivisation of transformation. There is anecdotal evidence, though it is not always as clear as it could be, that people do learn literacy capabilities through REFLECT, and that this can lead to powerful changes in their lives. As Cottingham, Metcalf and Phnuyal report about REFLECT pilot projects:

> *Participants cited a mixture of outcomes, from practical activities . . . skills . . . to attitudinal changes, such as increased self-confidence, and greater participation in their own family or community. In addition, 60–70 per cent of those enrolled achieved basic levels of literacy and numeracy, enabling them to write a one-page letter, read a passage, and carry out the four [arithmetical] operations . . . (1998, p. 30)*

It is important to note that although participation in community may have a collective dimension, all of these results are primarily individual. Very similar results were reported by Tagoe (2008) in Ghana, with outcomes in terms of literacy and personal attributes but little evidence of community mobilisation in the face of oppressive development practices. These results are consistent with many other reports, and while it is important to recognise the significance of individual benefits they do seem to cast some doubt upon the degree to which Freire-inspired literacy programmes lead to demonstrable political change.

In recent years, there has been a growth of literacy programmes influenced by social practices views of literacy. While they may not always aim to be as overtly political as the Freirian programmes, in practice many of the teaching approaches will be similar because of the shared commitment to recognising adults' prior knowledge and focusing on real life concerns. Examination of these programmes (e.g. Prins, 2007; Papen, 2005) suggests that sometimes people in developing countries are very clearly motivated to learn literacy capabilities by their pragmatic usefulness, and are less interested in the transformative political potential. In

Papen's (2005) study, learners were specifically interested in educational settings that were school-like, and saw this setting as the central mechanism for transmitting valuable knowledge. Again, this is consistent with issues arising in the REFLECT approach.

To be useful as a programme, instructional structures have to be formalised; there has to be a handbook or a system of some kind. While Freire's approach, when implemented by Freire in a region he knew well, may have led to community mobilisation, it is enormously difficult to take that approach and make it work in other parts of the world. The contradiction between the need to provide educators (and ultimately participants) with an instructional framework and the desire to ensure that participants shape the programme is strong and not at all easy to work within. Another dimension of the programmatic development of these ideas is the tendency to avoid defining and measuring outcomes. Sometimes outcomes are not clearly thought through, sometimes they are not stated in advance in order to recognise the extent to which participants can shape them, and sometimes it is a great deal more realistic to leave them undefined. After all, how many governments are likely to welcome programmes that aim for political transformation?

It would be misleading to suggest that literacy capabilities have no role to play in radical political transformation, and it would be overstating the case to argue that they are essential. While there is little direct evidence linking literacy and political outcomes, there does seem to be anecdotal indications that literacy education can play an important role within movements for social change, but it is certainly not an incontrovertible link.

Conclusion

The evidence indicates that literacy capabilities do not – in and of themselves – lead to more inclusive or self-directing communities. This is not particularly surprising, although it does fly in the face of the assumptions lying behind UNESCO and World Bank development programmes. This conclusion does not mean that literacy education lacks a critical role in social and political development, merely that it has to be conceived in more nuanced ways. The primary lesson from the review of the evidence is that literacy education is a tool for social change within contexts promoting social change, and that within those contexts the lines between literacy and political education can be extremely blurred. This is especially true for women, and it cannot be emphasised enough that in most of the world literacy is a very highly gendered issue.

Based on this review, there seems to be two primary uses of literacy capabilities within programmes setting out to change social structures. The first is to provide people with a reason to get engaged. For many people who have had little opportunity to develop their literacy capabilities the idea of gaining instrumental skills may well be attractive. As Robinson-Pant (2010) notes, providing formal education rather than informal education could be more attractive still, may be more effective in terms of personal capabilities, and may be a more sustainable model. Once again there is a tension between providing education in a form that has political significance and allowing it to collapse into a form that provides conventional education, simply to different sets of people. Done carefully, it seems that literacy education could be a useful and important starting point for individual and social change.

The second use is for communication, and there is more than one layer to this use. Literacy programmes provide a place for people to get together and talk to one another, often allowing women who might otherwise be isolated a legitimate reason and opportunity to share experience. This is not really a function of literacy capabilities, in my view, important though it is. A further layer is that literacy capabilities do directly allow communities to reach out to other communities around the world to offer and receive support. Reading and writing also provides people with the opportunity to record their history and tell their story, codifying their experience in a way that can reach across time and space.

Once again the answers to questions about the outcomes of literacy education reflect the notion that literacy capabilities are a resource, and that they will be used by different people in different situations in different ways. Literacy can be a mechanism to force people to accept a modernising agenda, or it can be a means to record and reinforce resistance to oppression. It can add to understanding, or obscure inequity under a veil of a strengthened meritocracy where those with the most highly developed formal skills reap rewards. It has enormous potential to create linkages between people driven apart by oppressive structures, but also to divide communities between those who embrace the value of these capabilities and those who value alternative means to reach solidarity. What seems strikingly clear, however, is that the enhancement of literacy capabilities does not guarantee a more enlightened or equitable society.

I would like to leave the last words in this chapter to a commentator on the use of literacy as a tool for women's empowerment in India, who I think sums up the position extremely well:

> *Literacy per se is of little relevance to poor women. However, literacy and education can be powerful tools to provide them with the very means of breaking out of the vicious cycle of powerlessness, poverty and marginalisation. In the twenty-first century development planners and educators face the challenge of harnessing the emancipatory potential of literacy and education by building upon rich knowledge, skills, experiences and practices of people and communities at the grassroots.* (Patel, 2003, p. 160)

PART THREE

REFLECTIONS AND CONCLUSIONS

CHAPTER TEN

Literacy matters

To get to this point in the book we have covered a lot of ground, some of it empirical and some theoretical. Throughout all of this, there have been strong central questions around the outcomes of literacy education in different domains of life, what we might expect those outcomes to look like, and how we can be sure we are really seeing them. In this chapter, I will pull together the strands of the argument. As I mentioned in the beginning of the book, my intention has not been to assess if literacy education matters, but to try to identify the ways in which it matters. One clear and consistent finding is that literacy learning matters in a number of different ways. Sometimes it matters in a direct way, and the ability to interact with text is the key to achieving a desired outcome. In many other cases, however, it seems that the effects are more indirect, and that the capability to achieve a goal derives not from literacy but from the context in which literacy is learned. Learning literacy may, for example, provide an opportunity for women to meet and discuss ideas when this would otherwise be difficult. Or being involved in learning could provide a boost in self-confidence and increase the feeling of control a person has over their life.

The perspective driving this book is that the significance of literacy capabilities is social and relational. In other words, understanding literacy capabilities is tied up with understanding the context in which they operate and what people want to do. I do not mean this in an oversimplified functional way, and certainly do not want to suggest that we should value learning only in terms of its potential utility, but I do take the position that application matters. In the case of communicative actions and resources

169

like literacy practices, the application is between people within a social context, and is shaped by the interests, perspectives and purposes of those people. As these can take a range of forms, from the most concrete to the most abstract, so can the valued outcomes of literacy capabilities. The capabilities model is an attempt to recognise those complexities, by recognising that literacy capabilities do not simply imply that people have strong skills in text use – there has to be a match with setting and purpose.

This perspective has underpinned the way I approached each area discussed in the book and tried to think through the evidence, looking at reasons why particular capabilities might manifest in particular settings. There is no single overarching message about why literacy matters, but on balance it seems that we can state with confidence that literacy, and literacy learning, has great significance for people in a variety of different ways depending on their circumstances. This chapter attempts to summarise and reinforce the key messages regarding the significance of literacy and literacy learning in the lives of adults. A good place to begin is by asking whether the capabilities model has been a useful organising framework. After that, I will present a summary of the findings of the discussion on the significance of literacy and literacy education for societies and for individuals.

Reflecting on the capabilities model

One useful question to start with is whether the capabilities model of literacy is consistent with the evidence gathered across the five areas of outcomes, and in general I believe that it is. It provides a way to conceptualise the loose articulation between people's literacy capabilities and the different types of outcomes. Perhaps the strongest example of this is the economic domain, where the outcomes attached to having or not having particular sets of abilities depend very strongly on the economic context. Yet even here, where the effects of literacy capabilities are so determined by external factors, we can state with some confidence that stronger capabilities are logically implicated in individuals' ability to attain better employment. It seems that the central claim of the model, that literacy capabilities are the ability to recognise and apply appropriate skills for a given context in order to achieve purposes, does fit well with the evidence reviewed. The model has certainly been useful in working through a considerable amount of evidence that all too often was highly contradictory.

The implications of this approach for understanding the way outcomes work are quite radical. It suggests that it is not possible to predict with any certainty what the outcomes of literacy learning will be for any individual, or even group of individuals. This is not a problem of instrumentation, of having the wrong tests or inaccurate information. It is more profound than this; it is a fundamental, irreducible unpredictability of the outcomes. The informal logical models developed in each of the five areas discussed helps to clarify what the outcomes might be, and how credibly they can be claimed as resulting from literacy education, but they certainly do not guarantee that certain things will definitely happen as a result of literacy learning.

Unfortunately, this is not a very helpful approach for people who are interested in promoting adult literacy education – it is unlikely to be well received when you tell a policymaker that investment in adult literacy education may produce some undefined benefits for an indeterminable group of people. There is a dilemma – is it better to state the outcomes of literacy of education responsibly, in which case they sound fuzzy, or state them more strongly, in which case they may be unobtainable.

The capability approach offers a different way to think through this dilemma. It shifts the argument around the outcomes of adult literacy education from the direct application of learning to the way that learning provides capacity to respond to changing demands and changing circumstances. Rather than offering the learner an enhanced grasp of a predetermined range of capabilities, literacy learning provides the opportunity to engage with a range of abilities that can be combined and augmented in a wide range of configurations reflecting the learner's social context. If this seems less clear than a model promising direct benefits from education, it is perhaps helpful to reflect that this is exactly the same logic that applies to initial schooling. The aim of schooling is not to predict all possible life courses for every schoolchild, but to equip all of them with a set of abilities that will allow them to respond creatively and effectively in the situations they are likely to encounter.

The ideas of social practices theory are really useful here, as they provide a way to frame the interaction between the individual and their context. Successful exercise of the social practices appropriate to a given setting requires both an understanding of the way those practices operate and the ability to participate in them. We could imagine this as a particular social context 'calling out' a set of social practices. If the person has the abilities needed to support those practices, they can be applied and the person demonstrates capability. This does not imply that people can potentially be equipped with a set of abilities appropriate to every possible context, because the process is much more subtle and much less determined than that. The key point to bear in mind is that individuals actively respond to their situation by negotiating a way to respond to the demands of that situation. In some cases, the response of the individual will be to turn away from a given situation, in others it will be an attempt to change the demands of the situation, and in yet others it will be a determination to learn the required abilities. When thinking about the way literacy capabilities operate, it is important to avoid the notion that individuals have a certain level of ability that can be placed somewhere on a single scale. Rather they have a complex set of skills and capabilities that can be added to, transformed and combined in new ways to help people to attain their goals.

This complexity goes a long way to explain why it is so hard to make definitive statements about the effects of literacy education. Even in the area where there is evidence that literacy learning has an effect, it is never a case of simply pointing directly to proof. A model has to be carefully constructed to link literacy learning to the outcomes that are hoped for, and in many parts of this book we have seen that the failure to prove a direct effect is not so much lack of evidence as a problem with the creation of this model. A good case is family literacy. Once the notion that literacy has to be either explicitly taught or not explicitly taught is accepted, then the problem is creating a model for how *changes* in adult literacy can be reflected in children. And, unfortunately, there does not seem to be a credible way to do so. If literacy is explicitly taught, then adults need to learn how to teach basic literacy more than strengthen their own skills. And if children learn through cultural osmosis, then the amount of change in adult literacy capabilities required to support this process might simply be infeasible.

Another interesting example is the relationship between literacy and health. Here there is considerable evidence that there is some kind of important link, and yet it still proves incredibly difficult to create a robust model of what is actually happening. The key gap, as mentioned in Chapter 7, is that we do not know very much about how or why people translate knowledge into action. Without understanding this step, all that it is possible to say is that stronger literacy capabilities may allow people to gain access to information about health more easily, but it is not really possible to say much about how this translates into concrete and measurable health outcomes.

A capability can also go unfulfilled if application of the appropriate skills does not happen for some reason. This could be simply because the person does not have these skills or because there is some other sort of interference. Perhaps the best illustration of this is the economic outcomes of literacy education once more. Here the simple expectation would be that 'more literacy = more money,' but as discussed in Chapter 6, it proves to be a great deal more complex than this. While there is a general indication that stronger literacy test scores and greater income tend to go together, there are a huge number of relevant factors that have to be comprehended. One very simple example is the case where a person has very highly developed literacy skills but does not have employment in which to apply them. In this case, the economic value of those skills is effectively zero and the literacy capability those skills represent is irrelevant to that economic context.

My intention in presenting this more nuanced model of literacy learning and its uses is not just to make things harder to understand. As I mentioned in the introduction, the adoption of oversimplified and over-ambitious goals for literacy education is extremely harmful to the field, reducing its credibility and value. When thinking about the benefits of a particular type of education in order to build strong accountability frameworks, it is critical to be as informed as possible about what those benefits are. There is a strong case that any linear assumption of literacy learning leading to pre-specified outcomes is simply not supported by the evidence.

What we can say about literacy learning is this. We know that literacy capabilities are associated with all sorts of outcomes that our societies would hope to promote, such as economic strength, health, positive emotional development, children who are engaged in education, and so on, but it is not possible to prove that literacy capabilities cause any of these outcomes directly. One way of getting some traction on the issue is to ask whether turning the question around helps at all – that is, what happens if we ask whether we could have these outcomes *without* literacy capabilities. The logic models we have explored in each of our five areas provide some unambiguous findings here. We can see this if we return to the example of health literacy above. While there is no way to guarantee that people with stronger literacy capabilities will definitely act in healthy ways, we can say with some certainty that people without these capabilities will find it harder to get to reliable health information. In the case of employment, whether the critical factor is signalling achievement or the exercise of textual skills, people who cannot access appropriate capabilities cannot take advantage of opportunities to attain economic security. Even in the case of cognitive effects, where there is little evidence that literacy capabilities really change the way people think, there is an argument that stronger capabilities allow far more effective expression of an individual's thinking than would be possible without those capabilities.

Appropriate application of literacy skills is a common factor across all of these areas, acting as a facilitative factor for people to achieve specific purposes. It makes sense to consider the emotional impact of literacy learning – about which we do have convincing evidence – as a product of the enhanced ability of individuals to achieve what is important to them. In a global society that is as strongly text-based as our own, literacy cannot fail to be an important component of communication. It is to be expected that literacy learning, as a means to enhance a critical communicative skill, will have individual and social significance beyond what can be captured by simple instrumental models. This can be illustrated by looking in more detail at the social impacts of literacy and literacy education.

How literacy education affects societies

In addressing this topic, I want to make it clear that I am not claiming any strong form of the literacy thesis, as discussed earlier. But it does seem reasonable to assume that social and individual effects are related to some extent. If there were no such relationship, it would suggest that everybody in a given society could have no literacy knowledge at all, yet the society would still maintain literacy as a key collective function. This does not make much sense, so even though it is difficult to be precise about the relationship there can be little doubt that there is one.

In earlier chapters, one clear message about literacy and society is that it might be best viewed as a tool or a resource, which will be called upon to serve specific social purposes as they arise within the society. The most important of those purposes will reflect the two great assets of written language compared to spoken language – its relative permanence and the ability to transcend space and time. Those interested in new media forms might respond immediately that these assets are shared by electronic media of various types, or even by established technologies such as film. While it may well be that in the future these types of media will do a lot of the work currently done by written language, there are several millennia of history supporting the effectiveness and relative accessibility of text archives. This matters a great deal because one of the main advantages of the key archival forms of a given society is trustworthiness – the idea that messages and ideas will be transmitted in the form in which they are recorded. It may be some time before electronic media reach this level of trust.

A second clear message is that literacy has little effect on the form of a society. There is very little to support the argument that a literate society is one in which people participate in political processes and feel as if they are part of a wider community. In fact, the balance of the evidence around the world probably suggests the opposite; that literacy is an important tool for ensuring compliance. Even within the Western societies, the people with the most developed literacy skills are rarely among those most actively working for social change.

Finally, the argument promoted by the OECD and a number of Western governments over the last decades, that literacy can be directly linked to productivity, also appears to lack a great deal of direct support. There is some evidence that higher levels of tested skills may be associated with wealthier societies, but the direction of this association is far from clear. If anything, the evidence once again points the other way, suggesting that wealthier economies can simply afford to provide their citizens with the education required to develop high skills levels. There may be some association with the types of work available in different types of society, so that wealthier societies have more symbolic work and call for more robust literacy abilities, but the details of this argument are not yet proven.

Given these rather negative findings, the question of why a government would want to invest in literacy education inevitably arises. After all, if it does not bring about political or economic development, what is the advantage to a society of offering this type of education at all? The answer comes back to the idea of literacy as a resource that can be called upon when needed.

In describing the capabilities model, I have gone to some length to point out that not everybody in a society will have the same path from cognitive processes to outcomes as expressed in particular social practices. However, it is quite reasonable to say that people who lack any part of these pathways will not be able to express the necessary capabilities. In a stable social form it would perhaps be possible to say that a particular person will need a specific set capabilities to get them through their life. But societies are not, and probably never have been, stable in this way. The social demands upon citizens change very significantly and very quickly, and societies have a responsibility to prepare their citizens for these changes whether this means providing the abilities they may need or supporting citizens' attempts to get them for themselves.

Based on the evidence reviewed, it is possible to state with some confidence that wealthy societies have well-developed literacy skills in their populations, but not that these skills lead to affluence. By once more turning the association around, however, it is possible to ask whether it is possible to have an affluent society without high skill levels. The evidence seems to suggest that it is not. This strongly supports the notion of literacy abilities as social resources, and is consistent with the notion that while societies with more developed literacy capabilities in the population are not necessarily richer, they may be in a better position to take advantage of changing technologies and other forms of opportunity when they arise. In other words, if governments are serious about the need for the working population to be ready for change and for 're-tooling' themselves in the face of evolving demands, then literacy capabilities need to be maximised across the population.

Leaving aside this somewhat speculative argument, the evidence that people are happier and more self-confident when they have stronger literacy skills should not be ignored. The cohort studies discussed at length in Chapter 4 point very strongly to literacy, and indeed learning more generally, as a component of a healthy lifestyle. Both physically and psychologically, literacy and health are linked. This is, of course, part of a wider cluster of factors that seem to run together and give some people great advantage in their lives. Even though the causational role of literacy cannot be known, it seems imperative to try to redistribute these factors as much as possible, and investment in adult literacy education would be a key strategy. This will be discussed in more length in the following chapter.

Changing the focus from developed economies to developing economies makes the arguments much clearer. The literacy resources within developing economies are not only more limited, they are distributed in less equitable fashion than within the developed economies (which is not to suggest that the distribution in the developed economies

176

is sufficiently equitable). While the claims of the OECD and UNESCO that increasing the literacy skills within the population of these countries will increase their affluence cannot be supported, it does seem reasonable to expect that the low literacy capabilities in these contexts could be a significant barrier to development. This does not mean that the Central African Republic should aim for a replica of an American or European school and adult education system – localisation and recognition of context remains a very important consideration.

The arguments for an adult education system in a developing economy are easier to make, in some ways, than in a developed context. People living in developing economies very often have not had initial schooling, especially if they are women, so the argument that 'they've had their chance' for education carries very little weight. In addition, as discussed earlier, adults within these societies often see education as a valuable resource for which they will put up with considerable inconvenience and discomfort. Within an increasingly globalised world, where economic and social factors are ever more frequently discussed on a transnational level, it certainly makes sense that a developing economy would want to support its citizens towards a level of capability consistent with a global economic and political presence.

The key social and political argument in support of adult literacy education is not that it is possible to prove advantages to a society in having such a system, but that there is strong evidence of the potential pitfalls on not having literacy education available. Such a failure would suggest that the earliest trajectories of advantage and disadvantage could not be changed throughout people's lives, leaving some citizens perpetually locked out of any developments that affect the society. But it is important to consider this argument more deeply by looking at the benefits of literacy learning for the individuals involved.

Individual outcomes of adult literacy learning

The individual effects of literacy learning are, in some ways, easier to identify directly than those for a society. There are a number of benefits that are supported by clear evidence and it is interesting to note that they are quite different from the benefits that circulate in policy discourse on the topic.

It should be stated very clearly early in this discussion that there is no evidence that individuals experience any sort of change in their cognitive processes as a result of learning literacy. It does not change long-term memory or short-term memory. Nor does it enhance people's ability to think in an ordered or disciplined way, because the demands for clear language use are not significantly different in spoken or written language. Certain cognitive tasks become more efficient as people become readers, but these are the very tasks that are practised in the process of reading. It is important to emphasise these findings in order to banish any last vestiges of the belief that any form of literacy intrinsically makes people more thoughtful or intelligent. As long as people have no specific reason to find literacy learning difficult, such as visual difficulties, there seems to be good evidence that anybody can expand their literacy capabilities as they find a need to do so. This is a very optimistic finding, and one that should underpin any discussion of the value of adult literacy learning irrespective of the context.

Among the clearest outcomes of adult literacy learning are a range of affective benefits. Even though these have not always been defined as rigorously as they might have been, the consistency with which they are mentioned in research projects is convincing. These benefits are often summed up as 'confidence,' and this seems to apply to both the confidence to learn and tackle new things within the classroom and or in people's broader lives. More specific terms include positive self concept, as learners become aware of the strength of their own abilities, increased self-esteem, as they realise they can learn, and self-efficacy, as their educational achievements demonstrate that they can achieve what they set out to achieve. The effect that engagement with literacy education can have upon the way that people view their whole lives is remarkable.

One of the more complicated areas of benefit is economic – whether people actually earn more money by developing their literacy skills. The background to this question is the considerable amount of evidence that, generally, stronger literacy skills and more extensive educational history are associated with higher earnings. Even though there are exceptions, such as CEOs who lack confidence in their reading, generally the pattern is very strong and consistent. The problem is that it is not clear how the association actually works. I am not referring to direction of causality here, but to the actual way that stronger skills translate to better paid employment.

It seems likely that the association of stronger skills and higher qualifications plays an important part here. It could well be that stronger literacy capabilities are rewarded in the labour market only if they are represented by a qualification that makes them visible to employers. The human capital people possess is not necessarily obvious to employers simply from an individual's work history, particularly if the individual has improved their abilities since getting their last job. This would underline the importance of learners having some way to represent their abilities accurately and clearly.

Here, the UK system of qualifications can, I suspect, both help and hinder learners. On the one hand, qualifications frameworks in both England and Scotland extend from a person's first learning to a doctorate, so that people can claim their place on the framework. On the other hand, the meaning of the frameworks and the levels on them are not always transparent to employers. For example, it is far from intuitive that 180 credits at Level 11 (in Scotland) is a Masters degree. The system in North America, where literacies learners aim for a Diploma of General Educational Development (GED) is far less sensitive to individuals' learning, but provides a far clearer signal to potential employers.

These issues raise the question of whether there is a threshold effect, in other words, whether people have to attain a certain level of qualification and concomitant skills to gain a labour market advantage. If this were the case, then people who want to improve their prospects would have to stick with literacy education until they reached a specific level. There seems to be some evidence that this is the case, and the available information seems to suggest that post-compulsory education is the critical level. But even here, it varies enormously by the type of qualification and, of course, by the type of employment being sought. So the answer to the question of whether learning literacy abilities can help people earn more money is, unfortunately, that it depends. There are some situations where a strong argument can be constructed, such as where an individual can take on more responsibility in their current workplace due to stronger capabilities, but there are also many cases where it is less obviously true. The clearest case is where gaining the certification needed for a specific job is likely to lead to specific rewards.

It is also critical to recognise the less direct effects of literacy learning on income. Increased literacy capabilities may not lead to enhanced work conditions, but may contribute to preparing an individual for further study or work based learning. For example, a cleaner in a hospital may be able to use their enhanced capabilities to achieve certification in more advanced hygiene techniques allowing them to move into more demanding and more highly paid areas of work. It would be incredibly difficult to track this type of indirect outcome of literacy learning, though it does fit well with the capabilities model.

In other areas of life, there is limited evidence of the effects of literacy learning. It may be that stronger capabilities allow people to engage in health care decisions with more agency and understanding, though there really needs to be more work done in this area. The dominant model of health literacy, which really means being able to understand and follow instructions, is not helpful in furthering understanding of how people use and relate to health information. Given the overall pattern of literacy engagement and other social advantages, however, it seems reasonable to assert that restricted access to literacy capabilities can contribute to perpetuating health inequalities.

One area where evidence is starting to accrue is the contribution literacy learning can make to networks of social capital. The theories of social capital are still very much in the early stages of development, but it is possible to discern how important they could become as they continue to receive attention. Literacy learning contributes significantly to people's social engagement and the links they have to other learners and people in other situations.

The political dimensions of literacy learning for adults are similarly nuanced. Claims that increased literacy capabilities lead automatically to social change and enhanced democracy are not supported by the evidence, but literacy learning can contribute to the infrastructures that permit these changes to happen. Enhanced capabilities seem to work primarily at an individual rather than a collective level, allowing people to engage in communication around issues that affect their lives and providing a reason to engage in the first place. Pulling those individuals together to act and lobby for their interests is a specific way to apply and animate of those capabilities rather than something inherent in reading and writing. While it is an important aspect of literacy capabilities that they can be developed and applied in such a way it should perhaps be considered as an indirect outcome.

Finally, the section on family literacy suggests that the direct impact of adult literacy learning on the literacy practices of the family may be limited, particularly when looking at the benefits of Evenstart 'four component' models. There is little hard evidence that changes in parental capabilities flow through to affect children's capabilities. However, a lot of the research on family literacy has examined only school-centred literacy, and it is probable that all sorts of other practices are being developed and applied that the existing research does not capture. More nuanced approaches to family literacy research that go beyond school-centred literacy could potentially capture some important and valuable interactions. The less direct effect, where literacy learning helps the adult to create a more 'literacy rich' environment for their family is likely to be extremely important, but there is a need to gather evidence on the mechanisms and the impacts of such effects. The importance of very simple changes such as learning to read in order to share books with one's children should not be overlooked in any way.

When looking across the evidence for the effects of adult literacy education on the lives of individuals there is a fair amount of evidence that it makes a real difference, but these differences tend to manifest in highly individual and subtle ways. This phenomenon challenges researchers, policymakers and educators to think beyond simple models of cause and effect, and find ways to capture and recognise the profoundly situated and embedded effects pervading learners' lives.

Conclusion

From this recapitulation of the evidence examined throughout the book there are a number of messages that emerge. The first is that literacy outcomes, and therefore the outcomes of literacy learning, are highly contextual. This means that they will also be varied and difficult to capture. It is simply not possible to make an overarching statement about a direct relationship between engaging in literacy learning and the outcomes people can expect to get out of that engagement. The relationship is inherently complex and varied.

A second message is that literacy is associated, to various degrees, with many outcomes that are desirable on a social or individual level. There are no instances where increased literacy capability is associated with a worse outcome. This implies that literacy capabilities can be considered as a resource that is highly desirable in contemporary societies, and that lack of this resource is a real disadvantage. This places a duty on governments to ameliorate this disadvantage by providing opportunities for people to gain the resource – through adult literacy education. This point is explored in more depth in the final chapter.

Overall, there are no easy answers regarding why adult literacy education matters. It shares with most other forms of education (except the most directly vocational) a loosely articulated relationship with a range of outcomes that are valuable and desirable. The lack of direct relationships need not be a disadvantage or an indication of weakness of adult literacy education; the far stronger message is the range of positive outcomes with which it is associated.

CHAPTER ELEVEN

Implications for adult literacy education policy and practice

The last chapter summarised the key messages that emerged from reviewing the evidence in the light of the capabilities model. Here I want to explore the implications of those messages for the way adult literacy education is conceived, and for policy and practice in the field. I begin by laying out a perspective on one of the most important on one of the most important historical and contemporary aspects of the field – the connection between literacy education and social justice.

Literacy and social justice

In most societies in the world, literacy is one of the fundamental capabilities and there is a great deal of merit in the basic argument that effective interactions with text are a central component of the individual's ability to exercise autonomy. This is shown, amongst other ways, by the appeal of literacy programmes in developing societies. Even though it is hard to find really convincing arguments for the economic or political advantages of literacy learning in these contexts the commitment and enthusiasm of learners cannot be denied, and this tells us something about the significance of the ability to interact with text.

When examining the way that people have the opportunity to attain resources that are considered valuable within a society one of the fundamental concerns is distributive justice. This principle of justice concerns whether these 'goods' are distributed in a fair way, and it is an important component of broader social justice framework. An obvious example is health care for babies. It is not fair or just that some babies born in the world's largest economy are provided with the best health care available while others have to settle for minimal attention – after all, at the age of a few days or weeks, the babies themselves are not going to have done anything to allow assessment of whether they deserve the best care or not. The only just action here is to provide the best possible health care to all babies, irrespective of where they are born in the world or the status of their parents. Similarly, it makes sense to pay two people equally for the same job whatever their gender, background or sexual preference. In other cases, distributive justice does not lead to the requirement to treat everyone equally. It does not make so much sense to pay everybody the same amount of money whatever their job, or to tax everybody equally however many dependents they have.

Most people would agree with distributive justice in principle; disagreements tend to arise when it has to be decided how these principles apply to different aspects of life. Affirmative action is a good example of this. Some people would claim that groups who have suffered historical disadvantage should be offered some form of redress, and that it is fair and effective to prioritise these groups in public sector hiring if all else is equal. Other people would see this practice as being discriminatory in itself, and as perpetuating the divisive potential of ethnicity. People on both sides of an issue such as this may have equally compelling and well thought out arguments, and a person's position on the 'right' thing to do may well be informed by their wider moral and ethical commitments.

Distributive justice is particularly relevant to literacy capabilities in two ways. The first is that different forms of literacy have different value attached to them. I discussed this to some extent in the chapter on family literacy, but briefly the issue is that school-centred forms of literacy capability and the skills that support them tend to be valued more highly – if other forms are valued at all. This represents an enormous bias in almost all of the research literature on literacy, with the exception of the work based on new literacy studies. This bias means that in nearly every case when the outcomes of literacy are examined only the formal, school-centred literacies are considered. If this limitation is made clear it is less of a problem, but many researchers seem to view school-centred literacy as the only form that has to be considered and fail to examine the implications of this assumption.

This blind spot in the research is even more troubling because it overlooks so many local forms of literacy not in favour of a universal form, but in favour of another local form that has been allocated considerable status. There is nothing inherent to school-centred literacy that means it should be the most valued form of text use. For example, few people realise how recent the development of standardised spelling in English really is – generally accepted spellings for most words did not really emerge until the 1800s, influenced to some extent by the spread of compulsory universal schooling. Really the notion of a standardised school-centred literacy in English has only been around for 150 years, and over that time it has managed to become the highest form of the language. The same process seems to be occurring in developing economies, raising interesting questions about the role of schooling in language development. This focus on school-centred language forms masks other forms of written language that cannot be captured in any sort of measure of standard text use, but which still act as critical resources for the people concerned. An example from an earlier chapter is the ability to use Spanish in the home, which may well not fit with the school's expectations but performs an important function in ensuring cultural and political solidarity in the family and wider community.

This becomes an issue of justice because different people have access to and use different forms of literacy. The people who have mastery of the valued forms of literacy tend to be people with privilege, and it would be naïve to think that this is a coincidence. In effect, people with power within a society get to select the form of literacy that has value and power attached to it; not surprisingly, they tend to select their own literacy form. The reason the United States speaks English is that the United Kingdom provided the colonial government that shaped the language practices of the early republic. In the same way Scotland, Ireland, Wales, India, several African nations, Australia, New Zealand, Canada and so on have had English as one of their official languages because of a specific colonial history.

These effects manifest on a far more local level. Within my own university, the most valued form of written language is academic English even though it would be completely indecipherable to many people living about 50 metres from the gates of the university. Their literacy practices would tend to be discounted by the university, even if they are brilliantly imaginative and effective, because they do not fit the university context. In other words, the power to decide what counts as an appropriate application of skills can be extremely important in shaping the practices in a specific context, and ownership of that power is an issue of justice.

The second issue of justice in the distribution of literacy capacities is related to the first, and concerns who has the opportunity to learn the valuable school-centred form of literacy. All the evidence I have presented earlier suggests that there are several gradients of school-centred literacy capability, and that they all point in the same direction. They show that advantage begets advantage. People with the strongest school-centred literacy capabilities tend to be from the most advantaged homes, as well as healthier, wealthier and better educated. Literacy capabilities seem to be one of the resources, among a number of others, that some people get a great deal of and others get very little of. I do not want to speculate here on the reasons these resources run together; for our purposes it is sufficient to note that they do. In fact they are so closely entwined that it would be quite feasible to reverse the usual forms of research and predict people's social class based upon their literacy test scores. Literacy is tangled up with a number of other fundamental indicators of a person's social position.

I believe it is important to recognise a number of implications of these social justice concerns. One important starting point is that it is imperative to avoid blaming the victim for limitations in literacy capabilities. Any factor that is distributed in a way that reflects social structures as closely as literacy does must have a fairly limited component of individual choice associated with it, and it is unjust to present arguments suggesting that people have more individual control over their literacy capabilities than is the case. This includes arguments implying that people are ignorant of more 'valuable' ways of doing things, as are sometimes found in family literacy. People act in ways that allow them to achieve their ends within their current context, and any evaluation of literacy practices must recognise that context.

It follows that in any society where there are strong demands for particular forms of literacy capability it is unjust to limit the ability of individuals to attain those forms of capability. This includes limiting that potential by restricting the forms of literacy people are able to learn to literacy designed to serve particular outcomes or a particular context. The overarching finding of this book is that it is not possible to predict how people will use literacy capabilities and to what ends they will apply them, and that to assume we know enough to define and measure outcomes is highly unrealistic. The same argument applies to the assumption that it is possible to define a certain level of literacy capability as the standard level – people will learn what they need to learn, when they need to learn it, provided that there is open and responsive adult literacy support available to them. Educators cannot predetermine the types of capabilities that people have to attain in order to enrich their lives.

Many of the measurement systems currently used in literacy are unjust because they privilege certain types of literacy over others even though people do not have equal opportunity to learn those forms of literacy. While defenders of these measures would argue that they reflect the demands of workplaces and other real life settings, this is not completely established. To some extent researchers may measure school-centred and formal literacy because they know something about how to measure it rather than because it is the only form that matters in people's lives.

Social justice arguments suggest that we can accept the outcomes of literacy education as they present themselves rather than trying to break them down into the effects of learning literacy and the effects of being in education. In this book I have tried to pull these apart a little because it is important in a study like this one to treat the evidence as rigorously as possible, but in practice I am far less convinced that it matters. We saw earlier that in many settings, literacy learning can work as a means to attract people to participate in educational programmes and gain benefits beyond the ability to interact with texts. It is unjust to the individuals involved to suggest that only the direct, instrumental benefits of adult literacy education should be considered legitimate when that contradicts their own experience so directly. If literacy learning leads to a range of outcomes that people value, it seems imperative to recognise those and acknowledge their origin.

In summary, I believe that a just approach to literacy learning is to view it as a way for people to gain access to capabilities that our global society values. If we take this seriously it means that everybody has to be provided with the opportunity to strengthen those capabilities whenever they need to. We know from the capabilities model that people recognise the need to learn when it is most pressing, and it is important to respond to that need. It is not going to be effective to limit the availability of support to certain types of literacy or certain times in people's lives because literacy learning simply does not work that way. Need for support with literacies arises when people interact with particular contexts and recognise particular areas that could benefit from being strengthened. It is a fundamental issue of justice that adults have the opportunity to strengthen these capabilities through literacy learning.

Implications for literacy policy

Pulling together the evidence gathered throughout this book in the light of a social justice framework can help to inform the development of policy around adult literacy learning. There are four central implications for policy that come out of this review of the evidence. Even though they are quite straightforward individually, taken together they imply significant changes in the way literacy education is structured and managed in developed and developing societies. These implications are underpinned by a single argument – simple, linear views of how literacy and literacy learning work are neither theoretically sound nor are they pragmatically helpful. The idea that people can be placed on a continuum of ability with good skills at the top and poor skills at the bottom not only misrepresents the workings of literacy, but more significantly for a pragmatic age it misleads us regarding the policy interventions that are desirable or likely to be effective.

I hope this discussion has made clear that measurement of literacy capabilities is an extremely challenging endeavour, and it is not certain that the approaches currently dominating this activity are necessarily the most useful. There are two aspects of the measuring systems that limit their utility. One is that their acceptance of literacy as a single continuum leads to a very narrow scope of measurement. There will be lots of types of literacy practice that really are not captured very well by these instruments. The second limitation is that they place people onto this continuum on the basis of very little concrete information. As discussed earlier in the book, placing people who have spiky profiles onto a unidimensional scale on the basis of limited information is unlikely to tell us a great deal.

What would be really useful for informed policy-making is a way to understand both the supply side of literacy capabilities and the demands for these capabilities. This suggests that there is a need for contextual measures that take into account the broader life situations of individuals rather than merely considering the distribution of mean scores on standardised tests. Good policy-making relies on good evidence, and when this is not available the quality of decision-making inevitably suffers.

It follows that international comparisons, such as that in the International Adult Literacy Survey, may not be very meaningful. Again, this hinges on the contextual nature of literacy capabilities. If skills requirements are specific to particular economies, for example, comparing measured skills levels across different economies is unlikely to tell us a great deal. Even though there is a great deal of interest in international league tables they mean very little if the contexts in which measurement occurs vary a great deal. Even within Europe, it may not be helpful to compare the UK outcomes (if we could measure them in a meaningful way) with those of Scandinavia. In the UK we have an extremely hierarchical society with markedly uneven distribution of social resources, including literacy capabilities, whereas historically Sweden and similar societies have had more open access to resources. So we need to ask what it tells us if we find that Sweden has higher test scores on the same scale as the UK when the two societies are starting from such different sets of assumptions.

The value of international comparisons – used responsibly – should not be dismissed, however. They do act as important and effective leverage points for policy change and for developing serious commitments to desirable goals. In the light of our discussion, perhaps it makes sense for the comparison to be based on the extent to which literacy learning is available to everybody in a given society whenever they need it. The closer a nation comes to universal offerings of adult literacy education the higher it should be in the comparison, exactly the same measure used in the UNESCO (2008) 'Education for All' programme for primary schooling. There is no obvious reason why education for adults should not be seen as having the same moral and political weight as education for children.

Reflecting both of these points, it follows that having targets for the literacy skills of a nation or a community is not very helpful. Setting aside the measurement issues, there is a really important question of identifying the problem that policies like this are trying to solve. If people do not perceive that they have a live reason to get involved in literacy learning they certainly will not do so just because government thinks it would be good for them. People's involvement in any form of education or training depends on some sort of demand for what will be learned, whether vocational or otherwise. The key to raising literacy skills across a population is to raise the demand for such skills in workplaces and everyday life. On an extremely pragmatic level, raising the literacy test scores or the capabilities of an entire population would require extraordinary investment.

It would be more useful to have broad targets for the number of people served by adult literacy learning, and measures associated with broader and more effective participation such as intensity of services received and satisfaction with those services. This places the responsibility for identifying and addressing any potential gaps in skills in the hands of the people living with those challenges rather than assuming they can be identified and addressed through a central mechanism. There is a need for universal support rather than universal measures.

The final, and perhaps the strongest, implication for policy is that functional literacy is simply not a useful concept. Engagement with text cannot be considered functional or not on a general level, there is always the need to ask 'functional for what, for whom?' One of the most common arguments for functional literacy is based on the economy, and the idea that people need to attain a certain level of skills to be employable. But even if we accept this as the central dimension of functional literacy, the key consideration is not the absolute level of skills in the population but the match between skills supply and skills demand. Functional literacy is not a constant or reliable measure, since changes in the demands can either increase or decrease the proportion of the population who can be considered to have functional levels of those capabilities.

Literacy capabilities is a more useful concept for policy-making than functional literacy. The policy concern here is not some predetermined level of idealised skills but the distribution of the capabilities associated with satisfactory lives, and theoretically there is no limit to the capabilities people could benefit from. Before it is pointed out that it would be incredibly expensive to provide everybody with perpetual education towards a receding horizon of infinite capability, I would like to suggest that it is unlikely that involvement in literacy learning would change that much. Just as people are essentially self-regulating in identifying needs, they are essentially self regulating in recognising when they can match the demands of their lives effectively. As mentioned earlier, most people are not that interested in education for its own sake. They are interested in education when it helps them to achieve their goals (Knowles, 1980).

The policy implications listed here seem rather idealistic in an age that is highly focused on the notion of measuring everything and attaching a price to it. I am arguing that we have to move away from outcomes-based management in literacy learning to a radically learner-centred system, where the learners have high degrees of control over what they learn and can decide when they have learned enough. Yet I am making this argument for the most pragmatic of reasons – the approach we are using now simply does not work very well. It has proven difficult, ineffective and expensive to measure literacy and develop literacy education as if capabilities can easily be measured, and policy needs to move away from its addiction to the refined sugar of quantification to re-engage with the complexities of literacy and learning.

Implications for the field of adult literacy education

The discussion in this book has interesting implications for the organisation and practices of the adult literacy education field. Literacy education has been influenced by many of the same forces that have affected education more broadly in the last few decades, including a focus on measured outcomes and a requirement for demonstrations of quality in the process itself. Yet the proportion of adults in any part of the world who actually engage with this form of adult learning remains relatively low even where there has been massive investment in adult literacy systems. One of the most useful questions to address would be how to ensure that people can get support with their literacy capabilities when they need it.

It seems important to reinforce what we know about the patterns of literacy learning that individuals get involved with. It is not really very helpful to imagine that adults are engaged in literacy learning only when they are in a class designed for that purpose. People learn literacies in a huge range of ways, varying from the formal to the most informal and casual, and it makes more sense to think of learners having a patchwork of learning strategies rather than any one specific approach to learning. Literacy education is one of those strategies, but so are the Internet, family support, friends and a whole rich network of other supports (Reder, 2009). People can also learn literacy capabilities in contexts that are designed to teach other things entirely, such as learning a better understanding of numbers through learning to cook. I believe it is important for literacy educators to recognise the range of supports people call upon, and not to believe that literacy classes are the only way to learn literacies.

In response to this, it makes sense to rethink what counts as participation in literacy learning. Most literacy education systems count hours of attendance, with many in the United States, for example, counting a participant only when they have attended 12 hours of classes. This is because the accountability mechanisms are focused upon a particular type of progress, and short participation is unlikely to lead to these particular outcomes. This means that many programmes are supplying services to individuals that they simply cannot represent in their statistics, which is unfair to the programmes and dismissive of the potential learning that is going on.

It is more consistent with the capabilities model to think about people's involvement in programmes on the basis of 'literacy support events' rather than hours in a programme or completion of a predetermined level of learning. This implies a radically learner centred approach to the teaching and learning process, driven by the participant's view of the capability they want to strengthen and reflecting a highly localised view of functional literacy. An example of a literacy support event might be an individual who comes to a local programme to get a little support with putting together a job application. They do not need or want a course in literacy or numeracy; they want to fill in a form. If this perspective is adopted, the meaning of hours of attendance is reversed, with an effective support event very possibly involving only a few hours of formal attendance rather than completion of dozens of hours of study. The key question is whether the individual was able to develop the capabilities they considered they needed.

There are implications for measurement with this approach. It is often seen as important to assess individual's capabilities when they enter a programme, in order to be able to measure the distance they have covered. This raises all of the same difficulties discussed in Chapter 4 regarding the way literacy abilities actually seem to work, and the impossibility of creating a meaningful universal scale. However, if the emphasis is placed on a discreet capability defined by the learner, it becomes far easier to measure progress. Instead of movement from *a* to *b* on a theoretical scale, measurement becomes a more pragmatic concern of working out whether the specific learner achieved their identified goal. An interesting side effect of this approach is that literacy education would become much cheaper because the costs would be spread across a larger number of participants and there would likely be a greater number of successful outcomes. So not only would it reflect the interests of learners more closely, it would also provide advantages for literacy educators and their funders.

A very similar system has been tried in Scotland, but has struggled to deal with a number of challenges (St.Clair and Belzer, 2007). One of the most difficult has been the need to deal with an audit culture that wants to count inputs and outcomes and connect them together in a simplistic way. This means that the system pivots on the definition of learner outcomes and how these are, in the most literal sense, counted. In addition, the school-centred model of what education should look like, with a curriculum designed by the educator and some form of testing to show achievement, has proven to be both pervasive and very difficult to shift. So while the possibilities for change are very substantial, so are the challenges.

One interesting point is how literacy education would show that it is doing a good job. At the moment this is extremely difficult. In most places in the world, it is based on the assumption that people enter literacy programmes at a certain measurable level of capability, complete a very substantial period in the programme (often more hours than an entire graduate degree) and leave with an increase in their measured capabilities. The measure of quality is generally how many people go through this process. If the field were to orientate itself towards literacy support events then quality concerns would be centred on making sure those events were as positive and effective as possible. What would matter would be that the participants felt that their needs were met well – surely the measure of quality that should lie at the heart of educational accountability.

This reorientation would require extremely skilled staff, and the requirement for effective professional development for literacy educators could not be overlooked. When educators are responding to the needs of individuals, which would necessarily be both broad and diverse, it is likely to be far more challenging than the delivery of a set curriculum. This reinforces the importance of deliberate development of careers in literacy education, with all the stability and long-term commitment that would require from funders, staff and the levels of government responsible.

It would be remiss not to mention the challenge of certification. As this discussion shows I am convinced that certification is important in signalling the level of skills that people possess, but I am less certain how best to design it. A unified competency-based system such as the European Qualifications Framework for Lifelong Learning (European Commission, 2008) offers a way to describe changes in ability and could potentially gain enough recognition to work as a signalling mechanism. Yet its very breadth can muddy the message it is trying to convey. For example, vocational qualifications achieved through years of work experience are considered essentially identical to academic qualifications that can be attained entirely through schooling. The type of person liable to have such qualifications, and their interests, are likely to be markedly different.

It is also possible that learners may not be interested in certification. They could very well already possess good qualifications and be involved in adult literacy education to address a specific area of learning, or they could be uninterested in the labour market. It is important that there are pathways available for these people to participate fully in literacy education and not feel that they are in any way valued less by adult literacy education providers. This can easily happen where agencies providing literacy education are paid on the basis of the qualifications learners achieve, which seems to be a growing trend internationally. While the rationale for such an approach, including an apparently built-in accountability framework, can appear convincing, the benefits can be outweighed by the unintended consequences of exclusion of potential learners and limitation of provision (Appleby and Bathmaker, 2006).

I would like to end this section with a few reflections on the political purpose and moral import of literacy education. I believe that it is important for literacy education to claim the broad set of outcomes that are associated with participation. While in this book I have tended to pull apart outcomes of *literacy* and outcomes of *learning* if I think they have been confused, when trying to understand the field as a whole I think it is more important to acknowledge that these are all effects of literacy learning. While it might be the case that the same effects would be seen if people learned watercolour painting or dog grooming they are not choosing to learn those things – they are choosing to learn about literacy. And that speaks to the importance and benefits associated with literacy learning.

I also believe the field should claim its contribution to social justice more strongly. If we accept the capability argument and take it seriously, literacy learning has an extremely important contribution to make to people across their lives and throughout their lives. While it may not lead directly to political transformation on a large scale, the key argument of this book is that literacy capabilities support people's capacity to decide for themselves, and to act on those things that they do see as important to change. Literacy capability is a good thing in a society premised on the ability to interact with text, and the more evenly and profoundly the capabilities can be distributed, the more just the society can be considered.

Each of these implications applies to both the developed nations and those in the process of development. The way they manifest will be considerably different, however. For the developed nations, the challenge is to move past the idea that adult literacy learning is second class education for people who missed out on schooling. While some participants have indeed not benefitted from initial education, many others will be going through some sort of transformation that changes the demands on their literacy capabilities. In developing countries, I see the challenge as moving beyond the assumption that traditional Western forms of literacy learning, possibly as school-like as possible, represent the most valuable form of learning. For both, the challenge is to find ways to resist school-centred models of engagement with text and find ways to build novel approaches recognising the power and diversity of written language in the lives of adults.

Last words

As we have reviewed the available evidence on literacy and literacy education, one message that seems to come across is how much more we have to learn about the operation of these capabilities. There is a great deal more that it would be useful to know, some of which we are close to knowing and some of which we will possibly never know. This does not mean that, in that cliché of academic writing, more research is needed; or at least not more of the same type of research. We have a great deal of information on literacy and the issue is not the amount but the form of that information. There is plenty of evidence on the association of literacy with other social resources, but little on how those associations work and what – if anything – we can do about those associations.

The data on literacy contains surprisingly little evidence on the direct effects of literacy learning, in the sense of a process aimed at strengthening capabilities. To some extent, however, this is balanced by the surprising extent and strength of evidence regarding outcomes broadly associated with literacy learning. So while it is hard to show that literacy capabilities definitely support positive health outcomes, for example, there is enough evidence to support an argument for the significance of strong literacy capabilities as a key form of capability tied up with a range of desirable outcomes.

Overall the message of this book is positive. There are indications that literacy capabilities are significant in a wide variety of ways. Even though this evidence is subtle and nuanced and not the stuff of indisputable cause and effect, when it is framed within the capabilities model it produces powerful arguments for changing the way we conceive both the outcomes of literacy learning and the process itself. On the other side, the evidence provides little reassurance that the current approaches we take to literacy learning – as educators, researchers or policymakers – help us to understand or strengthen the contributions of literacy learning. While the messages that emerge are nuanced, they are nonetheless messages that call for change.

I will end with the question of why literacy matters. The brief answer, albeit partial, is that literacy matters because we want it to matter. Our global society has orientated itself in such a way that literacy capabilities are fundamental and vital to our lives. In this book I have tried to find out if there is something about the acts of reading and writing that makes them inherently transformative, bringing about inevitable changes in our thinking or our politics or our health behaviours, and the answer seems to be clear that there is not. But there is such social and communicative significance attached to engagement with texts that to fail to see literacy capabilities as a central dimension of equity and social justice, and to fail to recognise the dimensions of deprivation that arise from their radically skewed distribution, is to misunderstand the nature of human society in the twenty-first century. We cannot say that everybody will do the same things with their literacy capabilities, or that a neat set of desirable outcomes will inevitably result. But we can, and must, recognise that restrictions in literacy capability constitute real deprivation of the resources people need in order to achieve their purposes. And the best tool we have to counter that deprivation is commitment to strong and open systems of support for literacy learning.

References

Action Aid Vietnam (2008). Literacy and community development programme. Retrieved December 10, 2009, from www.unesco.org/uil/litbase/?menu=4&programme=57.

Agence Nationale de Lutte contre l'illettrisme (undated). *Illiteracy: The Statistics*. Lyon, FR: Agence Nationale de Lutte contre l'illettrisme.

Aoki, A. (2005). 'Assessing learning achievements and development impact: Ghana's national functional literacy program.' *Australian Journal of Adult Learning, 45(1)*, 63–81.

Appleby, Y. and Bathmaker, A.M. (2006). 'The new skills agenda: increased lifelong learning or new sites of inequality?' *British Educational Research Journal, 32(5)*, 703–717.

Bailey, A. (2007). *Connecting the Dots . . . Linking Training Investment to Business Outcomes and The Economy*. Ottawa: Work and Learning Knowledge Centre.

Balatti, J., Black, S. and Falk, I. (2007). 'Teaching for social capital outcomes: the case of adult literacy and numeracy courses.' *Australian Journal of Adult Learning, 47(2)*, 245–263.

Barton, D. (1994). 'The social impact of literacy.' In L. Verhoeven (Ed.), *Functional Literacy: Theoretical Issues and Educational Implications* (185–197). Amsterdam: John Benjamins.

Barton, D. and Hamilton, M. (1998). *Local Literacies: Reading and Writing in One Community*. London: Routledge.

Barton, D., Hamilton, M. and Ivanic, R. (Eds) (2000). *Situated Literacies: Reading and Writing in Context*. New York: Routledge.

Barton, D. (2007). *Literacy: An Introduction to the Ecology of Written Language* (2nd ed.). Hoboken, NJ: Wiley-Blackwell.

Becker, G. S. (1975). *Human Capital: A Theoretical and Empirical Analysis, with Special Reference to Education*. New York: National Bureau of Economic Research.

Beder, H. (1997). 'Adult literacy and community development.' *Literacy Practitioner, 4(2)*, 1–7.

Beder, H. (1999). *The Outcome and Impacts of Adult Literacy Education in the United States*. Cambridge, MA: National Center for the Study of Adult Learning and Literacy.

Belzer, A. and St.Clair, R. (2005). 'Back to the future: Implications of the neo-positivist research agenda for adult basic education.' *Teachers' College Record, 107(6)*.

Berhane, Y., Högberg, U., Byass, P. and Wall, S. (2002). 'Gender, literacy and survival among Ethiopian adults, 1987–1996.' *Bulletin of the World Health Organisation, 80(9)*, 714–720.

Bernstein, B. (1990). *Class, Codes and Control: Volume 4 – The Structuring of Pedagogic Discourse*. London: Routledge.

Biddle, W. W. (1966). 'The "fuzziness" of definition of community development.' *Community Development Journal, 1(2)*, 5–12.

Bingman, M. B., Ebert, O. and Bell, B. (2000). *Outcomes of Participation in Adult Basic Education: The Importance of Learners' Perspectives*. Cambridge, MA: National Center for the Study of Adult Learning and Literacy.

Binkley, M., Matheson, N. and Williams, T. (1997). *Adult Literacy: An International Perspective*. Washington, DC: US Department of Education, Office of Educational Research and Development, National Center for Educational Statistics.

Blanche-Benveniste, C. (1994). 'The construct of oral and written language.' In L. Verhoeven (Ed.), *Functional Literacy: Theoretical Issues and Educational Implications* (61–74). Amsterdam: John Benjamins.

Blum, A., Goldstein, H. and Guérin-Pace, F. (2001). 'International Adult Literacy Survey (IALS): an analysis of international comparisons of adult literacy.' *Assessment in Education: Principles, Policy and Practice, 8(2)*, 225–246.

Blundell, R., Dearden, L., Meghir, C. and Sianesi, B. (1999). 'Human capital investment: The returns from education and training to the individual, the firm and the economy.' *Fiscal Studies, 20(1)*, 1–23.

Bourdieu, P. (1983). 'The forms of capital.' In J. G. Richardson (Ed.),

Handbook of Theory and Research for the Sociology of Education. Westport, CT: Greenwood.

Brannick, M. T. (Undated). 'Item Response Theory.' Retrieved June 22, 2009, from http://luna.cas.usf.edu/~mbrannic/files/pmet/irt.htm.

Brewer, K., Wyse, L., Lyle, K., McLean, P. and Perkins, K. (2006). *A Revised NRS: Towards an Essential Skills Framework.* Canberra: Commonwealth of Australia, Department of Education, Science and Training.

Brooks, G., Pahl, K., Pollard, A. and Rees, F. (2008). *Effective and Inclusive Practices in Family Literacy, Language and Numeracy: A Review of Programmes and Practice in the United Kingdom and Internationally.* Sheffield, UK: CfBT Education Trust, NRDC, University of Sheffield.

Bynner, J., McIntosh, S. A. V., Dearden, L., Reed, H. and Reenen, J. v. (2001). *Improving Adult Basic Skills: Benefits to the Individual and Society.* London: Department for Education and Employment.

Bynner, J. and Parsons, S. (2009). 'Insights into basic skills from a UK longitudinal study.' In S. Reder and J. Bynner (Eds), *Tracking Adult Literacy and Numeracy: Findings from Longitudinal Research* (pp. 27–58). London: Routledge.

Byrd, D. M. and Gholson, B. (1985). 'Reading, memory and meta-cognition.' *Journal of Educational Psychology, 77(4),* 428–436.

Chafetz, M. E. (2005). *Big Fat Liars: How Politicians, Corporations and the Media Use Science and Statistics to Manipulate the Public.* Nashville, TN: Nelson.

Chen, H. T. and Rossi, P. H. (1989). 'Issues in the theory-driven perspective.' *Evaluation and Program Planning, 12,* 299–308.

Chinca, C. and Young, C. (2005). 'Orality and literacy in the Middle Ages: a conjunction and its consequences.' In C. Chinca and C. Young (Eds), *Orality and Literacy in the Middle Ages* (1–16). Turnhout, Belgium: Brepols.

Coffield, F. (1999). 'Breaking the consensus: lifelong learning as social control.' *British Educational Research Journal, 25 (4),* 497–499.

Coleman, J. S. (1988). 'Social capital in the creation of human capital.' *American Journal of Sociology, 94S.*

Collins, J. and Blot, R. K. (2003). *Literacy and Literacies: Texts, Power and Identity.* Cambridge, UK: Cambridge University Press.

Comings, J. (2009). 'Student persistence in adult literacy and numeracy programmes.' In S. Reder and J. Bynner (Eds), *Tracking Adult Literacy* and *Numeracy Skills* (160–176). London: Routledge.

Cottingham, S., Metcalf, K. and Phnuyal, B. (1998). 'The REFLECT approach to literacy and social change: a gender perspective.' *Gender and Development, 6(2)*, 27–34.

Coulombe, S., Tremblay, J.-F. and Marchand, S. (2004). *International Adult Literacy Survey: Literacy Scores, Human Capital and Growth Across Fourteen OECD Countries.* Ottawa: Statistics Canada.

Crano, W. D. and Brewer, M. B. (2002). *Principles and Methods of Social Research* (2nd ed.). Mahwah, NJ: Lawrence Erlbaum.

Crowther, J., Hamilton, M. and Tett, L. (Eds). (2001). *Powerful Literacies.* Leicester, UK: National Institute of Adult Continuing Education (NIACE).

Cunningham, A. E. and Stanovich, K. E. (1998). 'What reading does for the mind.' *American Educator*, 1–8.

Davis, T., Long, S., Jackson, R., Mayeaux, E., George, R., Murphy, P., *et al.* (1993). 'Rapid estimate of adult literacy in medicine: a shortened screening instrument.' *Family Medicine, 25(6)*, 391–395.

De Haan, M. (2008). *The Effect of Parents' Schooling on Child's Schooling: A Nonparametric Bounds Analysis.* Amsterdam: Tinbergen Research Institute.

Deacon, T. W. (1997). *The Symbolic Species: The Co-Evolution of Language and the Brain.* New York: Norton.

Dearden, L., McGranahan, L. and Sianesi, B. (2004). *Returns to Education for the 'Marginal Learner': Evidence from the BCS70.* London: London School of Economics, Centre for the Economics of Education.

DeWalt, D., Berkman, N., Sheridan, S., Lohr, K. and Pignone, M. (2004). 'Literacy and health outcomes: A systematic review of the literature.' *Journal of General Internal Medicine, 19.*

EFF (2004). 'Equipped for the future.' From http://eff.cls.utk.edu/

Eldred, J. (2002). *Moving on with Confidence: Perceptions of Success in Teaching and Learning Adult Literacy.* Leicester, UK: National Institute of Adult Continuing Education (NIACE).

European Commission (2008). *The European Qualifications Framework for Lifelong Learning.* European Commission: Brussels.

Eysenck, H. J. (1971). *The IQ Argument: Race, Intelligence and Education.* New York: Library Press.

Facundo, B. (1984). *Freire-Inspired Programmes in the United States and Puerto Rico: A Critical Evaluation.* Reston, VA: Latino Institute.

Falk, I. (2000). *Human and Social Capital: A Case Study Of Conceptual*

Colonisation. CRLRA Discussion Paper D8/2001. Launceston, Tasmania: Centre for Research and Learning in Regional Australia.

Falk, I. (2001). *Literacy and Community: Social Capital and its Production of Human Capital. CRLRA Discussion Paper D6/2001.* Launceston, Tasmania: Centre for Research and Learning in Regional Australia.

Feinstein, L., Budge, D., Vorhaus, J. and Duckworth, K. (2008). *The Social and Personal Benefits of Learning: A Summary of Key Research Findings.* London: Centre for Research on the Wider Benefits of Learning.

Feinstein, L., Hammond, C., Woods, L., Preston, J. and Bynner, J. (2003). *The Contribution of Adult Learning to Health and Social Capital.* London: Centre for the Wider Benefits of Learning.

Fiedrich, M. and Jellema, A. (2003). *Literacy, Gender and Social Agency: A Research Report for Action Aid UK.* London: Action Aid UK and DFiD.

Fingeret, H. A. and Drennon, C. (1997). *Literacy for Life: Adult Learners, New Practices.* New York: Teachers' College Press.

Flower, L. and Hayes, J. R. (2004). 'A cognitive process theory of reading.' In D. Wray (Ed.), *Literacy: Major Themes in Education* (pp. 40–63). London: Routledge.

Freire, P. (1971). *Pedagogy of the Oppressed.* Harmondsworth, UK: Penguin.

Freire, P. (2004). *Pedagogy of Indignation.* Boulder, CO: Paradigm.

Gee, J., Hull, G. and Lankshear, C. (1996). *The New Work Order: Behind the Language of the New Capitalism.* St.Leonard's, N.S.W.: Allen and Unwin.

Goody, J. and Watt, I. (1968). 'The consequences of literacy.' In J. Goody (Ed.), *Literacy in Traditional Societies* (27–68). Cambridge, UK: Cambridge University Press.

Graff, H. J. (1994). 'Literacy, myths and legacies.' In L. Verhoeven (Ed.), *Functional Literacy: Theoretical Issues and Educational Implications* (37–61). Amsterdam: John Benjamins.

Graff, H. J. (1987). *The Legacies of Literacy.* Bloomington, IN: Indiana University Press.

Graff, H. J. (1995). *The Labyrinths of Literacy.* Pittsburgh: University of Pittsburgh.

Gray, W. S. (1956). *The Teaching of Reading and Writing: An International Survey.* Paris: UNESCO.

Greany, K. (2008). 'Circles in the sand: Challenge and reinforcement of gender stereotypes in a literacy programme in Sudan.' *Gender and Education, 20(1),* 51–61.

Green, A. and Howard, U. (2007). *Skills and Social Practices: Making*

Common Cause. An NRDC Policy Paper. London: National Research and Development Centre for Adult Literacy and Numeracy.

Grinyer, J. (2006). *Literacy, Numeracy and the Labour Market: Further Analysis of the Skills for Life Survey*. Nottingham: Department for Education and Skills.

Groot, W. and Massen van der Brink, H. (2006). *Dormant Capital: A Research into the Social Expenses of Low Literacy*. Amsterdam, NL: University of Amsterdam.

Hamilton, M. and Barton, D. (2000). 'The International Adult Literacy Survey (IALS): What does it really measure?' *International Review of Education*.

Han, S. (2008). 'Competence: Commodification of human ability.' *Asia Pacific Education Review, 9(1)*, 31–39.

Hankivsky, O. (2008). *Cost Estimates of Dropping out of High School in Canada*. Ottawa, Canada: Canadian Council on Learning.

Hannon, P. (1999). 'Rhetoric and research in family literacy.' *British Educational Research Journal*, 26(1), 121–138.

Hart, S.A., Petrill, S.A., DeThorne, L. S., Deater-Deckard, K., Thompson, L. A., Schatschneider, C., *et al.* (2009). 'Environmental influences on the longitudinal covariance of expressive vocabulary: measuring the home literacy environment in a genetically sensitive design.' *Journal of Child Psychology and Psychiatry, 50(8)*, 911–919.

Hartley, R. and Horne, J. (2006). *Social and Economic Benefits of Improved Adult Literacy: Towards a Better Understanding*. Adelaide: National Centre for Vocational Education Research.

Heckman, J. J. and LaFontaine, P. A. (2006). 'Bias-Corrected estimates of GED returns.' *Journal of Labor Economics, 24(3)*, 661–700.

Henderson, L. (1982). *Orthography and Word Recognition in Reading*. London: Academic Press.

Henningsen, I. (2006). *'Adults just don't know how stupid they are: dubious statistics in studies of adult literacy and numeracy.'* Paper presented at the Adults Learning Mathematics 13th International Conference, Belfast.

Jackson, S. (2007). 'Freire reviewed.' *Educational Theory, 57(2)*, 199–213.

Johnston, G. (2004). *Adult Literacy and Economic Growth*. Wellington, NZ: New Zealand Treasury.

Jones, S. (2009). 'Spurs eye Maxi, Everton back in for City's Jo, tug of war for Hammer Ashton, Sol reaches for parasol and who's going Balde?' *Daily Mail*. Retrieved from http://www.dailymail.co.uk/sport/football/article-1195462/THE-INSIDER-Spurs-eye-Maxi-

Everton-Citys-Jo-tug-war-Hammer-Ashton-Sol-reaches-parasol-whos-going-Balde.html.

Judkins, D., St. Pierre, R., Gutmann, B., Goodson, B., von Glatz, A., Hamilton, Webber, A., Troppe, P. and Rimdzius, T. (2008). *A Study of Classroom Literacy Interventions and Outcomes in Even Start. NCEE 2008–4028.* Jessup, MD: National Center for Education Evaluation and Regional Assistance.

Kerka, S. (2003). *Health Literacy Beyond Basic Skills. ERIC Digest 245.* Columbus, OH: ERIC Clearinghouse on Adult, Continuing and Vocational Education.

Kickbusch, I. S. (2001). 'Health literacy: Addressing the health and education divide.' *Health Promotion International, 16(3),* 289–297.

Kirsch, I. S., Braun, H., Yamamoto, K. and Sum, A. (2007). *America's Perfect Storm: Three Forces Changing our Nation's Future.* Princeton, NJ: Educational Testing Service, Policy Evaluation and Research Center.

Kirsch, I. S. and Guthrie, J. T. (1980). 'Construct validity of functional reading tests.' *Journal of Educational Measurement, 17(2),* 81–93.

Kirsch, I. S. and Murray, T. S. (1997). Introduction. In T. S. Murray, I. S. Kirsch and L. B. Jenkins (Eds), *Adult Literacy in OECD Countries: Technical Report on the First International Adult Literacy Survey* (13–22). Washington, DC: National Center for Education Statistics.

Knowles, M. S. (1980). *The Modern Practice of Adult Education.* Englewood Cliffs, NJ: Prentice Hall.

Ko, H.W. and Chan, Y.L. (2009) 'Family factors and primary students' reading attainment: a Chinese community perspective.' *Chinese Education and Society, 42(3),* 33–48.

Kutner, M., Greenberg, E., Jin, Y., Paulsen, C. and White, S. (2006). *The Health Literacy of America's Adults: Results from the 2003 National Assessment of Adult Literacy.* Washington, DC: National Center for Educational Statistics.

Labov, W. (1972). *Sociolinguistic Patterns.* Philadelphia, PA: University of Pennsylvania Press.

Laroche, M., Mérette, M. and Ruggeri, G. C. (1997). *On the Concept and Dimensions of Human Capital in a Knowledge-Based Economy Context.* Ottawa, ON: Economic and Fiscal Policy Branch, Government of Canada.

Lauritzen, C. (2007). 'William Scott Gray (1885–1960): Mr. Reading.' In S. E. Israel and J. Monaghan (Eds), *Shaping the Reading Field: The Impact of Early Reading Pioneers, Scientific Research, and Progressive*

Ideas. (307–326). Newark, DE: International Reading Association.

Lea, M.R. and Street, B.V. (2006). 'The "academic literacies" model: theory and applications.' *Theory into Practice, 45(4)*, 368–377.

Leigh, A. and Ryan, C. (2005). *Estimating Returns to Education: Three Natural Experiment Techniques Compared*. Canberra: Australian National University, Research School of Social Science.

Leu, D. and Kinzer, C. (1995). *Effective Reading Instruction K-8*. Upper Saddle River, NJ: Merrill.

Luebke, P. T. (1966). 'Towards a definition of literacy.' *Community Development Journal, 1(1)*, 33–37.

Lundborg, P. (2008). *The Health Returns to Education – What Can We Learn from Twins?* Amsterdam: Free University Amsterdam and Tinbergen Institute.

Lynch, J. (2009). 'Print literacy engagement of parents from low-income backgrounds: implications for adult and family literacy programmes.' *Journal of Adolescent and Adult Literacy, 52(6)*, 509–521.

Mace, J. (2001). 'Signatures and the lettered world.' In J. Crowther, M. Hamilton and L. Tett (Eds), *Powerful Literacies* (45–55). Leicester, UK: National Institute of Adult Continuing Education (NIACE).

Maclachlan, K., Tett, L. and Hall, S. (2009). 'The more you learn the better you feel: research into literacies, learning and identity in Scotland.' In S. Reder and J. Bynner (Eds), *Tracking Adult Literacy and Numeracy Skills* (329–348). London: Routledge.

Maclean, L. (1987). 'Emerging with honour from a dilemma inherent in the validation of educational achievement measures.' Paper presented at the American Educational Research Association, Washington, DC.

Maruatona, T. (2008). 'Reflections on policies for mass literacy education in Sub-Saharan Africa.' *International Review of Education, 54*, 745–754.

Maruatona, T. and Cervero, R.M. (2004). 'Adult literacy education in Botswana: planning between reproduction and resistance.' *Studies in the Education of Adults 36 (2)*, 235–251.

Metcalf, H. and Meadows, P. (2009). 'Outcomes for basic skills learners: A four-year longitudinal study.' In S. Reder and J. Bynner (Eds), *Tracking Adult Literacy and Numeracy Skills* (225–241). London: Routledge.

Miller, D. C. and Salkind, N. J. (2002). *Handbook of Research Design and Social Measurement* (6th ed.). London: SAGE.

NICHD (2000). *Teaching Children to Read: An Evidence-Based Assessment of the Scientific Research Literature on Reading and its Implications for*

Reading Instruction. Rockville, MD: National Institute of Child Health and Human Development.

Nutbeam, D. (1999). 'Literacies across the lifespan: health literacy.' *Literacy and Numeracy Studies, 9(2)*, 47–55.

Olson, D. R. (1989). 'Literate thought.' In C. K. Leong and B. S. Randhawa (Eds), *Understanding Literacy and Cognition: Theory, Research and Application* (3–16). New York: Plenum Press.

Organisation for Economic Co-operation and Development (2000). *Literacy in the Information Age: Final Report of the International Adult Literacy Survey*. Paris: Organisation for Economic Co-operation and Development, Statistics Canada.

Organisation for Economic Co-operation and Development (2009). 'Adult literacy.' Retrieved June 22, 2009, from www.oecd.org/document/2/0,3343,en_2649_39263294_2670850_1_1_1_1,00.html

Oxenham, J. (2004). *The Quality of Programmes and Policies Regarding Literacy and Skills Development: A Study Commissioned for the 2005 EFA Monitoring Report Draft 2*. Paris: UNESCO.

Pansiri, N. O. (2008). 'Improving commitment to basic education for the minorities in Botswana: a challenge for policy and practice.' *International Journal of Educational Development, 28*, 446–459.

Papen, U. (2005). 'Literacy and development: what works for whom? or, how relevant is the social practices view of literacy for literacy education in developing countries?' *International Journal of Educational Development, 25*, 5–17.

Parsons, S. and Bynner, J. (2007). *Illuminating Disadvantage: Profiling the Experiences of Adults with Entry Level Literacy or Numeracy over the Lifecourse*. London: National Research and Development Centre for Adult Literacy and Numeracy.

Parsons, S., Bynner, J. and Foudouli, V. (2005). *Measuring Basic Skills for Longitudinal Study*. London: University of London, National Research and Development Centre for Adult Literacy and Numeracy.

Partchev, I. (2004). 'A visual guide to item response theory.' Retrieved June 22, 2009, from http://www.metheval.uni-jena.de/irt/VisualIRT.pdf

Pasche, C. (2008). *What Is It about Schooling that the Labor Market Rewards: The Components of the Return to Schooling*. Bern, CH: The Swiss Leading House on Economics of Education.

Patton, M. Q. (1997). *Utilization Focused Evaluation: The New Century Text (3 ed.)*. Thousand Oaks, CA: Sage.

Perfetti, C. A. (1985). *Reading Ability*. New York: Oxford University Press.

Perfetti, C. A., Bell, L. C. and Delaney, S. (1988). 'Automatic (prelexical) phonetic activation in silent word reading: evidence from backward masking.' *Journal of Memory and Language, 27*, 59–70.

Phillips, B. M. and Lonigan, C. J. (2009). 'Variations in the home literacy environment of preschool children: a cluster analytic approach.' *Scientific Studies of Reading, 13(2)*, 146–174.

Pinker, S. (1994). *The Language Instinct: How the Mind Creates Language*. New York: William Morrow & Company.

Plato (360 BCE). *The Seventh Letter* (J. Harward, Trans.). Cambridge, MA: Massachusetts.

Power, M. (1999). *The Audit Society: Rituals of Verification*. Oxford: Oxford University Press.

Preece, J. and Houghton, A. (2000). *Nurturing Social Capital in Excluded Communities: A Kind of Higher Education*. Aldershot, UK: Ashgate.

Prins, E. (2007). '*Aqui no somos unidos*/We're not united here: Adult literacy and obstacles to solidarity in postwar El Salvador.' *International Journal of Qualitative Studies in Education 20(4)*, 401–431.

Prins, E., Toso, B. and Schafft, K. (2009). '"It feels like a little family to me": social interaction and support among women in adult education and family literacy.' *Adult Education Quarterly, 59(4)*, 335–352.

Putnam, R. D. (1993). 'The prosperous community: Social capital and public life.' *American Prospect, 4(13)*.

Quigley, B. A. (1997). *Rethinking Literacy Education: The Critical Need for Practice-Based Change*. San Francisco: Jossey-Bass.

Reder, S. (2009). 'The development of literacy and numeracy in adult life.' In S. Reder and J. Bynner (Eds), *Tracking Adult Literacy and Numeracy: Findings from Longitudinal Research* (59–84). London: Routledge.

Reder, S. and Bynner, J. (2009). 'Introduction.' In S. Reder and J. Bynner (Eds), *Tracking Adult Literacy and Numeracy: Findings from Longitudinal Research* (1–26). London: Routledge.

Reisenberger, A. and Sanders, J. (1997). 'Adult learners: pathways to progression.' *FE Matters, 1(12)*.

Reyna, V. F. and Brainerd, C. J. (2007). 'The importance of mathematics in health and human judgement: numeracy, risk communication, and medical decision making.' *Learning and Individual Differences, 17*, 147–159.

Ricciuti, A. E., St.Pierre, R. G., Lee, W. and Parsad, A. (2004). *Third National Even Start Evaluation: Follow-Up Findings from the*

Experimental Design Study. NCEE 2005–3002. Jessup, MD: National Center for Education Evaluation and Regional Assistance.

Robinson-Pant, A. (2010). 'Changing discourses: literacy and development in Nepal.' *International Journal of Educational Development, 30,* 136–144.

Rudd, R., Kirsch, I. S. and Yamamoto, K. (2004). *Literacy and Health in America.* Princeton, NJ: Educational Testing Service.

Rumelhart, D. E. and McClelland, J. L. (1981). 'Interactive processing through spreading activation.' In A. M. Lesgold and C. A. Perfetti (Eds), *Interactive Processes in Reading* (37–60). Hillsdale, NJ: Erlbaum.

Sandlin, J. A. and St.Clair, R. (2002). 'The unlettered state: illiteracy and intrusion in North American social policy.' Paper presented at the Standing Committee on University Teaching and Research on the Education of Adults, Stirling, UK.

Schnell-Anzola, B., Rowe, M. L. and LeVine, R. A. (2005). 'Literacy as a pathway between schooling and health-related communication skills: a study of Venezuelan mothers.' *International Journal of Educational Development, 25,* 19–37.

Schuller, T., Brassett-Grundy, A., Green, A., Hammond, C. and Preston, J. (2002). *Learning, Continuity and Change in Adult Life.* London: Centre for Research on the Wider Benefits of Learning.

Scottish Executive (2001). *Adult Literacy and Numeracy in Scotland.* Edinburgh: Scottish Executive.

Scottish Executive (2001). *Adult Literacy in Scotland: Analysis of Data from the 1996 Adult Literacy Survey.* Edinburgh: Scottish Executive.

Scottish Government (2007). 'Reduce number of working age people with severe literacy and numeracy problems.' Retrieved June 14, 2009, from http://www.scotland.gov.uk/About/scotPerforms/indicators/literacyAndNumeracy.

Scottish Qualification Authority (undated). 'Scottish Credit and Qualifications Framework.' Retrieved June 23, 2009, from http://www.sqa.org.uk/sqa/4596.html.

Scribner, S. and Cole, M. (1981). *The Psychology of Literacy.* Cambridge, MA: Harvard University Press.

Sen, A. (1979). *Equality of What? The Tanner Lecture on Human Values.* Palo Alto, CA: Stanford University.

Sen, A. (1999). *Development as Freedom.* New York: Alfred A. Knopf.

Sénéchal, M. (2006). *The Effect of Family Literacy Interventions on Children's Acquisition of Reading: From Kindergarten to Grade 3: A Meta-Analytic*

Review. Portsmouth, N.H.: RMC Research Corp.; Washington, D.C.: National Institute for Literacy, the Partnership for Reading.

Shohet, L. (2004). 'Health and literacy perspectives.' *Literacy and Numeracy Studies, 13(1)*.

Shufflebeam, D. L. and Shinkfield, A. J. (2007). *Evaluation Theory, Models and Application*. San Francisco: Jossey-Bass.

Silles, M. A. (2007). 'The returns to education for the United Kingdom.' *Journal of Applied Economics, X(1)*, 391–413.

Smith, M. K. (2002). 'Paulo Freire.' *The Encyclopaedia of Informal Education*. Retrieved from http://www.infed.org/thinkers/et-freir.htm.

St.Clair, R. (2005). 'Similarity and superunknowns: an essay on the challenges of educational research.' *Harvard Educational Review, 75(4)*, 435–453.

St.Clair, R. (2008). 'Reading, writing and relationships: human and social capital in family literacy programmes.' *Adult Basic Education and Literacy Journal, 2(2)*, 84–93.

St.Clair, R. (2009). *The Dilemmas of Accountability*. Toronto, ON: ABC CANADA Literacy Foundation.

St.Clair, R. and Belzer, A. (2007). 'National accountability systems.' In P. Campbell (Ed.), *Accountability in Adult Basic Education*. Edmonton: Grass Roots Press.

St.Clair, R. and Phipps, A. (2008) 'Ludic literacies at the intersections of cultures: an interview with James Paul Gee.' *Language and Intercultural Communication, 8(2)*, 91–100.

St.Pierre, R.G., Ricciuti A.E. and Rimdzius T. (2005). Effects of a family literacy program on low-literate children and their parents: findings from an evaluation of the Even Start family literacy program.' *Developmental Psychology, 41(6)*, 953–970.

Strauss, S. L. and Altwerger, B. (2007). 'The logographic nature of English alphabetics and the fallacy of direct intensive phonics instruction.' *Journal of Early Childhood Literacy, 7(3)*, 299–319.

Street, B. V. (1984). *Literacy in Theory and Practice*. Cambridge: University of Cambridge.

Street, B.V. (2004). 'Academic literacies and the 'new orders': Implications for research and practice in student writing in higher education.' *Learning and Teaching in the Social Sciences 1(1)*, 9–20.

Street, B.V. (2003). 'What's "new" in new literacy studies? Critical approaches to literacy in theory and practice.' *Current Issues in Comparative Education, 5(2)*, 77–91.

Styles, B. (2009). 'The future is random – why the RCT should often be the method of evaluation.' In R. St.Clair (Ed.), *Education Science: Critical Perspectives* (83–100). Rotterdam: Sense.

Tagoe, M. (2008). 'Challenging the orthodoxy of literacy: Realities of moving for personal to community empowerment through Reflect in Ghana.' *International Journal of Lifelong Education, 27(6)*, 707–728.

Tannen, D. (1985). 'Relative focus on involvement in oral and written discourse.' In D. R. Olson, N. Torrance and A. Hildyard (Eds), *Language, Literacy and Learning: The Nature and Consequences of Reading and Writing* (124–147). Cambridge, UK: Cambridge University Press.

Taylor, D. (1983). *Family Literacy: Young Children Learning to Read and Write*. Portsmouth, NH: Heinemann Educational.

Taylor, P. (1993). *The Texts of Paulo Freire*. Buckingham, UK: Open University Press.

Tett, L. (2000). '"I'm working class and proud of it" Gendered experiences of non-traditional participants in higher education.' *Gender and Education, 12 (2)*, 183–193.

Tett, L. and Maclachlan, K. (2007). 'Adult literacy and numeracy, social capital, learner identities and self-confidence.' *Studies in the Education of Adults, 39(2)*, 150–167.

Thompson, G. B. and Johnston, R. S. (2007). 'Visual and orthographic information in learning to read and the influence of phonics instruction.' *Reading and Writing, 20*, 859–884.

Tyler, J. H., Murnane, J. M. and Willett, J. B. (2000). 'Estimating the labour market signaling value of the GED.' *Quarterly Journal of Economics, 115(2)*, 431–468.

UNESCO (2002). 'Functional literacy.' Retrieved June 14, 2009, from http://www.uis.unesco.org/ev.php?ID=5014_201&ID2=DO_TOPIC

UNESCO (2008). *Overcoming Inequality: Why Governance Matters. EFA Global Monitoring Report 2009*. Paris: United Nations Educational, Scientific and Cultural Organisation and Oxford University Press.

Van der Gaag, M. and Snijders, T. A. B. (2003). *A Comparison of Measures for Individual Social Capital*. Groningen, Netherlands: University of Groningen.

Van Orden, G. C. (1991). 'Phonologic mediation is fundamental to reading.' In D. Besner and G. W. Humphreys (Eds), *Basic Processes in Reading: Visual Word Recognition* (77–103). Hillsdale, NJ: Erlbaum.

Verhoeven, L. (1994). 'Modelling and promoting functional literacy.' In L. Verhoeven (Ed.), *Functional Literacy: Theoretical Issues and Educational Implications* (3–34). Amsterdam: John Benjamins.

Vignoles, A., de Coulon, A. and Marcenaro-Gutierrez, O. (2008). *The Value of Basic Skills in the British Labour Market*. London: National Research and Development Centre for Adult Literacy and Numeracy.

W.K. Kellogg Foundation (2004). *Logic Model Development Guide*. Battle Creek, MI: W.K. Kellogg Foundation.

Walker, M. (2005). 'Amartya Sen's capability approach and education.' *Educational Action Research, 13(1)*, 103–110.

Walsh, C. (2007). 'Challenging the readiness myth: parents' involvement in early literacy development.' In B. J. Guzzetti (Ed.), *Literacy for the New Millennium. Volume 1: Early Literacy*. Westport, CT: Praeger.

Weiss, C. H. (1995). 'Nothing as practical as good theory: Exploring theory-based evaluation for comprehensive community initiatives for children and families.' In J. P. Connell, A. C. Kubisch, L. B. Schorr and C. H. Wiess (Eds), *New Approaches to Evaluating Community Initiatives* (65–92). New York: Aspen Institute.

Wickens, C. M. and Sandlin, J. A. (2007). 'Literacy for what? Literacy for whom? The politics of literacy education and neo-colonialism in UNESCO- and World Bank-sponsored literacy programmes.' *Adult Education Quarterly, 57(4)*, 275–292.

Willis, P. (1977). *Learning to Labour*. Aldershot, UK: Gower.

Winchester, I. (1985). 'Atlantans, Centaurians, and the litron bomb: some personal and societal implications of literacy.' In D. R. Olson, N. Torrance and A. Hildyard (Eds), *Language, Literacy and Learning: The Nature and Consequences of Reading and Writing* (34–49). Cambridge, UK: Cambridge University Press.

Wolf, A. (2002). *Does Education Matter? Myths about Education and Economic Growth*. London: Penguin.

Wolf, M. and Bowers, P. G. (1999). 'The double-deficit hypothesis for the developmental dyslexias.' *Journal of Educational Psychology, 91(3)*, 415–438.

Wong, J. (1999). *Jan Wong's China: Reports from a Not-so-Foreign Correspondent*. Toronto: Doubleday.

World Bank (1993). *World Development Report: Investing in Health*. Washington, DC: World Bank.

Zinn, H. (1999). *A People's History of the United States*. New York: Perennial Classics.

Index

212

216